The Master Chefs of
Britain Recipe Book

The Master Chefs of Britain Recipe Book

Over 250 recipes
from the Great Chefs of Britain
compiled with the cooperation of Carte Blanche®

A Publication of
The Master Chefs Institute
Sandy Lesberg, Director

DAVID & CHARLES
Newton Abbot   London

Illustratons: Judy Parenio
Graphic Production: Filmar Graphics, Inc., San Diego, CA

ISBN: 0-7153-8240-3

Printed in the United States of America

Preface

There can be no doubt that the following work, for which I have the honour of being asked to subscribe a preface, will turn out to be both a tangible and an invaluable aid for the lady of the house, the gourmet, and also for the professional.

It is a great pleasure to discover throughout this book chefs of different nationalities carrying out their chosen profession in all kinds of restaurants scattered all over Great Britain. They offer a wide selection of international yet personalised dishes, ranging from the most simple to the most sopohisticated and from the most economical to the most sumptuous.

The wealth of colour and variety herein is reminiscent of an artist's palette from which the pupil can indulge either his own tastes or exploit the possibilities of the moment, to choose his master, and to cook in the knowledge that what he has cherished and pampered will always receive the acclaim that it rightly deserves, and that very often he will be agreeably surprised by the final result. Could there be any greater satisfaction than witnessing the hum of conversation around a dinner table being brought to a sudden halt by the presentation, the colours, the texture, and the sophistication of a culinary creation?

The British chefs included in this work deserve a special and encouraging mention. They have no reason to be envious of their European counterparts, as they too are truly masters of their trade. The public is only too often either unaware of them or adopts a disdainful attitude towards them. Let us hope that, one day, measures at government level will restore the former professional prestige to this hard but noble vocation. If this were to happen, we could well one day see British chefs in action, not only in their own country, but all over the world.

My culinary philosophy and my everyday working attitude since the age of fourteen have led me to certain positive conclusions and have given me a great deal of satisfaction. Without a certain amount of sacrifice and a constant striving towards new goals, however, life would be empty and meaningless. My brother and I have understood this, and without doubt, the most concrete and the strongest vindication for us lies in the strength of our "association." It is this, and this alone, that constitutes the success from which I draw my faith, my respect, and my love.

The recently created Master Chefs Institute is an association that will serve to strengthen the bonds between professionals. Let us hope that as many chefs as possible understand its significance and decide to join, lending their strength to its purpose. Its aim is the further promotion of our splendid profession, and this can be nothing but an advantage for the discerning public.

This book is a splendid initiative and provides us with an important and much needed glimpse of the serious side of gastronomy in Great Britain.

Michel Roux
Director, Roux Restaurants, Ltd.

Publisher's Note: To avoid any possible diversion from the precise intentions of the chefs we are printing the recipes exactly as they were written. "Spoons" in the list of ingredients usually mean "tablespoons," but do use your own judgment. You must decide for yourself what liberties, if any, you will take. I strongly recommend that you stay fairly close to the chefs' instructions for at least the first try at any of the recipes. There is much to be said for freedom of action in the kitchen but with a collection of pedigree recipes such as these a modicum of conservation would, I suggest, stand you in good stead.

Contents

Introduction

The Master Chefs Institute is an international affiliation of great chefs and restaurateurs whose primary function is to provide a bridge between the professional working chef and the public. THE MASTER CHEFS OF BRITAIN RECIPE BOOK represents the finest cuisine in the country presented by her greatest chefs and restaurateurs. Through their membership in the Institute they share the secrets of their speciality recipes with you, some more challenging than others, but all worthy of your attention and eminently adaptable to your household kitchen.

You will note that after the names of some of the chefs there are printed the letters M.C.G.B. They stand for the title "Master Chef of Great Britain" and while every chef represented in this book has, by dint of his or her membership in the Institute, achieved an unassailable position in the culinary world, the relatively limited number of those declared Master Chef of Great Britain are to be considered at the very zenith of their art and profession.

A final word about the Institute: we have a limited number of public memberships available in each country where the Institute functions. These members receive special discounts for most publications (i.e. THE MASTER CHEFS OF FRANCE RECIPE BOOK in French or English, THE MASTER CHEFS OF AMERICA RECIPE BOOK, etc.). From time to time receptions are held at various sites around Britain where Master Chefs demonstrate their specialities, to which the public members receive special invitations. A chef-to-chef newsletter is sent to public members — they are entitled to reduced tuition rates for our cooking school in Cannes, etc., etc. If you would like more specific information about public membership in the Institute write to me personally and I promise you a prompt reply. My London address is:

> The Master Chefs Institute
> The Tower Hotel
> St. Katherine's Way
> London E1 9LD
> ENGLAND

Here, then, is a collection of the most exciting recipes from the greatest restaurants of Britain. There are many wonders to be worked from these pages. It's time to begin!

> Sandy Lesberg
> Director, The Master Chefs Institute

Bagatelle

Bagatelle is a pretty and elegant restaurant situated in Chelsea, near the Kings Road that is renowned for its trendy clothes shops. The restaurant is now five years old.

Daniel Marrocco, the owner, attended the École Hotelière de Paris, worked in the managing departments of different hotels in France, then moved to London where he worked as a cook for five years. Having gained full experience in both the management and the cooking side, he bought a two-storied restaurant with a vaulted cellar, fully refurbished and redecorated it, and opened Bagatelle. It is now a light and airy yet warm restaurant, accented with house plants, with a lovely garden at the back offering the possibility of having lunch or dinner under a trellis.

With his team of Japanese chefs headed by Osamu Ono, he produces a small regular menu of both very classical French cuisine as well as some *nouvelle cuisine*, together with a wide variety of daily specialities according to the availability of the day's market. The wine list is limited to 15 well selected French wines, and the cheese board offers a wide variety of French cheeses. Speciality recipes are presented on the opposite page.

**5 LANGTON STREET
LONDON, SW10**

01-351-4185

**LUNCH: 12 TO 2 P.M.
DINNER: 7 TO 11 P.M.
MONDAY — SATURDAY**

**PROPRIETOR: DANIEL MARROCCO
CHEF: OSAMU ONO**

Roulade de Poisson au Beurre Blanc

70 ml milk

1 whole egg

25 g flour

1 tsp chopped parsley

250

25

10

1

4

2

200 g girolle mushrooms (or any other kind if not available)

2 large measures Madeira wine

fond de veau (veal stock), as needed

1 tsp chopped tarragon

few drops of lemon juice

Cook first 4 ingredients together in a hot pan with butter to make 1 square crepe.

To prepare white mousseline: liquidise 170 grams white fish. Add 2 egg whites, then add pepper and cayenne pepper. Add 125 millilitres cream, little by little, then finish with salt.

To prepare red mousseline: liquidise the salmon trout with tomato purée, then add 1 egg white and proceed as before only adding 50 millilitres cream little by little.

To prepare green mousseline: liquidise remaining white fish, then add spinach, whole egg, peppers, remaining cream, and salt.

Lay crepe out flat. Without mixing colours, arrange as follows: red mousseline in centre, green around red, white around green. Roll up crepe and wrap with aluminum foil. Cook on low heat in a double boiler in oven for ½ hour.

To prepare white butter sauce: reduce wine and shallot by ½, add butter, little by little, then add tomato, tarragon, lemon juice, salt, and pepper. Serve sauce over finished crepe.

Volaille Sous-Bois

To prepare gâteau de volaille: liquidise 1 chicken breast with cooked spinach, add whole egg and egg whites, then gradually add cream. Pour mixture into 6 small buttered moulds and put 1 egg yolk in the middle of each. Double boil in oven for about 10 minutes.

Cut each remaining chicken breast into 4 thin slices, add salt and pepper, and sauté in butter on both sides until cooked. Remove chicken. In the same pan, add chopped shallots, mushrooms, and girolle mushrooms. Deglaze with Madeira and veal stock and reduce a little. Add seasoning and finish with butter.

Serve chicken on plate with the gâteaux and sauce.

Serves: 6

GRILLED MARINATED
SWORDFISH WITH
AVOCADO BUTTER

8 servings

Swordfish

  8 small swordfish steaks
  ½ cup vegetable oil
  ⅓ cup soy sauce
  ¼ cup fresh lemon juice
  1 teaspoon grated lemon peel
  1 garlic clove, crushed

Avocado Butter

  ½ cup (1 stick) butter, room temperature
  ½ cup mashed ripe avocado
  5 tablespoons fresh lemon or lime juice
  2 tablespoons minced fresh parsley
  2 garlic cloves, minced
  Salt

  8 lemon or lime wedges
  8 parsley sprigs

For fish: Pierce fish on both sides with fork. Arrange in single layer in shallow baking dish. Blend oil, soy sauce, lemon juice, lemon peel and garlic in medium bowl. Pour over fish. Marinate in refrigerator 2 hours, turning occasionally.

For butter: Beat butter in small bowl until soft and creamy. Beat in avocado, lemon juice, minced parsley and garlic. Season with salt. Cover with plastic wrap and refrigerate until ready to serve.

Prepare barbecue grill or preheat broiler. Drain fish, reserving marinade. Grill fish 9 minutes per 1-inch thickness, brushing often with marinade and turning once. Transfer fish to plates. Top each with spoonful of avocado butter. Garnish with lemon wedges and parsley sprigs and serve. □

—Compiled by Karen Kaplan

Boulestin Restaurant Francais

Boulestin Restaurant Francais was opened in 1925 by a French journalist called Boulestin. With the success of his cookery books and his knowledge of classic French cuisine, this man, who had also been an interior decorator and a Great War interpreter to the British forces, had a strong influence on British cooking and culinary taste. When he died during the 1939-45 war, the restaurant changed hands shortly afterwards and its standards dropped.

It wasn't until late 1978 that it reverted back to its original glory. It was bought by Grand Metropolitan Hotels, and Kevin Kennedy was put in charge. Kevin Kennedy is Chef de Cuisine et Directeur. He has been a professional chef for more than 16 years, is a graduate from the Westminster Hotel School, and is of the new school. One meal at Boulestin will tell you that he is a master of French sauces. In fact, such is his culinary background that he is a master of all departments.

Boulestin Restaurant Francais is located in London's Covent Garden. The decor of the 1930s has been retained, even to the colour prints in the lobby: 1920s cartoons with archly-flirty girls, smooth men, and culinary captions. It has a truly friendly ambiance — the feeling you are walking into a friend's home.

Brioche d'Oeufs de Caille aux Girolles à la Porto

1 oz unsalted butter

1 oz wild girolle mushrooms

1 tsp chopped shallots

    salt and milled black pepper, to taste

2 fl oz port wine

2 fl oz thick dairy cream

1 round *brioche à tête*

1 tbsp duxelles of girolle mushrooms

1 tbsp spinach purée

4 quail eggs

To prepare sauce: heat butter, add girolles, and cook quickly over fast heat. Add shallots, season, and stir well until all is cooked. Add port and reduce by ⅔. Add cream, stir, and cook to correct consistency. Check seasoning. Hollow out the brioche and warm in oven. Heat the purée of girolles and purée of spinach together, mixing well. Check seasoning. Poach the eggs and drain onto cloth or kitchen paper. Fill brioche with purée, top with eggs, and coat with sauce.

Serves: 1

Andouillette de Saumon en Habit Vert

3 tbsp finely chopped shallots

    butter, as needed

5 fl oz plus ¼ bottle dry white wine

    sea salt and freshly ground black pepper, to taste

15 fl oz thick cream

2 fl oz chicken stock

8 oz blanched watercress

1 tbsp chopped chives

4 fl oz water

1 tbsp lemon juice

8 oz salmon fillet

2 egg whites

4 × 4 oz fillets of salmon

    blanched spinach leaves, as needed

    fish stock, as needed

    watercress, to garnish

To prepare *crème de cresson* sauce: sweat ⅔ shallots in butter until translucent. Add 5 ounces wine, salt, and milled pepper and boil until reduced to 2 tablespoons of purée. Boil ⅔ cream with the chicken stock until reduced by ⅔. Let cool. When cold, put into a liquidiser with blanched watercress, chives, water, and lemon juice. Check seasoning and store, covered, in refrigerator until required.

To prepare mousse of salmon: pass the 8 ounces of salmon fillet through a food processor with egg whites, salt, and black pepper for 1 minute. Add remaining cream and run for 30 seconds. Allow to rest in refrigerator 1 hour.

Gently flatten the 4 salmon fillets into a rectangle by placing them between 2 sheets of cling film and gently tapping with a smooth meat hammer. Place onto a single layer of overlapping spinach leaves. Season the salmon and spread a ⅛ inch layer of mousse on the salmon. Roll up like a Swiss roll. Butter a heavy ovenproof dish and place the salmon on the bottom, sprinkle with remaining shallots, add ¼ bottle white wine, and enough fish stock to cover the sides of the salmon by ⅓. Cover and cook for 15 minutes in an oven at gas mark 5 (375°F/190°C). Drain and keep warm between 2 plates. Reduce the cooking juices by ⅔, add the prepared crème de cresson sauce, and boil to a thick but pouring consistency. Pour sauce onto warm plates and dress salmon on top with a small sprig of watercress.

Serves: 4

Salade des Fruits Brouille (Mixed Fruit Salad)

    ripe fruit, prepared for use: kiwi fruit, orange segments, strawberries, banana slices, grapes, etc.

    a little liquor of your choice

    whipped, unsweetened thick dairy cream

    soft light brown sugar (Demerara), as needed

Mix fruit together then sprinkle with only a little liquor. Fill china dishes (just a little larger than a tea cup) with fruit to within ½ inch from the tops. With a palette knife or plastic scraper, fill remaining space with cream. Level off at top. (May be refrigerated for up to 24 hours.) Coat the top liberally with sugar (about ⅛ inch thick) and gently flatten. Use a flattened kitchen serving spoon or a salamander (a long metal rod with wooden grip and a round, thick heavy metal disc attached) and place in a hot fire until red hot and tops of sweets burn to a golden brown. Serve.

Capital Hotel

Brian Turner is the executive chef of the **Capital Hotel**'s restaurant. He was born and brought up in the West Riding of Yorkshire. His father owned and ran a transport cafe of a very high standard. Brian's interest in cooking stemmed from this, and at the age of 16, he enrolled at Leeds College of Technology for the Chefs' course and got his first job in London at Simpson's as a *commis tournant*. After 18 months, he went on to become *commis saucier* at the Savoy. After more schooling, a year working in Switzerland, and a year at Claridge's, he came to the Capital Hotel.

Chef Turner enjoys running the small attractive ten-year-old French restaurant at the hotel. It is modern and imaginatively decorated in quiet beige and brown, with well spaced tables. His kitchen is small but superbly organised and has a grill section. His staff is a happy group, all young English lads. He reports, "We have everything scaled down to what we can do, and we do what we can do best. We stay within the framework of our ability."

The quality and presentation of a meal at the Capital Hotel supports Chef Turner's philosophy, which is "You have to put a lettuce leaf on the plate as if you cared about it. The good Lord who made it cared, so you should."

Salade de Coquilles St. Jacques

12 scallops

butter, to sauté

4 oz white button mushroom caps

lemon juice, as needed

seasoning, to taste

curly endive, to garnish

chives and parsley, to garnish

Sauté cleaned scallops in butter very lightly (with colour on the outside). Leave to drain slowly; collect the juice. Slice the scallops across the grain and lay them around the outside of a small plate. Slice the washed mushrooms thickly and marinate in lemon juice for 5 minutes. Drain, sauté in melted butter, season, and add the juice from the scallops. Be careful that the mushrooms do not cook but just warm through. Lay them on a leaf of curly endive, sprinkle with chives and parsley, and serve just slightly warm.

Serves: 4

Noisettes d'Agneau à la Crème de Basilic

1 loin of lamb, boned and trimmed of fat and gristle

butter, to sauté

¼ pt port

1 bunch finely chopped fresh basil, reserve leaves for garnish

¼ pt white wine

½ pt veal stock

½ pt double cream

4 oz butter

seasoning, to taste

Tie lamb into a roll and cut into 12 slices 1 inch thick (3 per person). Sauté the noisettes in butter to a pink colour, remove, and leave to stand in a warm place.

Remove excess fat from pan. Add port, chopped basil leaves, and white wine and reduce until almost completely disappeared. Add veal stock and reduce. Add cream. Boil all these ingredients gently, skimming all the time, until the sauce has reduced enough to give correct consistency and amount of "body." Add knobs of butter and shake the pan until butter is absorbed by the sauce. Check seasoning and consistency. Pass noisettes through the oven to reheat. Put lamb onto a serving dish and nap sauce on top. Serve immediately.

Serves: 4

Tarte aux Poires Bordeloue

1 lb puff pastry dough

¾ pt pastry cream

2 oz ground almonds

zest of 1 orange

10 × ½ poached pears, sliced

¼ pt whipped double cream

4 oz egg white made into meringue

toasted ground almonds, for topping

double cream, to serve

Line 10 × 3 inch tart moulds with puff pastry. Fill each ¼ full with ½ pint pastry cream mixed with ground almonds and orange zest. Leave to rest ½ hour. Fill tarts with slices of poached pears in an attractive design. (Half a pear should fill each tart.) Bake at 380°F (195°C) for 20 minutes. Remove from oven and let cool.

Mix remaining pastry cream with whipped double cream and spread on each tart. Crumble meringue over the top, sprinkle with toasted ground almonds, and serve with double cream.

Carlton Tower Hotel

Bernard Gaume, who has been the executive chef at the **Carlton Tower Hotel** for 12 years, was born into the restaurant business. He comes from Vichy where his family owned a hotel, and he served his apprenticeship in some of France's best restaurants, as well as at a number of hotels around the world. His talents have been largely the reason for the success of **The Chelsea Room** restaurant.

Mr. Gaume is an expert of *la nouvelle cuisine*, which he introduced to the Carlton Tower in 1976. All of his ingredients are fresh, and each dish is cooked to order. Many of the ingredients and delicacies, such as goose livers, are delivered daily from France, straight to the restaurant.

Each year, Mr. Gaume and Jean Quero, Maître d'Hotel, make a journey to France to observe their fellow professionals in Rennes, Lyons, and Valence. In this way, new dishes find their way onto the Chelsea Room menu, which changes with the seasons.

It's not just the food that Messrs. Gaume and Quero are concerned with, it's the total ambiance of a restaurant, the way the food is served as well as how it's prepared. Jean Quero and his staff ensure that the service is first class, while Chef Gaume continues to receive accolades for his superb cuisine.

This elegant restaurant, overlooking Cadogan Gardens, is spacious, with modern decor. The atmosphere is further enhanced by the live piano music at night. The Chelsea room features a quality wine list, several house wines, and a cocktail lounge.

Thornbury Castle

The Lygon Arms

Chewton Glen Hotel

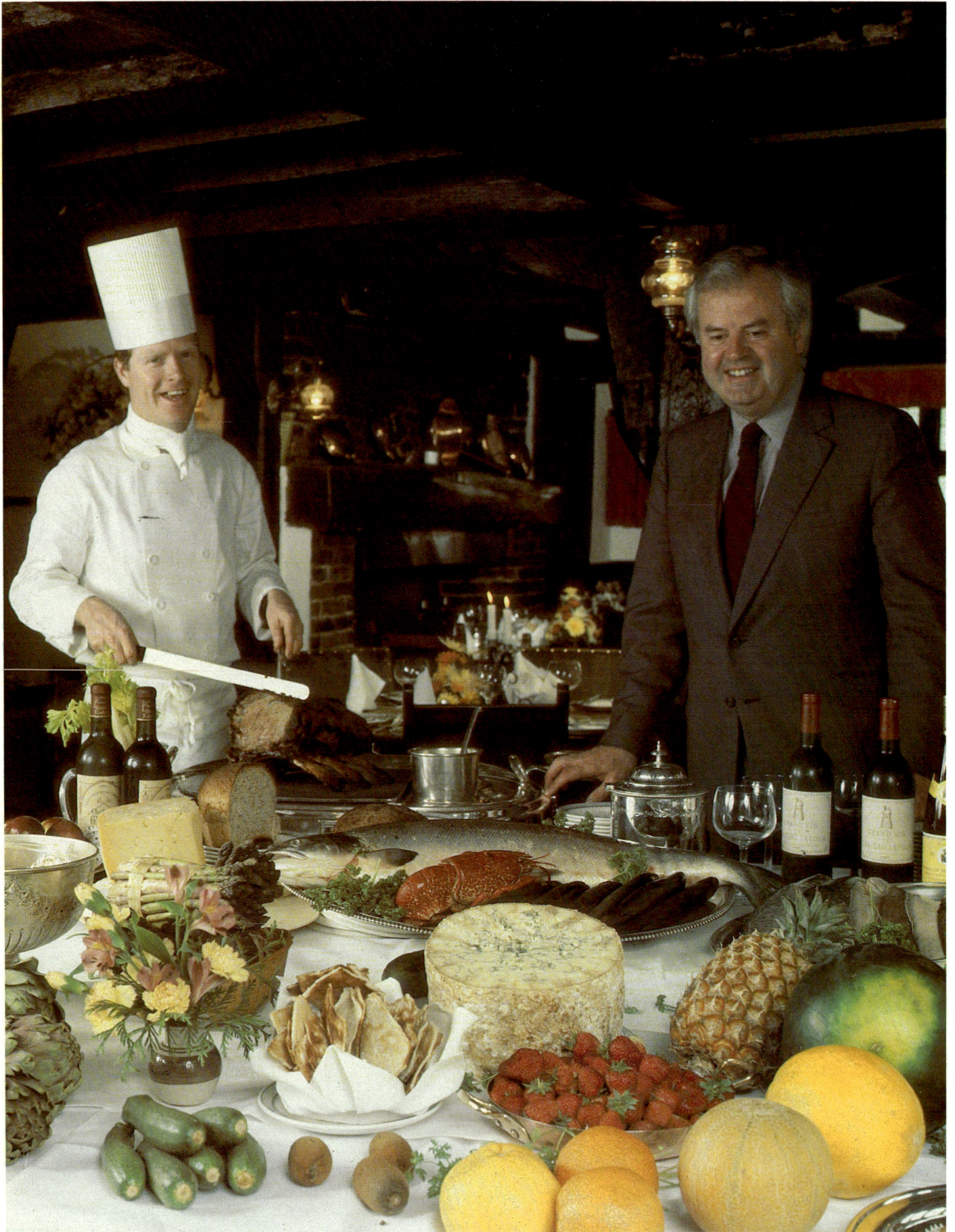

Le Talbooth Restaurant

Huîtres de Whitstable Chaudes

24 Whitstable oysters

2 medium shallots, chopped

    butter, to sauté

1 oz shredded sorrel

1 oz green peppercorns

2 oz white wine

2 oz double cream

    shredded and slightly cooked leeks, carrots, turnips, and mushrooms, enough to cover oysters

2 oz butter

Open the oysters and remove from shells. Put washed shells in a warm place and keep hot.

Toss shallots in melted butter in a wide, shallow pan for 2 minutes. Add oysters and poach them for 1 minute only over low heat. Remove oysters and ½ cooking juices. Put sorrel, peppercorns, and wine in the pan and reduce the rest of the cooking liquor. Add cream and reduce again until only ¼ cooking liquid remains (should yield enough sauce for 12 oysters). Pour remaining juice of cooked oysters into sauce, add shredded vegetables, and cook for a few minutes. While sauce is simmering, add butter, a few small pieces at a time.

Put oysters back in hollow, hot shells. Cover 12 oysters with vegetables and 12 oysters with sorrel sauce. Serve at once.

Serves: 4

Filet d' Agneau au Basilic et au Tomate

2 best ends of lamb

75 g butter

2 chopped shallots

2 medium-sized Dutch tomatoes, peeled and roughly chopped

1 bunch fresh basil

100 ml dry white wine

100 ml lamb stock made with the bone and strained

Cut lamb meat from bone and trim off all fat. Put ⅓ butter in a pan, add lamb fillets, and cook very slowly (lamb should be served pink or medium pink). Remove fillets and keep warm.

Strain off fat, add shallots and cook for a few minutes. Add tomatoes and basil. Add white wine and let reduce a little, then add strained lamb stock. Bring sauce to a boil, then finish it with the remaining butter cut into 4 pieces and added a little at a time.

Pour the sauce onto a serving dish, cut the fillets of lamb diagonally and lay them on top of the sauce, and serve.

Serves: 4

CHEF'S TIP

HERBS SUCH AS CHERVIL AND BASIL SHOULD BE FRESH AND CUT AT THE LAST MINUTE USING SCISSORS.

Wine: *Louis Tadot Reserve Couent des Jacobins, 1978*

Flan aux Pruneaux (Prune Meringue Pie)

180 g flour mixed with pinch of salt and sugar

150 g unsalted butter

2 egg yolks

1 tbsp milk

100 g sugar

900 g dried prunes, soaked then cooked in port and stoned

250 g double cream

4 egg yolks

6 egg whites

250 g sugar

4 tbsp hot apricot purée

Prepare short pastry with the first 5 ingredients, then line 2 flan rings with it. Bake at 375°F (190°C) for 10 minutes. Fill the bottom of the rings with the cooked prunes.

Mix the double cream and 4 yolks together to make an egg custard and cover prunes with the mixture. Bake at 350°F (175°C) until set.

Prepare meringue by beating egg whites with remaining sugar and cover the flan with meringue about ½ inch thick. Return to oven at 350°F (175°C) to set the meringue.

Coat the meringue with the hot apricot purée and serve.

Wine: *Tattinger Comtes de Champagne Rose, 1971*

Chez Moi

Chez Moi is a small genteel French restaurant situated in one of the elegant Victorian houses in the exclusive London district of Holland Park. Fourteen years ago, it was taken over by Colin Smith, who now runs the restaurant with confident efficiency, and Richard Walton, who is now a widely acclaimed chef. The two men worked together at another establishment before venturing out on their own.

The restaurant is small, yet somehow seats 50. The á la carte menu is by no means extensive, yet it capably offers a goodly number of choices in each category. Several special dishes are always present and are changed every two weeks.

There is a fairly broad wine list available with many French regions represented, and there are also two fine house wines from which to choose.

Chef Walton is a native of Rhodesia who originally was interested in hotel management, but after a year in the kitchens of London's Savoy and six months at Lausanne, he decided his first love was cooking. It is to his credit that the food served at Chez Moi is imaginatively and always deliciously prepared.

Chez Moi

**3 ADDISON AVENUE
HOLLAND PARK, LONDON, W11**

01-603-8267

**DINNER: MONDAY - SATURDAY
RESERVATIONS**

**PROPRIETORS:
COLIN SMITH, RICHARD WALTON
CHEF: RICHARD WALTON**

Oeufs à la Pomme d'Amour

6   very firm tomatoes

1   tbsp olive oil

1   finely chopped onion

2   large cloves garlic, finely chopped

1   tbsp white wine

    salt and freshly ground black pepper, to taste

6   egg yolks

    grated Parmesan cheese, as needed

6   croissants

    butter, as needed

Cut the tops off the tomatoes and scoop out the flesh. Turn tomatoes upside down on a plate to drain.

Heat olive oil, add onions and garlic, and sauté for about 1 minute. Add scooped out tomato flesh, white wine, salt, and pepper, and continue to cook until sauce is fairly thick. Cool.

Place a little sauce in the bottom of each hollowed out tomato. Gently slip an egg yolk into each tomato, add more sauce, top with grated cheese, and dot with butter. Put into a very hot oven at mark 7 (425°F/220°C) for 10 minutes (no longer or the tomatoes will collapse). Serve each on a croissant dotted with butter and gently warmed in the oven for 1–2 minutes.

Serves: 6

Crêpes de Palourdes Chez Moi

1½   oz butter, and as needed

1½   oz flour

5   fl oz clam juice

5   fl oz double cream

    juice of 1 lemon

1   oz gelatine

1   tbsp white wine

    pinch of salt

5   fl oz dry champagne

2 × 10 oz tins baby clams

4   oz white button mushrooms, sliced

4   oz white grapes, peeled and pitted

1   finely chopped shallot

6 × 6 in crepes

    grated Parmesan cheese, as needed

Melt butter over gentle heat and add flour to make a roux. Cook the roux about 1 minute. Add clam juice, cream, and lemon juice and continue to whisk over gentle heat. As mixture thickens, add gelatine dissolved in white wine and a pinch of salt and continue cooking for 5 minutes. Remove from heat, whisk in champagne, and allow to cool.

Drain clams from the 2 tins, discard bits of shell, and mix clams together. Add mushrooms, grapes, and shallot. Divide mixture among crepes, roll up, sprinkle with grated cheese, dot with butter, and place in a hot oven for only 5–6 minutes (no longer or champagne sauce will ooze out). Lift off with a spatula onto plates and serve.

Serves: 6

Glace de Canneberge (Fresh Cranberry Ice Cream)

½   pt rosé wine

½   pt red wine

6   oz sugar

1   cinnamon stick

8   cloves

3   thick slices lemon

3   thick slices orange

2   drops vanilla essence

1   good dash Angostura bitters

¼   pt glycerine

2 × 7 oz punnets fresh cranberries

½   pt double cream

3   egg yolks

Make a syrup by reducing the wines with sugar, cinnamon, cloves, lemon and orange slices, vanilla, Angostura bitters, and glycerine to ½ original quantity. (Temperature should be 240°F, 115°C, or "Jam" on a cooking thermometer.) Strain syrup, add cranberries, and bring back to a boil. Continue to cook until about ½ the cranberries have popped (about 1 minute). Allow to cool, then refrigerate.

Whisk double cream with yolks. When thick, slowly strain in syrup from the berries. Finally, add berries, whisking only for a short period. (Mixture must be thick when berries are added.) Freeze.

CHEF'S TIP

TO MAKE THE ICE CREAM A BIT LIGHTER, FOLD IN 3 STIFFLY BEATEN EGG WHITES LAST OF ALL.

Chez Nico

On 14 June 1973, proprietor/chef Nico Ladenis first opened the doors of **Chez Nico** on Lordship Lane in East Dulwich. According to him, "The only things going for us were low rent and total optimism." From the very first, he decided not to advertise, but instead, to rely on word of mouth. This was the longest road, but he believed it to be ultimately the best. To this day, even after a change of location (to the Queenstown Road address on 21 April 1980) and a break of five months, Chez Nico has retained customers who came in within a month of the first opening.

The restaurant's small interior is dressed in what Chef Ladenis calls '"feminine" decor. The colors are pretty pinks and apricot, the seating is snug but comfortable, and the lighting is subdued.

The menu, which features modern French cuisine, is small but well-balanced. Says the chef, "Our policy on food is to always get the finest quality regardless of cost. In fact, portion control and stock control are non-existent words for us."

Chez Nico is basically a husband and wife operation, with a small, but devoted staff that is most efficient. There is a short list of excellent French wines available.

Chez Nico

**129 QUEENSTOWN ROAD
LONDON, SW8**

01-720-6960

**DINNER: 7 TO 10:45 P.M.
TUESDAY — SATURDAY
RESERVATIONS**

PROPRIETOR/CHEF: NICO LADENIS

Les Filets de Sole au Beurre de Champagne

fish fumet made from water, wine, butter, shallots, chives, bay leaf, and peppercorns, as needed

4 × **10 oz Dover soles, skinned and filleted, cut in 4 pieces each**

2 c **fish stock** (*fond de poissons*)

2 c **Noilly Prat vermouth**

9 oz **butter**

1¼ pt **double cream**

1 c **water**

2 **chopped leeks**

½ **bottle good quality champagne**

salt, as needed

chives, to taste

Bring fish fumet to a boil. Roll the sole fillets and secure them with cocktail sticks. Drop fillets into fumet and remove from heat. Leave in a warm place.

Place fish stock, vermouth, 2 ounces butter, and 1 cup cream in one saucepan. Place water, 3 ounces butter, leeks, champagne, and a little salt in a second saucepan. Cook second pan's contents for 20 minutes, then place contents into first pan and reduce over fast heat until syrupy. Add remaining butter in pieces and remaining double cream, adjust seasoning, and cook very gently for 5 minutes to make a sauce. Add chives to sauce; stir together.

Pour sauce on each plate and arrange fillets, 4 on each plate, on top. Do not pour sauce on top of fillets.

Serves: 4

CHEF'S TIP

OVEN TEMPERATURES AND COOKING TIMES CAN BE MEANINGLESS. MUCH DEPENDS ON YOUR OWN OVEN, HOW OLD IT IS, IF IT'S GAS, ELECTRIC, ETC. KNOW YOUR OWN OVEN AND PLAN ACCORDINGLY.

Mousse Glacée au Caramel, Sauce Framboise

2 pt **double cream**

1¾ lb **sugar caramelised without water**

1 pt **water**

½ lb **sugar**

18 **eggs, separated**

Sauce Framboise (*recipe follows*)

To prepare mousse: bring the double cream to a simmer, then very slowly mix in the caramelised sugar (very difficult), mix together properly and leave to cool. Prepare sugar syrup by heating the water with sugar. Beat the egg yolks in a mixer on high speed for 3 minutes. Slowly add hot syrup until yolks have risen and are hard. Mix this with the cream and caramel mixture. Whip the egg whites, blend into the main mixture slowly, then pour into 50 × 3 inch ramekins. Freeze for 12 hours. Serve with Sauce Framboise.

Serves: 50

Sauce Framboise

¼ lb **sugar**

½ pt **water**

1 lb **puréed raspberries**

lemon juice, to taste

To prepare sauce framboise: mix sugar and water together to make a syrup. Strain the puréed raspberries to obtain maximum juice. Mix the syrup and raspberries together and add lemon juice to taste. Serve with mousse glacée au caramel.

Dorchester Hotel, The Grill Room

The Grill Room at the **Dorchester Hotel**, which opened in 1931, is an elegant comfortable restaurant with period Spanish-style decor and spacious positioning of the tables. The room has recently been made smaller and the kitchen modernised, so it gives Chef Anton Mosimann full scope to put into practice many of his own ideas for the international cuisine he considers suitable for the present day.

Anton Mosimann was born in Solothurn, Switzerland, and knew at the age of six that he wanted to be a chef. He became an apprentice at the Hotel Baeren in Twann at age 15 and was considered its best student by the time he turned 17. Later, he travelled the world, working in many hotels at all levels and, thus, gaining all his experience. He was the youngest chef ever to gain the "Chef de Cuisine Diplome," the highest culinary award in Switzerland.

Chef Anton was working at the Palace Hotel, Gstaad, as commis patissier ("the humblest role of the pastry kitchen, just to gain further experience in patisserie") when he was asked to come to the Dorchester as Maître Chef des Cuisines.

Simplicity, precision, and perfection are the basis of his art. "Take the ingredients, cook them to perfection and present them with simplicity. The whole secret of successful cooking — more, the very essence of culinary perfection — is, or should be, simplicity."

The Dorchester

**PARK LANE
LONDON, W1**

01-629-8888

**OPEN EVERY DAY. BREAKFAST 7 TO 11 A.M.
LUNCH 12:30 TO 3 P.M.
DINNER 6 TO 11 P.M.**

**GENERAL MANAGER: UDO SCHLENTRICH
CHEF: ANTON MOSIMANN, M.C.G.B.**

Grill Room

Rendezvous de Fruits de Mer

60 g butter

30 g julienne of celery, carrot, and leek

60 g fresh salmon

60 g scallops

60 g lobster

60 g turbot

100 ml Noilly Prat vermouth

100 ml fish stock

400 ml double cream

10 g basil, julienne

seasoning, to taste

Place ⅓ butter into a hot pan and add julienne of vegetables. Cut fish into ½ inch cubes and add to pan. Swill with vermouth and cook for a few more seconds. Remove fish. Add stock to pan, reduce, then pour in double cream. Bring to a boil. Whisk in butter. (Make sure sauce is very thin.) Add julienne of basil, return fish to sauce, and heat but do not boil. Season to taste and serve.

Serves: 4

Entrecôte Sautée Dorchester

4 × 180 g entrecôte steaks

well crushed white and black peppercorns, as needed

salt, to taste

50 ml peanut oil

40 ml cognac

200 ml brown veal stock

200 ml double cream

40 g butter

freshly ground pepper, to taste

3 g green peppercorns

3 g pink peppercorns

Season the well-trimmed entrecôtes with white and black peppercorns and salt. Sauté them on both sides in hot oil. Remove entrecôtes and keep warm.

Skim the fat, flame the cooking juices with cognac, add veal stock, and reduce to ½ original volume. Add cream and reduce to required consistency. Finish with butter and season with salt and pepper. Add the green and pink peppercorns just before serving or sauce will be too spicy. Cover the entrecôtes with the sauce and serve.

Serves: 4

Bread and Butter Pudding

100 g butter

20 slices bread without crusts

100 g currants

5 egg yolks, whisked

2 eggs, whisked

200 g sugar

1200 ml milk

nutmeg, to taste

50 ml apricot glaze

Butter 2 oval pudding dishes and the bread. Cut the bread diagonally and place in layers with the currants in the dishes. Sieve the whisked eggs and mix with the sugar and milk. Pour mixture over the bread, sprinkle with grated nutmeg, and cook in a bain-marie in the oven until done. Brush the top with apricot glaze and glaze gently under a salamander.

Serves: 10

Wine: *English Adgestone or Lamberhurst Priory*

Eatons Restaurant

Eatons Restaurant was opened in December of 1975 with a very clear aim: to establish itself as the neighbourhood good value "local." The location on Elizabeth Street was chosen because of its famed village atmosphere and its proximity to the large residential areas of Belgravia and Chelsea.

The restaurant was originally smaller than it is today, which worked to its advantage initially in establishing an intimate atmosphere. The floor space was subsequently enlarged, so Eatons now seats 40. More than a third of the dishes appearing on the menu are changed every week to give the long-standing regular customers some variety. This formula seems to have worked well as many of their clientele have been "regulars" since the restaurant's opening.

The menu features Continental cuisine prepared and, in most cases, created by Chef Santosh Bakshi, who was trained at the Savoy and served as head chef at several establishments. At one such appointment, he worked with Shayne Pope for seven years, just prior to both of them opening Eatons. Their relationship continues to be most rewarding because Eatons has indeed become a successful "local."

The wine list at Eatons is small but comprehensive. It features only French and German wines. There are also two fine house wines available.

Eatons

**49 ELIZABETH STREET
BELGRAVIA, LONDON, SW1**

01-730-0074

**LUNCH: MONDAY - FRIDAY, 12 TO 2 P.M.
DINNER: MONDAY - FRIDAY, 7 TO 11:15 P.M.
RESERVATIONS**

**PROPRIETOR: SHAYNE POPE
CHEF: SANTOSH BAKSHI**

Fresh Herrings with Sauce

8 large fresh herring fillets, washed and scaled

1 Spanish onion, sliced

1 carrot, grated

salt and pepper, to taste

2 spoons vinegar

1 c water

2 apples

1 pickled cucumber

4 oz sour cream

paprika, to taste

chopped parsley, to garnish

Place the herring fillets flat on an ovenproof dish and cover with ½ sliced onion, grated carrot, salt, and pepper. Add vinegar and water. Bring to a boil and leave in a cool place for at least 12 hours. When thoroughly cool, place in refrigerator for another 12 hours to set, still in stock.

To prepare sauce: peel and grate apples and cucumber and squeeze out excess liquid. Add sour cream and salt and pepper to taste.

Remove herring from stock and put in serving dish. Cover with remaining onion and top with sauce. Sprinkle with a little paprika and chopped parsley and serve chilled.

Serves: 4

Pork Escalope with Red Cabbage and Raisins

2 lb red cabbage sliced thinly

2 apples, peeled and diced

½ onion, sliced

2 spoons sugar

1 oz sultanas

1 spoon vinegar

1 c red wine

4 lb loin of pork

salt, as needed

horseradish, to taste

bread crumbs, as needed

butter and vegetable oil, to fry

Put cabbage, apples, onion, sugar, and sultanas in a small saucepan and cook slowly for 1½ hours in the vinegar and red wine. Allow to cool for 12 hours.

Clean pork thoroughly of all fat, bones, and skin, then cut in 4 equal pieces. Slit every piece down the middle, but do not cut through. Open out and flatten into a thin envelope. Beat very thin. Sprinkle with a little salt and brush with a little horseradish. Cover inside of "envelope" with a generous amount of red cabbage mixture, then fold closed. Press down the edges to seal and cover outside with bread crumbs. Fry in a shallow pan with a mixture of butter and oil. Serve hot.

Serves: 4

Sherry Punch Bombe

12 eggs

14 oz sugar

5 oz cocoa powder

9 oz flour

3 measures sherry, and as needed

3 oz crushed dark chocolate

2 oz raisins

½ pt whipped double cream

icing sugar, to garnish

To prepare sponge mixture: beat eggs and sugar together until fluffy and increased about 4 times in volume. Add

cocoa powder and flour and mix gently with a wooden spoon. Turn out into a large nonstick cake tin and bake at gas mark 4 (350°F/175°C) for about 40 minutes or until cooked. Allow to cool.

Break sponge into a crumb-like texture in a bowl and add sherry, chocolate, raisins, and cream. Mix in thoroughly. Add more sherry if required to help mixture stick together. Turn out into a mould or pudding basin and press down well. Turn mould over and stand the "bombe" on a serving plate. Sprinkle a little icing sugar on top and serve cold.

Serves: 4–6

The English House

The English House, located in the heart of Chelsea, is an elegant townhouse that has been stylishly decorated by interior designer Michael Smith. Its rooms are accented in rich, warm fabrics and are most conducive to enjoying a quiet, intimate, and first-rate repast.

The goal of proprietor Malcolm Livingston, who opened The English House two years ago, is to emphasize personal service and good taste and to foster a renewed appreciation of classical English cuisine. The recipes prepared in his restaurant are almost all drawn from historical cookery books; the remainder are contemporary dishes created by Chef Martin Lam, who throughout his career has strived to promote the renaissance of English food. To that end, he tries to use mainly English ingredients, and only the finest that London's markets can provide. His Capon Stuffed with Saffron Rice, covered in saffron sauce, is one such Old English recipe. It is the house speciality and it is excellent. Also offered is a broad selection of English and French wines.

From the moment the restaurant opened, the response from customers, both English and foreign, was extremely favourable. Today, The English House is renowned for its accomplishments.

The English House

3 MILNER STREET
LONDON, SW3

01-584-3002

LUNCH: 12:30 TO 2 P.M.
DINNER: 7:30 TO 11:30 P.M.
MONDAY - SATURDAY
RESERVATIONS

PROPRIETOR: MALCOLM LIVINGSTON
CHEF: MARTIN LAM

Tomato, Orange, and Ginger Broth

4½ c chicken stock or tinned broth

½ c orange juice

   rind of 1 orange, julienne

2 tbsp drained stem ginger, julienne

1 tbsp tomato paste

4 tomatoes, peeled, seeded, julienne

¼ tsp ground ginger

   salt and pepper, to taste

chopped fresh mint leaves and orange slices, to garnish

In a large stainless steel on enamelled saucepan, combine the chicken stock or broth, orange juice, orange rind, ginger strips, and tomato paste. Bring to a boil and simmer for 5 minutes. Stir in the tomatoes, ground ginger, and salt and pepper to taste. Heat the soup over moderate heat for 5 minutes or until heated through. Ladle soup into heated bowls and garnish with mint leaves and orange slices.

Serves: 4–6

Leg of Lamb with Spinach and Apricot Stuffing

½ lb dried apricots

3 lb spinach

1 large onion, chopped

2 c fresh bread crumbs

½ c butter, cut in bits and softened

2 large eggs, lightly beaten

1 tbsp grated lemon rind

1 tbsp salt, and to taste

½ tsp ground mace

   pepper, to taste

1 × 6 lb leg of lamb, boned

   butter and vegetable oil, as needed

½ c brown stock or beef broth

To prepare stuffing: let apricots soak in enough cold water to cover for 4 hours, then drain and chop them. In a kettle of boiling salted water, blanch the spinach for 2 minutes, drain in a colander, and refresh under cold running water. Squeeze the spinach to remove as much water as possible, then chop coarsely. In a large bowl, combine spinach, onion, and apricots. In a food processor, grind the mixture coarsely in batches, then transfer to a bowl. Stir in bread crumbs, butter bits, eggs, lemon rind, salt, mace, and pepper.

Sew up the opening at the larger end of the lamb; leave the smaller end open. Sprinkle inside of lamb with salt and pepper, stuff it loosely with about 1½ cups stuffing, and transfer remaining stuffing to a buttered 1 quart baking dish. Sew up second opening of lamb with kitchen string; brush lamb with vegetable oil. Roast lamb in an oiled flameproof roasting pan in a preheated moderate oven (350°F/180°C) for 1¼ hours for medium-rare, or until meat thermometer registers 130°F (55°C). During the last 30 minutes of roasting, bake the stuffing in the baking dish covered with foil. Transfer lamb to a cutting board; keep warm and covered.

To prepare the sauce: skim fat from pan juices, add stock or broth, and deglaze pan over high heat. Season sauce with salt and pepper.

Cut lamb into ½ inch slices, arrange slices on a heated platter, and nap them with sauce. Serve lamb with the stuffing.

Serves: 6–8

Flummery

2½ c double cream

¼ c sugar

2 tbsp grated lemon rind

1 tbsp unflavoured gelatine

¼ c water

1 tbsp orange flower water

   strawberries or raspberries, to garnish

In a large stainless steel on enamelled saucepan, combine double cream, sugar, and lemon rind. Heat mixture to just below boiling. In a small bowl, sprinkle gelatine over water and let soften 10 minutes. Set bowl in a pan of hot water and stir until gelatine is dissolved. Add gelatine to cream mixture, add orange flower water, and strain mixture into 4 × 6 ounce wine glasses. Chill until set, garnish with fruit and serve.

Serves: 4

Le Français

In March 1967, two French gentlemen, Jean-Jacques Figeac and Bernard Caen (respectively chef and headwaiter at a well-established restaurant), left their employ to open their own French restaurant in Chelsea, an area of London that became fashionable in the Sixties. In establishing **Le Français,** their aim was to promote the cooking of the various regions of France on a weekly basis. That is to say, each week they would prepare a different menu representing one particular part of France served with the wine of that same region.

Mr. Figeac, who has been a chef for more than 30 years, and Mr. Caen, better known by the customers as "Mr. Bernard," have been most successful in the endeavor.

The room space of the restaurant had 45 seats at the beginning, but after being extended, it now offers at least 75 seats divided into two sections. Two years ago, the entire restaurant was again altered, and now it offers a full length bar counter with the two dining sections becoming a restaurant room and a bar lounge. Furnishings have all been imported from France.

The staff employed is exclusively French "upstairs and downstairs," and the ingredients used in the cooking are imported from France. Both of these facts are a great source of pride for the owners of Le Français and is reflected in the service they bestow on their customers.

Le Français

**259 FULHAM ROAD
LONDON, SW3**

01-352-4748

**LUNCH: 12 TO 2 P.M.
DINNER: 7 TO 11:15 P.M.
MONDAY - SATURDAY
RESERVATIONS**

**PROPRIETORS:
JEAN-JACQUES FIGEAC, BERNARD CAEN
CHEF: JEAN-JACQUES FIGEAC**

Stewed Lobster Provençal

2 × 800 g lobsters

oil, as needed

4 medium-sized onions

4 cloves garlic, well minced

10 g flour, to sprinkle

8 medium-sized tomatoes, peeled and chopped

4 wine glasses dry white wine

1 wine glass water

1 liqueur glass cognac

Cut the lobster in pieces, cook them in oil, and keep hot.

In a separate pan, sauté the onions and garlic until onions are clear. Add flour and tomatoes. Dilute the mixture with a mixture of wine and water and let reduce. (The sauce should be well thickened.) Add the pieces of lobster. Before serving, add cognac.

Serves: 4

Partridge with Cabbage "Limousine"

4 partridges

seasoning, to taste

2 or 3 white cabbages

4 × 30 g slices lean bacon

2 tbsp oil

4 medium-sized carrots, sliced

4 medium-sized onions, sliced

275 g sausage meat to make 8-10 meat balls

bouquet garni, as needed

broth, as needed

bacon or pork rind, as needed

Season the partridges and roast for 10 minutes to brown them. Keep warm.

In a separate pan, blanch the white cabbages for 20 minutes, then cool them, drain, and grind them coarsely, pulling back the leaves that are too large.

Put slices of lean bacon in a large stew pot with oil, carrots, and onions. Add part of the cabbage, meat balls, and bouquet garni. Lay a layer of cabbage in the pot, then put partridges on top. Cover with the rest of the cabbage. Dilute some broth, bring to a boil, rectify the seasoning, and cover with a large slice of bacon or a piece of pork rind. Cover the stew pot and cook on moderate heat for at least 2 hours, then serve.

Serves: 4

Crème Bretonne

1 pod vanilla

500 ml milk

500 g chocolate

60 g butter

50 g cream of rice

Put vanilla in the milk and heat milk to bubbling stage. Melt the chocolate in the bubbling milk. Keep warm.

Put the butter and cream of rice in an earthenware pot. Beat the mixture with a wooden spatula, in a warm place, until very smooth. Gently add the warm milk and chocolate mixture, stirring gently. Pass this mixture through a cheesecloth or muslin into another casserole. Place back on heat and cook for about 10 minutes. Refrigerate and serve cold.

Frederick's

Frederick's was originally a public house built in 1789 and called "The Gun." Upon its rebuilding in 1834, it was renamed "The Duke of Sussex" in honour of George III's sixth son, Prince Augustus Frederick (1773-1843), from whom Frederick's takes its present name.

Frederick's, as we know it today, is now 11 years old. Its proprietor is Louis Segal, who has been associated with the restaurant since its opening. Kitchen operations are supervised by Chef Jean-Louis Pollet, who enjoyed extensive experience in many hotel and restaurant kitchens before joining Frederick's five years ago.

Frederick's is a smart, pleasant restaurant that is surprisingly large. It has separate dining areas providing for various moods. The dining room is split-level and overlooks a white-walled conservatory that leads out into a garden room. The gardens are extensive and patio dining is offered in the summer.

The menu shows a varied range of starters (soups, duck terrine, taramasalata), with fish, poultry, and game represented in mainly French-style main courses. Carefully cooked vegetables and sweets from the trolley are all prepared to a high standard, and everything is attentively served.

FREDERICK'S

CAMDEN PASSAGE
ISLINGTON, LONDON, N1

01-359-2888

LUNCH: 12:30 TO 2:30 P.M.
DINNER: 7:30 TO 11:30 P.M.
MONDAY - SATURDAY
RESERVATIONS

PROPRIETOR: LOUIS SEGAL
CHEF: JEAN-LOUIS POLLET

Le Suprême de Turbot au Sabayon de Poireau

6 × 200 g skinned turbot fillets

    fresh lemon juice, as needed

    salt and milled pepper, to taste

150 g unsalted butter, and as needed to grease

100 g shallots, chopped

  6 large, tender leeks, sliced

300 g small white button mushrooms, sliced

  6 egg yolks

    pinch of nutmeg

  6 large iceberg lettuce leaves, blanched

  1 bottle dry white wine

    pinch of cayenne pepper

    sliced truffle, to garnish

Brush the fillets with lemon juice, season with salt and pepper, and reserve in refrigerator to firm.

To prepare *appareil* of shallots, leeks, and mushrooms: melt ⅓ butter in a flat sauté pan and, without colouring, gently fry ½ shallots, ½ leeks, then add mushrooms. Season. Cover with a lid and sweat about 10 minutes to soften them. Allow to cool.

Place appareil of shallots, leeks, and mushrooms in a large bowl, add 2 egg yolks and pinch of nutmeg, then mix well. On the middle of each lettuce leaf, place 2 full spoons of appareil and fold to form a small cushion about the size of each fillet. Melt another ⅓ butter in a small sauté pan and add lettuce packets. Keep on very low heat, cover with a lid, and keep turning from time to time.

Place turbot fillets in a buttered baking tray. Season, add wine, cover with greaseproof paper, and bake in a moderate oven about 15 minutes. Remove from tray and keep hot. Reserve cooking liquid.

To prepare leek purée: heat remaining butter, and soften the remaining leeks and shallots without browning, about 10 minutes. Purée mixture in a liquidiser and keep warm.

To prepare leek sabayon sauce: reduce cooking liquid from the fillets to the quantity of a teacup; pass through an étamine. Put remaining egg yolks in a large stainless steel bowl. Add part of the reduced cooking liquid, drop of lemon juice, salt, pepper, and pinch of cayenne pepper. Beat over low heat with a wire whisk until mixture is increased in volume and is foamy. Add gradually to the hot leek purée.

With a brush, slightly butter a silver serving dish. Arrange hot lettuce packets on the dish and on each place a portion of turbot fillet. With a spoon, nap each portion with leek sabayon. Glaze under the grill, garnish with truffle, and serve very hot.

Serves: 6

Wine: *Pouilly Fuissé*

Les Rognons de Veau en Laitue

  3 large milk-fed veal kidneys cut in 6 slices each, fat and skin removed

200 ml Mandarine Napoleon liqueur

    juice of 1 lemon

  1 large juicy orange

    milled pepper, to taste

  1 large onion, sliced

250 g unsalted butter

 18 large leaves iceberg lettuce, blanched but still crisp

  1 kg small white button mushrooms, chopped

    salt, to taste

250 ml fresh cream

  2 large young leeks, julienne, blanched

  2 large young carrots, julienne, blanched

    clarified butter, as needed

Slightly brush veal kidney slices with a mixture of liqueur, lemon juice, and orange juice. Season with pepper and firm in refrigerator.

Put onion in melted butter, then add mushrooms and lemon juice and season with salt and pepper. Cover duxelle with greaseproof paper and cook gently When duxelle is half-cooked, drain through a mousseline cloth and keep the mushroom juice. Reserve in refrigerator.

Add salt to kidneys then fry each slice in hot butter, keeping them fairly pink. Coat each slice with a soupspoon of duxelle. Wrap each slice in a lettuce leaf and keep warm.

Remove fat from pan in which kidneys were fried. Deglaze with mushroom juice. Add cream and reduce very gently. Season with salt and pepper. When sauce is reduced enough, check seasoning and add 140 millilitres Mandarine Napoleon and 60 grams butter, a piece at a time, whisking continuously until all butter is incorporated. Pass sauce through an étamine cloth onto the serving dish.

Warm the julienne of vegetables in boiling water. Arrange kidney slices on the serving dish with some julienne on top of each. Seconds before serving, lightly brush julienne and lettuce with clarified butter to give life to the colours.

Serves: 6

Wine: *Nuits St. Georges Faiveley*

Le Gamin

Le Gamin is the third of the Roux brothers restaurants located in the City. It was opened in 1971 and offers middle-priced, fast, friendly service of well-cooked and prepared French cuisine. The decor of the restaurant was carefully chosen to give it, as much as possible, a French air; chilled bottles of Kronenbourg or Stella d'Artois add to the Brasserie atmosphere. The striking floor tiles, marble-topped tables, and wicker chairs were all imported from France.

Le Gamin is open for lunch only. The menu and wine list are short to help keep the prices down, but the standard of cooking remains constantly high under the auspices of Chef Denis Lobry. Among his offerings are onion and watercress soups, avocado stuffed with seafood in a home-made sauce, moules cooked in white wine, and tomatoes and garlic as starters. The main courses are predominantly French provincial dishes: Boeuf Bourguignon, Choucroute Alsacienne, and Petit Sale aux Lentilles, to name just a few. Or you could choose the classic French Entrecôte Bearnaise with Pomme Frites. The best desserts are home-made pastries or sorbets, and the cheese board is one of usual high standards. The menu changes every six weeks.

The upstairs of the restaurant is run as a very good "fast food" snack bar offering excellent sandwiches and other cold food such as quiches, salads, and pâtés to take away.

Le Gamin

32 OLD BAILEY
LONDON, EC4

01-236-7931

LUNCH ONLY TO 3:30 P.M.
MONDAY - FRIDAY
RESERVATIONS

PROPRIETOR: ROUX RESTAURANTS
CHEF: DENIS LOBRY

Feuilleté d'Escargot Bourguignon

butter, to sauté

24 small onions

100 g mushrooms, sliced

50 g bacon, cut in small pieces

3 large shallots, chopped

1 clove garlic, chopped

24 snails

½ bottle Bourgogne red wine

salt and pepper, to taste

50 g butter

6 vol-au-vents (pastry shells)

Melt butter in a frying pan and cook onions in it until crisp. Add mushrooms and bacon to the onions and cook for a couple of minutes.

Place shallots and garlic in a separate frying pan and cook until half transparent. Add snails, deglaze with wine, and reduce slowly. Add the 50 grams butter, mix onion and mushroom mixture with snails, and season with salt and pepper.

Fill the *vol-au-vents* with the mixture and serve.

Serves: 4

Scampi Citi d'Antin

5 large tomatoes

3 shallots

150 g mushrooms

butter, to sauté

600 g scampi

pinch of mixed herbs

1 tsp Ricard

250 ml double cream

salt and pepper, to taste

Blanch the tomatoes then put them in cold water. Cut tomatoes in 2 and remove seeds. Chop shallots and mushrooms into small pieces. Melt the butter in a frying pan, add the scampi, and sauté.

Add the shallots, herbs, tomatoes, and mushrooms. Flame with Ricard. Add the double cream and bring to a boil. Remove immediately. Season with salt and pepper and serve in an ovenproof dish.

Serves: 4

Sorbet aux Pommes (Apple Sorbet)

500 ml water

500 g sugar

100 g glucose

200 g stewed apple

1 tsp Calvados

Put water, sugar, and glucose in a pan and boil for 5 minutes to make a syrup. Mix with a spatula and cool. Whisk the syrup, stewed apple, and Calvados together. Pour this mixture into a mixer and mix for 10 minutes until medium thick.

Serving suggestions: either pour the mixture into 4 scooped out apples or into a previously chilled crystal bowl.

Serves: 4

Le Gavroche

Le Gavroche, opened in 1967 and run by the Roux brothers, features outstanding French cuisine. It was at first situated in Chelsea, but has recently moved to Mayfair where it has been carefully decorated.

The restaurant is divided into three main areas: the bar and reception lounge, decorated in moss green with deep green sofas and brown chairs; the large dining room, situated on the lower-ground floor and tastefully decorated, predominantly in green with circular tables and bronze-coloured chairs; and the coffee area, adjoining the dining room, furnished with coffee tables and deep red sofas. The atmosphere and service in the large dining area are formal. There are fresh flowers, crystal glasses filled with Malvern water, and handsome cutlery on each perfectly damasked table.

The menu offers a choice of carefully selected classical French specialities prepared by the celebrated chef Albert Roux. Appetizers include Papillote de Saumon Fumé Claudine and the genuine foie gras frais made by the Roux brothers. The main courses, such as Rognons de Veau aux Trois Moutardes, pot au feu sauce Albert, and Côtes d'Agneau au Vinaigre d'Estragon, are served with crisp and perfectly prepared vegetables. Then comes the excellent cheese board, the sable framboise, or the soufflé à l'orange.

The extensive wine list includes an impressive number of estate-bottled Burgundies and clarets.

le Gavroche

43 UPPER BROOK STREET
LONDON, W1

01-499-1826

LUNCH TO 2 P.M.
DINNER TO 11 P.M.
MONDAY - FRIDAY
CLOSED BANK HOLIDAYS AND
24 - 30 DECEMBER
RESERVATIONS

PROPRIETOR: ROUX RESTAURANTS
CHEF: A.H. ROUX, M.C.G.B.

Caneton Gavroche

2 × 1¾ kg oven ready ducklings

400 g carrots with leaves

600 g turnips

300 g butter

    water, as needed

    salt, as needed

50 g sugar

6 shallots

1 dessertspoon white wine

    bouquet garni

    pepper, to taste

200 g chicken liver, chopped in large pieces

100 g foie gras, goose or duck, must be fresh

1 tsp thyme

2 tsp cognac

4 slices white sandwich bread

Roast ducklings, without fat, in an oven at 465°F (240°C) for 20 minutes. Remove and keep the fat and juices. Let duck sit 10 minutes. Remove legs and breast. Set aside. (Reserve legs for a second meal.)

Slice ⅔ carrots and turnips in oval shapes; reserve carrot leaves. Place sliced vegetables in separate deep frying pans, each containing 50 grams butter, a little water, pinch of salt, and ½ the sugar. Boil down liquid, remove vegetables, and set aside. Slice remaining carrots and turnips julienne with a shredder. Put another 50 grams but-

ter in a deep frying pan, add julienne carrots. When half-cooked, add turnips. Keep julienne separate.

Mince remaining bones and meat from ducks. Put in oven tray and place in oven for a few minutes, then add 4 shallots and carrot leaves and put all into a casserole. Deglaze baking tray with white wine, reduce by ½, mix with minced bones, etc. Add enough water to cover bones, add bouquet, and boil. Leave for 1 hour on low heat but use skimmer frequently over surface. After 1 hour, strain through muslin. Put juices in pan over medium heat, reduce to syrup consistency, mix in another 50 grams butter, salt, and pepper.

In a frying pan, on medium heat, add 4 soupspoons duck fat, remaining 2 shallots, duck livers, and chicken livers. Add foie gras in large pieces, thyme, salt, and pepper. Flambé with cognac. (Do all this very quickly to keep livers medium rare.) Put all into a sieve and grind with a pestle, place in a bowl, put in a bain-marie, and mix for 1 minute.

Cut bread into 4 duck shapes with a pastry cutter. Melt ½ remaining butter in a frying pan and fry bread on both sides.

Remove skin from breast. Cut 4 slices from breast and place on a plate, one on top of the other. Cover with greaseproof paper and return to oven at 375°F (190°C) for 5 minutes to reheat.

Remove the mixture from the bain-marie, add 2 tablespoons duck stock, and spread on each breast. Put breast on plate. Place oval-shaped vegetables, julienne vegetables, and duckling-shaped bread around breast on each plate. Pour ⅓ duckling stock on bottom of plate. Serve remaining stock in a sauce boat.

Serves: 6

Roule Marquis (Raspberry Cake Roll)

3 egg yolks

175 g icing sugar

4 egg whites

50 g cocoa powder

15 g potato flour

1 tsp butter

    pinch of flour

300 ml fresh cream

250 ml thick sauce of red fruits or Melba sauce

2 tbsp raspberry eau de vie, optional

250 g raspberries

120 g coffee beans in alcohol

Mix yolks with 80 grams sugar until fairly stiff. Beat whites. When hard, add 45 grams sugar and mix well for

1 minute. Mix yolks and about ⅓ whites and, when smooth, carefully add remaining ⅔. When smooth, sift in cocoa and potato flour and mix well. Spread on greaseproof paper coated with butter and flour in a rectangular shape of 12 by 20 centimetres about ¾ centimetre thick. Bake in 375°F (190°C) oven for 8−10 minutes. Put upside down on cooling tray, remove paper, and let cool 5−10 minutes.

Beat cream with remaining sugar. Mix fruit sauce with raspberry eau de vie and coat cooled cake mixture with ⅓ this mixture. Spread beaten cream on cake, then raspberries, then coffee beans. Roll cake into shape of a roll. Refrigerate 2−3 hours before serving. (Will keep refrigerated 24 hours.)

To serve: slice roll. Serve on cold plates with remaining red fruit sauce in a sauce boat.

Serves: 6

The Gay Hussar

The Gay Hussar opened on Greek Street in 1928. In 1953, it was purchased by its current owner, Victor Sassie. Mr. Sassie has been in the restaurant business for more than 50 years. After serving his apprenticeship in London in 1930, he spent eight years picking up practical experience by working in restaurants in Hungary, Germany, and the United States. This was followed by seven years in the Army. In 1948, he opened his first Hungarian restaurant, Budapest. The Gay Hussar, as previously mentioned, was taken over in 1953, and his third restaurant, La Princess, opened in 1961. The Gay Hussar is the only one that survived, and it has been very successful.

This small restaurant provides authentic Hungarian atmosphere in addition to authentic Hungarian cuisine. The extensive menu features a vast array of delicious traditional Hungarian dishes that are all prepared by Chef Martin Howe, who, after receiving an extensive formal and practical education, joined The Gay Hussar in 1970 and became its head chef in 1977. His speciality is Smoked Duck with Scholet. It is a traditional winter dish in Budapest that is similar to cassoulet. It is one among many excellent preparations. The dessert list should not be overlooked either; it features many unusual and delicious treats.

The wine list at The Gay Hussar offers an extensive choice of modestly priced clarets and a good selection of Tokays. There is also a choice of house wines.

The Gay Hussar

**2 GREEK STREET
SOHO, LONDON, W1V**

01-437-0973

**LUNCH: 12:30 TO 2:30 P.M.
DINNER: 5:30 TO 11:30 P.M.
MONDAY - SATURDAY
CLOSED BANK HOLIDAYS
RESERVATIONS**

**PROPRIETOR: VICTOR SASSIE
CHEF: MARTIN HOWE**

Bogracs Gulyas (Original Cauldron Goulash)

4 oz lard

½ lb onions, chopped finely

1½ lb shin of beef, cut in small cubes

1 oz paprika

1 clove garlic

1 good pinch caraway seeds

½ fresh green chili

¼ tsp white pepper

1 tsp salt

2 pt stock

2 lb diced potatoes

4 ripe tomatoes, peeled and seeded

2 green peppers, sliced lengthways

4 oz flour

1 egg

Melt lard in a saucepan. Add onions and fry until translucent. Add meat, paprika, garlic, carraway seeds, chili, white pepper, and salt. Add a little stock, stir, and allow to simmer. Add more stock as liquid evaporates. When meat is half-cooked (about 40 minutes) add potatoes, tomatoes, and green peppers. Add rest of stock (should cover all ingredients) and cook another 10 minutes until almost tender.

Mix flour and egg into a stiff paste. With fingers, tear paste into tiny irregular shapes or snippets (*csipetke*) and drop into pan of boiling salted water and cook 2–3 minutes. Strain and add pellets of dough to the goulash and cook another 5–10 minutes. Serve.

Serves: 4

Somloi Delice

3 egg yolks

2 oz sugar

¼ tsp vanilla essence

1 tsp grated lemon rind

3 egg whites

2 oz plain flour

3 egg yolks

2 oz sugar

¼ tsp vanilla essence

1 tsp grated lemon rind

1 oz plain flour

1 oz cocoa powder

1 pt milk

2 large egg yolks

2 oz sugar

1 oz flour

½ tsp vanilla essence

¼ pt double cream

2 stiffly beaten egg whites

3 oz walnuts

3 oz sultanas

3 tbsp water

3 tbsp rum

¼ pt rum

1 tbsp apricot jam

½ oz sugar

¼ oz cocoa powder

¼ pt double cream

2 oz melted chocolate

Prepare vanilla sponge with first 6 ingredients. Beat yolks and sugar vigorously in a warm bowl, add vanilla and rind. Beat whites until stiff. Fold whites and yolks together. Shake in flour through a sifter. Fold gently together and pour into a slightly greased baking tin. Bake 7–8 minutes in centre of a preheated oven at gas mark 6 (400°F/200°C) with door slightly ajar. Test by slightly pressing centre; if it springs back, sponge is cooked.

Prepare chocolate sponge with next 6 ingredients. Method is same as for vanilla sponge but add cocoa powder with flour.

Prepare vanilla pastry cream with next 7 ingredients. Heat milk. Beat yolks, sugar, flour, and vanilla together. Slowly pour hot milk onto beaten mixture and continue beating to avoid lumps. Pour back into saucepan; reheat, but don't boil. Allow to cool a little, then beat in cream. Fold in beaten egg whites.

Prepare walnut base with next 4 ingredients. Chop walnuts and sultanas finely. Place in small dish and pour on water and rum. Let steep.

To assemble dish: place vanilla sponge in any straight-sided dish. Sprinkle with ½ rum. Spread walnut base on sponge. Lay chocolate sponge on top and sprinkle with remaining rum. Heat jam and spread on top of chocolate sponge. Spread with cooled vanilla pastry cream. Mix sugar and cocoa together and sprinkle on vanilla cream. Let stand several hours.

To serve: spoon onto plate, whip double cream and pipe around, and trickle melted chocolate on top.

Serves: 4

Hotel Inter-Continental Le Souffle Restaurant

Le Souffle Restaurant, located in London's **Hotel Inter-Continental**, is a luxurious art deco dining establishment that opened in July of 1975. It offers exquisite, unusual soufflés and French speciality dishes which are highly complemented by pastries and other desserts of distinction. Emphasis is placed on soufflés, as the name of the restaurant implies, and most are the creation of Executive Chef Peter Kromberg, whose experience includes an apprenticeship in Germany followed by many years working for hotels and restaurants in Switzerland, Greece, Thailand, and other countries before he joined the Hotel Inter-Continental in 1971.

The restaurant is warm and relaxing and very classy. Skillful service is provided by a team of young waiters, all most competent and helpful. They are supervised by a manager, A.C. Belment, who previously worked for several hotel organisations before coming to Le Souffle two years ago.

Week night diners can choose from an extensive à la carte menu. On Saturday evenings, the restaurant puts on a dinner dance with live music and a special menu. Sunday brunch is a family affair, and it too offers live music.

An extensive wine list featuring more than 200 choices is available at your table, and there is also a luxurious cocktail bar on the premises.

Gâteau de Foie Blond a l'Oseille et Langoustines

150 g fat chicken liver

150 g fresh goose liver

50 g sieved bone marrow

50 ml double cream

350 ml boiled and recooled milk

4 whole eggs

salt, pepper, and nutmeg, to taste

20 g fresh sorrel

60 g butter

20 ml Noilly Prat vermouth

10 ml tarragon vinegar

100 ml strong chicken stock

200 ml double cream

1 tbsp glacé américaine sauce

20 cooked langoustine tails, shelled

fresh tarragon leaves, to garnish

To prepare the gâteau: liquidise the first 6 ingredients, season with salt, pepper, and nutmeg, and fill into buttered ramekin dishes. Poach in a bain-marie in the oven, covered with aluminum foil, for about 35 minutes at 300°F (150°C).

To prepare the sauce: sauté the sorrel in ½ butter, add vermouth and vinegar and let reduce to ½. Add chicken stock and gradually add cream. Reduce to sauce consistency, add glacé américaine, finish with butter, and season.

Place the sauce on plates, turn out the liver gâteau, and place into the middle of each plate. Garnish with warm langoustine tails and 2–3 fresh tarragon leaves.

Serves: 6–7

Wine: *a light Sauterne or a vintage Gewürztraminer*

Soufflé de Homard (Lobster Soufflé)

9 egg yolks

10 tbsp dry vermouth

salt and pepper, to taste

6 soupspoons whipped cream

2 × 600 g cooked lobsters

20 ml glacé américaine sauce, reduced

cayenne pepper, to taste

drop of lemon juice

12 egg whites

80 g butter

20 g flour

Make a sabayon by whipping egg yolks and vermouth over boiling water until it thickens. Season with salt and pepper; add cream. Slice lobster tails and claws. Keep 12 nice slices aside and make a ragout (*salpicon*) with the rest mixed with the glacé américaine. Season with salt, pepper, cayenne pepper, and a drop of lemon juice. Whip whites with a pinch of salt but not too stiffly. Butter and flour 6 soufflé dishes.

Mix the lobster ragout with the sabayon and gradually add the egg whites. Place mixture into dishes and bake for 5 minutes in the oven at 350°F (180°C). Remove from oven and place 2 slices of remaining lobster on top of each soufflé. Bake again for 8 minutes. Serve immediately.

Serves: 6

Fraises au Poivre Vert

80 g caster sugar

60 g butter

300 g fresh small strawberries

milled pepper, as needed

20 ml cherry spirit

20 ml Grand Marnier

10 g green peppercorns, crushed

50 g Melba sauce

juice of 1 lemon

8 scoops vanilla ice cream

50 ml whipped double cream

Caramelise the sugar in a fairly large non-stick pan, add butter and stir until foamy. Add strawberries, 3–4 twists of peppermill, and then flambé with cherry spirit first and then with Grand Marnier. Cook for about 2 minutes over rapid heat, add crushed green peppercorns, Melba sauce, and lemon juice.

Pour some strawberries and sauce on a large plate, place ice cream in the middle, coat with remaining sauce, twist peppermill over it again, and serve whipped cream on the side.

Serves: 4

Wine: *Vintage Champagne Brut*

Interlude de Tabaillau

Interlude de Tabaillau was opened in 1979 by Jean-Louis Taillebaud, who came to England nine years ago to work for the Roux brothers at Le Gavroche; for six years he was their head chef. He is an advocate of classical French cuisine, and the choice of dishes at this establishment range from a simple fish and leek tart to perfectly cooked fricassee de canard au Beaujolais.

The decor of this restaurant is "thirties-as-seen-by-the-eighties." The walls are stippled salmon pink with a blue line as a decorative feature. The low ceiling is covered in rough-textured tiles, and the windows are obscured with bamboo blinds.

The menu offers specialities of the house or a choice from the daily menu. The first course specialty is Feuilleté d'Agneau Sauce Moelle or, from the daily menu, a choice of consommé with port, Venison Mousse with tomato, or Ragout de St. Jacques et Huître au Sauternes. The main course specialties are Barbue Karpinski (brill),and Supreme de Caneton Juliette. The daily menu has a choice of a further half-dozen dishes.

The cheese board is excellent, offering a choice of about 25 different cheeses, all in peak condition. The desserts are mouthwatering, which makes the choice difficult. The service is smooth, professional, and friendly.

Interlude de TABAILLAU

**7-8 BOW STREET
LONDON, WC2**

01-379-6473

**LUNCH: MONDAY - FRIDAY, 12:30 TO 2 P.M.
DINNER: MONDAY - SATURDAY, 7 TO 11 P.M.
RESERVATIONS**

**PROPRIETOR/CHEF:
JEAN-LOUIS TAILLEBAUD**

Feuilleté d'Agneau Sauce Moelle

250 g lamb meat, middle neck

50 g fresh goose liver

2 egg yolks

salt, pepper, port, and Madeira wine, to taste

300 g double cream

puff pastry dough, as needed

egg yolks, as needed

To prepare filling: pass lamb meat, goose liver, 2 egg yolks, and seasoning through a cutter and *tamis* (strainer). Add double cream, make it quite firm, check seasoning, and refrigerate about 1 hour.

Roll out the dough to a thickness of 2 millimetres, then cut 12 rounds of 10 centimetres in diameter. Lay down 6 rounds and coat with some yolk. Put 2 soupspoons of filling in the middle of each round then cover each with a second piece of pastry. Make sure sides stick together well. Cover tops with egg yolk and decorate with scraps of dough. Cook in the oven at gas mark 7 (425°F/220°C) for 10–15 minutes.

Serves: 6

Wine: *Côtes du Ventoux Rouge*

Barbue Karpinski (Brill Karpinski)

6 × 150 g fillets of brill

butter, as needed

2 sliced shallots

100 g chopped chives

4 chopped tomatoes

150 ml Noilly Prat vermouth

500 ml fish stock

250 g cream

50 g butter

2 medium-sized carrots

200 g French beans

200 g turnips

18 small tartlets

Cook the fillets gently in butter without colouring them. Cook the shallots, chives, and tomatoes together with vermouth and fish stock until it is reduced ⅓. Add some cream and let it boil for about 5 minutes. Finish sauce with butter, pass it through a strainer, and add tomatoes and chives.

Make 3 kinds of purées with carrots, beans, and turnips. Put a fillet in the centre of each plate, cover with sauce, and put 3 tartlets filled with the different purées around each fillet.

Serves: 6

Lemon Tart

500 g flour

400 g caster sugar

200 g butter

pinch of salt

2 egg yolks

7 eggs

225 g caster sugar

juice and skin of 3 lemons

1750 ml whipped double cream

Form 2 pastry cases with the first 5 ingredients. Bake until slightly brown.

To prepare the lemon filling: mix the 7 eggs, sugar, lemon juice, and grated lemon skin together. Gently add the whipped cream.

Fill the pastry cases with the lemon filling and cook in the oven at gas mark 3 (340°F/170°C) for 20 minutes.

Serves: 8

CHEF'S TIP

IMAGINE THAT EVERYTHING YOU COOK AND SERVE IS GOING TO BE SERVED TO YOU IN A RESTAURANT.

Ivy Restaurant

In 1911, Abel Giandellini, an acknowledged master of the culinary art, opened the small **Ivy Restaurant** in the heart of London's theatreland. His aim was to provide fine French cuisine for cultured palates.

His clientele were, from the first, selective and distinguished. Although predominantly theatrical, they also included men and women high in the counsels of the nation, artists, and men of letters.

Among the famous figures of the Twenties, the Ivy was a synonym for quality; it became an exclusive meeting place. The theatrical patronage remained predominant, and at the Ivy's tables Noël Coward and Marie Tempest could be seen regularly. They were joined by scores of other theatre and screen personalities, men and women celebrated in the arts and letters, kings and queens of sport, and newspaper editors.

At the time of the outbreak of the Second World War, the Ivy had acquired something of the position of an institution in the artistic and social life of London. Its fame had spread to the United States and Europe, and today, distinguished men and women from abroad seldom fail to include visits to the Ivy to sample the offerings of Chef Guissepe Pedri who came to England from the Tyrol 30 years ago and has been maître chef at the Ivy for the past eight years.

Ivy Restaurant

1-5 WEST STREET
LONDON, WC2

01-836-4751

LUNCH: MONDAY - FRIDAY,
12 TO 3 P.M.
DINNER: MONDAY - SATURDAY,
6 P.M. TO 12:30 A.M.
RESERVATIONS

PROPRIETOR: THE LADY GRADE
CHEF: GUISSEPE PEDRI

Avocado Trianon

3 ripe avocados

3 oz chopped smoked salmon

3 oz peeled prawns

3 tbsp fresh mayonnaise

dash of Worcestershire sauce

juice of ½ lemon

seasoning, to taste

mayonnaise, as needed to coat

3 chopped hard-boiled eggs, to garnish

chopped parsley, to garnish

12-15 prawns, to garnish

6 lettuce leaves

Cut avocados in half and remove stone. Spoon out flesh, being careful not to damage the shells. Put flesh into a basin and mash with a fork. Add smoked salmon, prawns, mayonnaise, Worcestershire sauce, lemon juice, salt, and pepper and mix thoroughly. Return mixture to shells and smooth. Spread a thin layer of mayonnaise over the top. Decorate each half with a chopped hard-boiled egg, parsley, and 2–3 prawns. Serve each stuffed avocado half on a lettuce leaf.   Serves: 6

Escalope de Veau Delysia

6 scallops of veal, sufficient for 6 portions

bread crumbs, to dust

fat, to sauté

18 cooked asparagus tips

sliced cooked mushrooms, as needed

6 spoonfuls tomato concasse (roughly chopped tomato)

jus lie (thin meat sauce), as needed

6 knobs nut butter, heated

Dust veal with bread crumbs and fry quickly in hot fat until crisp and light golden brown on both sides. Arrange on a large dish. Place 3 asparagus tips diagonally across each scallop. To one side, place a few sliced cooked mushrooms. On the other side, put a spoonful of tomato concasse. Put under a grill for 2 minutes to warm garnish. Pour a little *jus lie* over the vegetables and put a knob of hot nut butter on the veal.

Serves: 6

Trifle

1 × 4 egg sponge sandwich, prepared

2 tbsp strawberry jam

apples, pears, oranges, peaches, and cherries, cut up as needed for fruit salad

½ glass sherry

1½ pt strawberry jelly

1 pt milk

1 oz custard powder

1 oz sugar

Spread strawberry jam over sponge sandwich and cut into strips. Line the bottom of a serving dish with ½ sponge. Peel and core the fruit and cut into small cubes. Place in a bowl together with their own juices. Put a layer of the fruit salad on top of the sponge, cover with the remaining sponge, and sprinkle generously with sherry. Pour strawberry jelly over and allow to set.

To prepare custard: make a roux by mixing a little cold milk, custard powder, and sugar in a jug. Heat the remaining milk until nearly boiling, then pour heated milk into the roux and stir vigorously. Return to pan and bring to a boil again, stirring constantly. Remove from heat.

Pour 1 pint custard over the sponge and allow to set. Chill in the refrigerator.

Serving suggestion: decorate with sweetened whipped cream, toasted nuts, and glacé cherries and angelica.

Kundan Restaurant

Kundan Restaurant specialises in selected Indian and Pakistani dishes prepared in the traditional manner favourite to both kings and Nawabs.

The chef at Kundan is Aziz Khan. Mr. Khan learned his cooking in Pakistan where he worked in restaurants for eight years. He then came to England where he cooked in a number of top Eastern restaurants before joining the Kundan when it opened four-and-a-half years ago.

Chef Khan's use of the many spices is subtle and sophisticated to insure that no menu selection will be unkind to the stomach. Managing director Nayab Abbasi adds, "The spices are not only used for developing taste and flavour in our food, but also as blood purifiers and for producing heat in the body, for cleaning and burning out cold, etc. For instance, the use of turmeric, ginger, clove, and so on maintain health or correct body disfunctions."

The restaurant is very spacious and comfortable and is elegantly decorated in smart shades of brown and gold. Indian/Pakistani food is traditionally eaten with the fingers, but to accommodate Western needs, each table is set with silver service. To round out the atmosphere, there are candles and soft background music. A modest but excellent wine list is available, as is a cocktail lounge.

kundan
restaurant

**3 HORSEFERRY ROAD
LONDON, SW1**

01-834-3434

**LUNCH: 12 TO 3 P.M.
DINNER: 7 P.M. TO 12 A.M.
EVERY DAY
RESERVATIONS**

**PROPRIETOR: NAYAB ABBASI
CHEF: AZIZ KHAN**

Tikka Kabab Lamb

1 dessertspoon Worcestershire sauce

juice of ¼ lemon

juice of ½ in fresh root ginger

juice of 1 garlic clove

½ tsp dry mustard

½ tsp white pepper

1 tsp paprika

salt, to taste

1 lb meat from a marcel of lamb (leg of lamb), cut into 1 in cubes

1 large onion

4 firm tomatoes

2 oz clarified butter

Combine liquid ingredients with the mustard, spices, and salt in a bowl, add meat, and allow to marinate for at least 8 hours (or, preferably, overnight). Just before cooking, cut onion and tomatoes into bite-size pieces and arrange on skewers by alternating a cube of lamb with a piece of onion, cube of lamb with piece of tomato, etc. Cook under a hot grill for approximately 8 minutes (2 minutes per side) and baste with a little butter during cooking.

Serves: 3

Murgh Korma with Polao Arasta

oil, to fry

6 cloves

2 cinnamon sticks

2 cardamoms

2 large onions, sliced

2 cloves garlic, chopped finely

1 very small piece fresh root ginger, chopped finely

1 medium-sized chicken, skinned and cut in 12 pieces

1 × 4-5 oz carton natural yogurt

pinch of saffron

1 lb tomatoes, chopped

2 red chilis, cut in ¼ in pieces

salt, to taste

pinch of *jaifal* (mace) and *javatri* (nutmeg)

Polao Arasta *(recipe follows)*

Heat a little oil in a saucepan and fry cloves, cinnamon, and cardamoms. Add onions and fry until golden brown. Add garlic and ginger and fry another 5 minutes. Add chicken and fry until brown.

Put yogurt in a bowl, add saffron and beat until smooth. Add to chicken mixture along with tomatoes, chilis, and salt. Cover saucepan tightly and cook over low heat until chicken is tender. Uncover and cook another 5–10 minutes. Garnish with a little powder of *jaifal* and *javatri*.

Serving suggestion: serve with Polao Arasta.

Serves: 3

Polao Arasta

1 large onion

8 oz butter

2 lb bones with meat

1 in fresh root ginger

4 cloves garlic

2 tsp coriander seeds

2 tsp aniseed

4 cloves

3 large cardamoms

6 whole black peppercorns

2 × 1 in sticks cinnamon

1½ tsp salt

3 pt water

1 lb Basmati rice

fried onion rings, to garnish

Brown the onion in butter until golden. Add meat bones and fry for 5 minutes, then add all remaining ingredients except rice and onion ring garnish. Bring the water to a boil and simmer gently until ¼ of the liquid has evaporated. Strain the stock.

Wash the rice thoroughly in running water until the water runs clear. Soak the rice in water for 35–40 minutes, then drain.

Reheat the strained stock, add the rice, cover, and simmer until the rice is cooked and the stock has evaporated. Serve decorated with golden fried onions.

Lacy's

Lacy's was the result of a journalist interviewing a chef for *Gourmet* magazine. Margaret Costa, then food and wine editor of *The Sunday Times Magazine*, deeply impressed by Bill Lacy's haute cuisine when he was head chef of the Empress Restaurant in Berkeley Street, invited him to be photographed with other London gastronomic luminaries for the magazine in a feature about London's restaurants, their chefs and their critics. They joined forces some two years later and Lacy's restaurant was born.

With Bill Lacy's formidable culinary expertise and Margaret's lifelong passion for good food and wine, the restaurant took off with some élan, after opening quietly with no trumpets sounding. Her *Gourmet* articles brought many American visitors to the restaurant — Londoners were already aware of Bill Lacy's reputation. He cooked, she welcomed the guests and bought the wines. They are not quite so compartmentalised today, but these are still their basic roles.

It is a little difficult to describe the cuisine. Officially French, it is now a personal kind of cooking with some very idiosyncratic recipes which have become so popular that chef Lacy can now allow his imagination free rein. There is always a personal welcome at Lacy's and the service is friendly, too, but unobtrusive.

LACY'S

**26-28 WHITFIELD STREET
LONDON, W1**

01-636-2323

LUNCH: MONDAY - FRIDAY,
12:30 TO 2:30 P.M.
DINNER: MONDAY - SATURDAY,
7:30 TO 11 P.M.

PROPRIETORS:
WILLIAM AND MARGARET LACY
CHEF: WILLIAM LACY

Scallop and Artichoke Soup

1½ Spanish onions, chopped

2 oz butter

1½ lb Jerusalem artichokes, peeled and sliced

2 medium-sized potatoes, peeled and chopped

1¾ pt well-seasoned chicken stock

salt and freshly ground pepper, to taste

4 large or 6 small scallops

½ pt milk

2 egg yolks

6 tbsp cream

chopped parsley, to garnish

Cook the onions in butter until soft and transparent. Add artichokes and potatoes and stir until all are buttery. Cook gently for about 15 minutes. Add chicken stock, cover, and simmer about 20 minutes longer, then put through a liquidiser, a sieve, or a vegetable mill. Return to pan and season well with salt and pepper.

Lightly poach the scallops in milk, then cut the white flesh into dice. Reserve the coral. Add the scallops and milk to the soup and heat through. Beat the egg yolks with cream and stir into soup. Let soup thicken without boiling.

Just before serving, add the uncooked scallop corals, cut into 2 or 3 pieces, and scatter lavishly with chopped parsley.

Serving suggestion: serve with crisp oatcakes.

Serves: 4

Best End of Lamb with Apricot Sauce

6 - 8 oz dried apricots

medium dry white wine, as needed

2 best ends of lamb (6 - 8 cutlets according to size), trimmed

salt and pepper, to taste

chicken stock, as needed

sugar, if needed

zest and juice of 1 orange

2 fl oz brandy or apricot brandy

1 pt espagnole sauce, heated

Soak the apricots overnight in white wine.

Preheat oven to 450°F (230°C), put in the lamb seasoned with salt and pepper, and reduce heat to 350°F (180°C). Roast to the desired degree.

Simmer the soaked apricots in the wine and a roughly equal quantity of good chicken stock until soft. Sieve or put through a blender. Add sugar if the purée does not taste distinctly sweet and reduce it if the flavour is not sufficiently concentrated. (If you are using apricot brandy, sugar may not be needed.) Stir in the orange rind and juice and brandy. Stir the apricot mixture into the hot espagnol sauce, a little at a time, tasting until sauce has a definite and unmistakeable apricot flavour. (The amount needed varies on the quality of the dried fruit.) Serve with the roast lamb.

Serving suggestion: serve with spiced arborio rice.

Serves: 6 − 8

CHEF'S TIP

WHEN COOKING A SAUCE, RECTIFY OVER-THICKENING BY SLOWLY BEATING IN ONE OR TWO EGG YOLKS AND A TABLESPOON OF HOT WATER.

Everlasting Lemon Syllabub

1 lemon

brandy, as needed

3 oz caster sugar

½ pt double cream

¼ scant pt any sweet white wine

blanched strips of lemon rind, to decorate

Peel the lemon very thinly with a potato peeler. Squeeze out the juice and put into a bowl with the rind and enough brandy to make ⅛ pint. Leave overnight. Strain, then add sugar until totally dissolved. Whip the cream with a wire balloon whisk until it just holds its shape. Gradually add the brandy, lemon juice, and wine. (The cream should absorb it all and still stand up in soft peaks. Add only a very little at a time to insure success.) Pile the cream into little cups or glasses.

The syllabub will keep for several days in a cold larder or the refrigerator; it is best made the day before serving.

Sprinkle a few blanched strips of lemon rind in a little cluster on top before serving.

Langan's Brasserie

Langan's Brasserie is "an unholy alliance of a chef, an actor, and a drunk." It opened four and a half years ago and has become one of London's most talked about restaurants.

The partners are Peter Langan, a self-proclaimed "soak with spots of spasmodic genius," celebrated actor Michael Caine, and Richard Shepherd, one of England's best chefs. While Caine is acting and Langan drinking, Shepherd does most of the work and produces a good standard of cooking at a price that most still consider okay.

If there is a cafe society in London, it's here. The *frisson* of actors, journalists, and everyone-who-wants-to-be-someone is what this "happening" is about. And it is an artists' restaurant: Hockney, Francis Bacon, *et al.* seem to live here permanently. Hockney drew the menu, and many pictures crowd the restaurant's walls. What is wrong with many restaurants is that they take themselves too seriously and one ends up eating in a church; by comparison, this place is a rock opera.

The food is quite good. Shepherd's Artichaut Farci à la Nissarda; Soufflé aux Epinards, Sauce Anchois; Carré d'Agneau; and Crème Brûlée can hardly be bettered. A modest but excellent list of wines and two quality house wines are available. Seating is extensive at 175.

Langan's Brasserie

**STRATTON STREET
PICCADILLY, LONDON, W1**

01-493-6437

**LUNCH: MONDAY - FRIDAY, 12:30 TO 3 P.M.
DINNER: MONDAY - FRIDAY, 7 P.M. TO 12 A.M.
AND SATURDAY, 8 P.M. TO 1 A.M.
RESERVATIONS**

**PROPRIETORS: PETER LANGAN,
MICHAEL CAINE, RICHARD SHEPHERD
CHEF: RICHARD SHEPHERD, M.C.G.B.**

Gravetye Manor

Le Gavroche

Central Hotel   Malmaison Restaurant

Sharrow Bay Country House Hotel

Artichaut Farci à la Nissarda

white wine, as needed

water, as needed

few coriander seeds

few peppercorn seeds

lemon juice, as needed

thyme, bay leaf, and salt, to taste

6 globe artichoke hearts rubbed with lemon juice

1¼ lb duxelles of mushrooms

double cream, optional

2 oz chopped shallots

3 oz diced ham

pepper, to taste

½ pt Hollandaise sauce

chives, to garnish

Make a bouillon of ¼ white wine and ¾ water. Add a few coriander and peppercorn seeds and a little lemon juice, thyme, bay leaf, and salt. Cook artichokes in bouillon until tender. (Test with point of small knife.)

Cook the duxelles until all moisture has evaporated. (If mushrooms are a little bitter, add a drop of cream.) Reduce the shallots in white wine. Add shallots, ham, salt, and pepper to the duxelles.

Dress the artichokes on a serving dish and fill with the mushroom mixture. Cover with Hollandaise sauce, sprinkle with chives, and serve hot.

Serves: 6

Poulet Sauté Safrané

6 oz butter

oil, as needed

2 × 3½ lb chickens cut in 16 equal pieces

salt and pepper, to taste

2 large finely chopped onions

good pinch of saffron, leaves preferred, *not* ground saffron

½ bottle white wine

2 pt veal stock, slightly thickened, or use stock cubes

½ pt double cream

chopped parsley, to garnish

Heat butter and just enough oil to prevent burning in a thick-bottomed pan. Season the chicken with salt and pepper and sauté the pieces until golden brown. Remove chicken, strain fat, and wipe out pan.

Return fat to pan, add onions, and sweat without colouring them. Add saffron and white wine and reduce by ½. Add stock, return chicken, and cover and cook for 20 minutes. If necessary, add more stock.

Remove chicken and skim off any grease from top of sauce. Reduce sauce if needed to get correct flavouring. Add cream and stir until sauce returns to boil.

Dress chicken on serving dish, cover with sauce, and sprinkle with chopped parsley. Serving suggestion: serve with boiled or plain rice.

Serves: 4

Crème Brûlée

1 litre double cream

5 egg yolks

200 g caster sugar

vanilla essence, as needed

Demerara sugar, to sprinkle

Bring ¾ double cream to a boil and remove from heat. Mix the rest of the cream, egg yolks, caster sugar, and a little vanilla essence thoroughly together. Add to the boiled double cream. Return to heat and stir constantly with a wooden spoon until just at the boiling point.

Remove pan from heat and pour into 8 × No. 1 ramekin dishes. Allow to go cold and set.

Sprinkle each mould with Demerara sugar and glaze quickly under a salamander. Return to refrigerator, allow to set, and serve.

Serves: 8

Lichfield's

Lichfield's is a small and simply decorated restaurant run by its chef/patron Stephen Bull to appeal to people for whom the quality and variety of the food is the most important aspect of a restaurant. The menu is small and changes frequently, particularly with reference to the changes in the seasons. Everything used is fresh; the vegetables are cooked to order for each customer, and even the ice creams and sorbets are made on the premises.

The food is, on the whole, French with some emphasis placed on the developing fashion for the lighter and more adventurous styles known as *la nouvelle cuisine*, but traditional methods and some of the better dishes from other national cuisines are also featured occasionally.

Stephen Bull is an ex-advertising man whose long-standing and intense interest in cooking inspired him to open his own restaurant one day. Before starting Lichfield's three years ago, Chef Bull was the proprietor and chef of a restaurant in North Wales. He has a noticeable tendency to innovate, which may be due to his lack of formal training. He is self-taught and subscribes to no one set of principles that have been passed on from a mentor; therefore, all styles and approaches can be seen as potential influences upon him. He has also developed an imaginative list of predominantly French wines from which to choose.

Lichfield's

**LICHFIELD TERRACE, SHEEN ROAD
RICHMOND, SURREY**

940-5236

**DINNER: TUESDAY - SATURDAY
RESERVATIONS**

PROPRIETOR/CHEF: STEPHEN BULL

Ragout of Scallops with Dill

8 large or 12 medium scallops

2 oz butter

white of 2 medium leeks, julienne

½ large carrot, julienne

½ stick celery, julienne

¼ pt fish stock

¼ pt white wine

⅛ pt double cream

salt, to taste

1 tbsp chopped fresh dill

Wash and clean scallops, retaining only white meat and orange coral. If large, slice horizontally into 3, if medium, into 2; remove coral.

In a large heavy pan, melt ½ the butter, add prepared vegetables, cover, and cook over low heat for 5 minutes. Do not let brown. Uncover, add stock and wine, and reduce by fast boiling to about ⅛ pint. Add cream and boil for a few moments until it thickens. Season lightly with salt. In a heavy frying pan, melt remaining butter and pour in scallops and coral. Salt lightly and sprinkle with most of the dill. Cook 1 minute on each side until just becoming opaque. Do not let brown. Pour off a small amount of the liquid released into the other pan, shake to mix thoroughly.

Divide the sauce and vegetables among 4 dishes. Arrange the scallops on top of the sauce, sprinkle the remaining dill on top, and serve.

Serves: 4

Rosettes de Boeuf Persillées

1 fist-sized bunch of parsley, finely chopped

rind of 1 lemon, grated

4 cloves garlic, finely chopped

½ tsp thyme

8 slices middle cut fillet steak, ½ in thick

butter, to sauté

⅛ pt meat glaze or ¼ pt beef or veal stock

2 oz anchovy butter

watercress, to garnish

Mix the parsley, lemon rind, garlic, and thyme together to make a *persillade*. Press both sides of each slice of beef into the mixture and cook them in hot butter for 2 minutes per side without scorching the coating. Remove beef and keep hot.

Deglaze the pan with meat glaze or stock, reduced to a thin syrup, and thicken with anchovy butter, cut into small pieces and added piece by piece. (Shake the pan to incorporate butter smoothly into the sauce.) Pour sauce over the beef slices, garnish with watercress, and serve.

Serves: 4

Rum and Brandy Mousse

8 eggs, separated

7 oz caster sugar

3 tbsp brandy

2½ tbsp rum

5 tsp gelatine dissolved in a little water

¾ pt double cream

grated chocolate or toasted almonds, to garnish

Whisk the yolks and sugar until pale, then add brandy and rum and whisk for 30 seconds. Add gelatine. Beat the cream until thick, beat the egg whites until soft peaks form, then gently fold whipped cream, then the egg whites, into the gelatine mixture. Put mixture into glasses, chill, and serve with some grated chocolate or toasted almonds on top.

Ma Cuisine

Ma Cuisine is a small, unpretentious six-year-old French restaurant located on Walton Street. Its proprietor/chef is Guy Mouilleron. Following an apprenticeship at the Ritz in Paris, Chef Mouilleron's determination to succeed brought him to London. Here he worked at the Savoy and subsequently spent several years working as Maître Chef at the Cafe Royal. However, Chef Mouilleron's dream had always been to be able to dedicate his energy, enthusiasm, and skills to his own "cuisine." This ambition was realised in 1975 when, with the addition of the organised efficiency of his wife, Lucette, he opened Ma Cuisine.

Potential customers should not be put off by the fact that the sign on the door permanently reads "closed" — it is simply an indication that Ma Cuisine is always fully booked. This is because the ambiance, service, and food are all faultless. The atmosphere is intimate without being overcrowded; the service — presided over by Lucette — is personal and friendly, but at the same time, highly professional.

The consistently imaginative menu, whilst being varied depending on what the morning's market has to offer, always includes a choice of Guy's tried and tested favourites. Ingredients that are unobtainable in England, or of a quality not up to Chef Mouilleron's standards, are imported from France. A modest but good quality wine list is available.

Ma Cuisine

**113 WALTON STREET
LONDON, SW3**

01-584-7585

**LUNCH: 12:30 TO 2 P.M.
DINNER: 7:30 TO 11 P.M.
MONDAY - FRIDAY
RESERVATIONS**

**PROPRIETOR/CHEF:
GUY MOUILLERON, M.C.G.B.**

Oeuf Vert Galant

4 eggs

   boiling salted water, as needed

2 tbsp white wine vinegar

1 nut butter

4 tbsp sweet corn

   salt and milled pepper, to taste

4 cooked pastry tartlets

   warmed Béarnaise sauce, as needed

Poach the eggs in gently boiling salted water with vinegar added. Carefully shape the eggs until the yolk is completely enclosed in the white. When lightly poached, remove eggs with a perforated spoon, place them in iced water, and set aside.

Melt the butter in a frying pan and sauté the sweet corn without colouring them. Season with salt and pepper. Place the cooked tartlets in a warm place to heat through. Immerse the eggs in hot water. Take each tartlet and fill with a tablespoon of sweet corn. Drain each egg, which should be hot but still soft, on a dry cloth. Place an egg on each bed of sweet corn. Coat each egg with the warm Béarnaise sauce and glaze under a very hot salamander.

Serves: 4

Noisette d'Agneau Pastourelle

1 large onion, peeled

1 tbsp parsley

4 tbsp bread crumbs

   fresh mint, to taste

   salt and milled pepper, to taste

1 egg yolk

1 pair best ends of lamb, prepared and completely boneless

   oil, to sauté

To prepare onion purée: wrap the onion in foil paper and bake in a hot oven until thoroughly cooked. Remove from foil while still hot and discard any brown pieces. Place in a liquidiser with the parsley, bread crumbs, mint, salt, pepper, and egg yolk. Mix well, then transfer the purée to a small bowl.

Remove most of the fat and gristle from the best ends and cut each into 8 pieces. Flatten slightly and season well. Sauté in very hot oil for about 1 minute per side (depending on desired degree of pinkness). Remove from frying pan and arrange on a fireproof dish. Coat each eye of meat with a teaspoon of the purée and place under a very hot grill to glaze to a golden colour.

Serves: 4

Mousse Brûlée

125 g granulated sugar

3 gelatine leaves or equivalent in powder

   cold water, as needed

3 egg yolks

150 ml double cream

6 egg whites

1 tbsp icing sugar

Place granulated sugar in a clean, heavy-bottomed pan and cook over strong heat. Soak the gelatine in water. Whisk the yolks and ½ cream together. Warm the remaining cream with the drained gelatine until it is completely dissolved. When the sugar reaches a very dark caramel, add the warm cream and gelatine mixture carefully. This should be thoroughly blended and then whisked into the yolks and cream mixture. Allow this mixture to cool. When cool, whisk the whites until firm, add icing sugar, and continue to whisk until very firm. Pass this caramel mixture onto the whites through a coarse sieve and fold in carefully. When completely blended, place the mousse into 4 soufflé moulds. Serve cold.

Mes Amis

Mes Amis is a sunny, airy, garden-fresh, green and white "Provençal" restaurant located just behind Harrods, the famous London store. Knightsbridge businessmen, handsome Arab families, and well-dressed shoppers make a pretty picture under the dark rustic beams, arched whitewashed walls, and hanging pots of ferns and ivies. There is a beautiful arrangement of fresh vegetables, cheeses, herbs, and sausages on a table that welcomes you just inside the entrance. The wooden tables all have rush mats, candles, and more fresh flowers.

The pretty menu is sensibly divided into hot and cold hors d'oeuvres, potages, poissons entrées, grillades, légumes, and desserts. The experienced chef, Martin Cunningham, makes sure every dish is properly prepared, in a large portion, and using only ingredients of the highest quality. Chef Cunningham's Cotelettes en Croûte, for example, are absolutely perfect; the pastry is light and flaky. Fillet steaks are also excellent, and the duck is deliciously honey-roasted. Portions of vegetables are equally large and very fresh. Salads are crisp and fresh, the cheese board is impressive, the desserts are delicious, and the waiters, dressed in fresh green, are always attentive.

There is an extensive wine list in all price ranges available, and there is a cocktail lounge on the premises.

mes amis

**31 BASIL STREET
LONDON, SW3**

01-584-4484

**LUNCH: 12:30 TO 3:30 P.M.
DINNER: 7:30 TO 11:30 P.M.
DAILY
RESERVATIONS**

**PROPRIETOR: JOHN PARNES
CHEF: MARTIN CUNNINGHAM**

Cassolette Cap Ferrat

1 oz unsalted butter

1 oz shallots, diced

2 oz fresh prawns, shelled and diced

2 oz fresh scallops, shelled and diced

2 oz scampi, shelled and diced

fresh basil, to taste

1 gill French white wine

1 gill *fumet de poisson* (fish stock)

2 oz crawfish

½ oz lobster butter

½ gill double cream

seasoning, to taste

Melt butter in a sauté pan. Add shallots, prawns, scallops, scampi, and fresh basil. Pour white wine and fish stock over the ingredients and poach. After 2 minutes, add crawfish. Cook for 6–8 minutes. Remove all ingredients from pan, place in a dish, and keep warm.

To prepare sauce: reduce liquid in pan by ½, add lobster butter and double cream and season.

Return ingredients to finished sauce, correct seasoning, and serve.

Serving suggestion: decorate with fresh prawns with shells on.

Serves: 2

CHEF'S TIP

DON'T RUSH YOUR SAUCE — BE PATIENT, EXERCISE CARE, AND DON'T BE AFRAID OF THE RECIPE.

Côtelettes d'Agneau

1 lb prime best end of lamb, cut into 2 cutlets

2 oz unsalted butter

½ oz diced shallot

2 oz diced mushrooms

herbs, to taste

1 oz strudel paste

fresh watercress, to garnish

Seal the lamb cutlets in butter. Set aside to cool.

To prepare mushroom duxelles: place diced shallot, mushrooms, and herbs into a deep frying pan and cook quickly. Remove from heat.

Roll out strudel paste very thinly then place in melted butter. Put enough mushroom duxelles on each cutlet, then carefully wrap each cutlet in strudel paste. Cook in oven for 15–20 minutes.

Decorate with fresh watercress. Serving suggestion: serve with sauce vin blanc.

Serves: 2

Vacherin Mont Blanc

1× 1 oz meringue base

1 whole chestnut

1 oz vanilla ice cream

2 oz crème chantilly

1 oz chocolate sauce

½ oz flaked almonds

Fill the meringue base with vanilla ice cream, top with whole chestnut, and surround with crème chantilly. Coat with chocolate sauce, sprinkle with flaked almonds, and serve.

Serves: 1

Mirabelle

Mirabelle is situated on Curzon Street in London's fashionable area of Mayfair. When you arrive, the doorman will look after your car and you can go straight down into the silvery-oak panelled bar for newspapers and nuts with your drink. Or you can wait on a soft banquette in an ante-room filled with mirrors and alcoves of china.

The dining room is large and airy, has brocade or tapestries on the walls, and opens onto a patio planted with flowering shrubs and plants. The tables are decorated with flower arrangements of red, yellow, and glossy green touches which blend in beautifully with the surroundings.

The two chefs, Jean Drees and Edward Robinson, have both been with Mirabelle for 26 years. Jean Drees, a Frenchman, is polite, self-assured, and obviously dedicated. Edward Robinson is very English, gently spoken with a shy, genuine smile. He is as dedicated, self-assured, and as positive in his views on food as his colleague.

They work closely together, yet apart in two separate domains. Jean Drees governs the meat, fish, poultry and game cookery, while Edward Robinson creates trifles and dresses the desserts and pastries. They both agree that you should never overlay the inherent flavours and subtleties of good food with heavy sauces, strong flavours, or artifical brightness. Testimonies to their philosophy appear on the opposite page.

Mirabelle

56 CRUZON STREET
MAYFAIR, LONDON, W1

01-449-4636

LUNCH AND DINNER:
MONDAY - SATURDAY AND PUBLIC HOLIDAYS

PROPRIETOR:
DE VERE RESTAURANTS, LTD.
CHEFS: JEAN DREES, EDWARD ROBINSON

Gratin de Crabe

2½   lb cooked crab, fresh or cooked

3   oz cooked mushrooms

½   pt double cream, and as needed

1   small glass sherry

1   coffeespoon English mustard

    salt and pepper, to taste

    pinch of cayenne pepper

1   egg yolk

    bread crumbs, as needed

Remove every scrap of flesh from the crab by breaking the inside. Put the brown and white flesh, which is mostly from the claws, in separate bowls. Reserve the shell for serving.

Purée the mushrooms with ¼ pint cream and line the shell. Gently simmer the white flesh in a small pan with sherry and another ¼ pint double cream for about 10 minutes.

Pound the brown flesh with a wooden spoon, mix it with mustard, salt, pepper, and pinch of cayenne pepper. Warm the brown flesh without boiling it, then mix it with the yolk and a little double cream until mixture is of a smooth, soft consistency for spreading.

Lay the white flesh on the mushroom purée in the shell, then spread brown mixture on top. Cover with bread crumbs and grill until coloured.

Serves: 2

Wine: *Chablis Fourchaumes, Louis Jadot, 1977-78*

Côtelettes d' Agneau Prince de Galles

3   oz mushrooms

3   sprigs of tarragon

    salt and pepper, to taste

1-2   dessertspoons brandy

½   c double cream

½   lb veal

3   thin lamb cutlets, trimmed

    butter, to sauté and as needed

    thinly sliced raw potatoes, as needed

    button mushrooms and artichoke hearts, to garnish

    Madeira or Perigourdine sauce, prepared

Purée the mushrooms and season with tarragon, salt, pepper, and brandy. Mix in the double cream. Mince the veal and add it to the purée. Consistency should be stiff. Spread the mixture on both sides of the cutlet (crumb if desired, but it's not necessary). Sauté the cutlets in butter for 5 – 6 minutes per side. Sauté the potatoes in a separate pan and spread them on a dish. Lay the cooked cutlets on top. Warm the button mushrooms and artichoke hearts in butter, cover them with Madeira or Perigourdine sauce and use them to garnish the dish.

Serves: 1

Wine: *Chateau Lynch Bages, Pauillac*

Coupe Glacée Mirabelle

4   oz caster sugar

    water, as needed

1   tsp glucose

    sponge fingers, as needed

    strawberry ice cream, 2 scoops per person

    cream, as needed

    chopped fruit marinated in Grand Marnier, as needed

    whipped cream and flaked almonds, to garnish

To prepare caramel sauce: put sugar in a pan and just cover it with water. Add glucose and bring to a boil, stirring all the time. (Glucose prevents crystallising.) Boil furiously. Watch mixture carefully and lower heat as soon as colour begins to change (can happen very quickly). Put into the sink and add cold water, a drop at a time, until you've added about 2 tablespoons. Return to stove and mix well. If you see a slight thread of spun sugar when you lift a little boiled sugar on the end of the spoon, the consistency is right. (This keeps well refrigerated.)

Put 2 tablespoons caramel sauce in bottom of a tall glass, preferably a sundae glass, and insert a sponge finger. Add a small scoop of ice cream, pipe cream around, then add marinated fruit with Grand Marnier. Place another scoop of ice cream on top and decorate with a rosette of cream and garnish with flaked almonds. Serve extra sponge fingers with it.

Oslo Court Restaurant

Oslo Court Restaurant is a family owned and operated restaurant that features international cuisine. Rajko Katnic is the chef and has a team of three chefs trained by himself. The restaurant is run by Megan Katnic and her daughter June.

The menu offers many dishes created by the chef, and daily items appear according to season and availability. The menu has a strong bias toward fish dishes. Among the many original hot hors d'oeuvre offerings are the unique Crab la Rochelle (a fresh crab blended with cream and brandy, folded into a flaky pastry, and served with sauce) and Stuffed Onions Kostrena (onions stuffed with sea bass and salmon trout cooked in an egg and lemon sauce).

Of the main dishes, Salmon Trout Mama Zora is very popular, as is Sole Halibut Papa Augustine (fish baked with mushrooms, tomatoes, and herbs in foil). It is very moist and tasty. The dessert menu features a choice of hot sweets that change daily. They include hot Cheese Pancakes, which are particularly light and delicate, Hot Strawberries grilled with cherry brandy and served with home made lemon ice cream, and Tangerine or Raspberry Soufflé.

The wine list is extensive and has been built up over a number of years to cater to almost every palate. Offered are selected years from a wide variety of vineyards in full and half bottles. Table settings are Royal Albert china and fine crystal glasses; service is friendly and attentive.

OSLO COURT

PRINCE ALBERT ROAD
REGENTS PARK, LONDON, NW8

01-722-8795

LUNCH: TUESDAY - FRIDAY, 12:30 TO 2 P.M.
DINNER:
TUESDAY - SATURDAY, 6:30 TO 10:30 P.M.
RESERVATIONS

PROPRIETORS:
RAJKO, MEGAN, AND JUNE KATNIC
CHEF: RAJKO KATNIC

Salmon Quenelles

½ lb finely minced Scottish salmon
   salt and pepper, to taste
   pinch of nutmeg
3 egg whites
½ pt double cream, whipped lightly
   fish stock or salted water, to poach
½ pt fish stock
1 tbsp white wine
3 tbsp cream
   grated cheese, as needed

Thoroughly beat minced salmon until smooth. Add salt, pepper, and nutmeg, then gradually add egg whites until blended. Gradually fold in double cream. Mould mixture with 2 dampened dessertspoons to desired size, then gently poach in simmering fish stock or salted water for about 6 minutes.

To prepare sauce: bring ½ pint fish stock to a boil and thicken until it coats the back of a spoon. Simmer for 5 minutes, add wine, cream, and season to taste. Coat cooked quenelles with sauce and top with a little grated cheese. Glaze until golden under a grill. Serve immediately.

Serves: 6

Salmon Trout Mama Zora

  2 medium onions, finely chopped
 60 g butter
250 g mushrooms, finely chopped
  1 small sprig fennel, finely chopped
  4 tsp Pernod
  5 g flour
  2 whole eggs
     salt and pepper, to taste
2 × 2 kg salmon trout, cleaned and boned
275 g puff pastry dough
     egg wash, as needed
250 ml double cream

To prepare stuffing: gently fry the onion in butter until transparent. Add mushrooms and cook another 5 minutes, stirring occasionally. Stir in ½ fennel and ½ Pernod. Fold in the flour and cook 2–3 minutes. Beat in eggs, one at a time. Season with salt and pepper.

Open the fish, sprinkle with salt and pepper, and spread the stuffing inside. Brush with butter and place on a greased baking dish. Cook in oven at gas mark 5 (350°F/175°C) for 10 minutes.

Roll out pastry dough to 4 millimetres thick. When fish is done, remove from oven and carefully peel away skin on both sides. Wrap dough around fish. Decorate top, brush with egg wash, and replace in oven until golden brown.

To prepare sauce: heat cream until almost boiling. Stir in remainder of fennel and Pernod. Serve with fish.

Serves: 6–8

Wine: *Meursall Perrier, 1971*

Raspberry Soufflé

  1 pt puréed raspberries
  ½ pt milk
  ¼ lb sugar, and as needed
  3 oz flour
  3 oz butter, and as needed
 12 eggs, separated
 2½ fl oz orange liqueur

Place ½ raspberries in a saucepan, bring to a boil, and cook slowly for about 10 minutes. In another saucepan, boil milk with sugar. Blend flour and butter to a smooth paste then slowly add to the milk until mixture can support itself. Cook slowly for 10 minutes (until mixture comes away from sides of pan). Remove both pans from heat and add 6 egg yolks to each, one at a time, beaten in well. Mix the 2 mixtures and orange liqueur together and let cool. Whisk egg whites until stiff and fold into cold mixture. Prepare 8 × 7 inch soufflé dishes with butter and sugar, then place soufflé mixture into each, ¾ to the top. Carefully place in middle of oven at gas mark 7 (425°F/220°C) and cook for 35 minutes without opening the door.

Sweeten the remaining raspberry purée to taste with sugar and serve cold with the soufflés.

Serves: 8

Parkes

The joy of discovery was one of the principles of Ray Parkes when he founded the **Parkes** restaurant in 1959. To him, the enjoyment of food had been stifled by formality, suffocated by snobbery, and bludgeoned by a reliance on traditional dishes whose design might have been grand but had since been reduced to mediocrity by repetition. Innovation soon became his by-word, and he became a pioneer in not only creating new dishes, but also in allowing his customers to watch him as he created.

When Tom Benson became his assistant in 1960, Ray Parkes had already stripped away the pretentiousness that had straight-jacketed too many other restaurants. He had introduced informality with elegance (the personal choice of flowers on the plate, a menu that teases rather than dictates), creating an atmosphere that was both intimate and yet casual, one that would make a customer feel relaxed both before and after the meal.

After Mr. Parkes died in 1963, Chef Benson took over the restaurant, realising that only a fool would change what had already been established.

Although the restaurant has since been extended twice and a bar introduced on the ground floor, the fundamental ideas remain. New dishes are still created and old customers still return. Only the finest and freshest ingredients are employed in all preparations, and there is also an excellent list of wines in all price ranges available.

Parkes

4-5 BEAUCHAMP PLACE
LONDON, SW3

01-589-1390

LUNCH: MONDAY - FRIDAY,
12:30 TO 2:45 P.M.
DINNER: MONDAY - SATURDAY,
7:30 TO 11 P.M.
RESERVATIONS

PROPRIETORS:
TOM BENSON, BEECHER MOORE
CHEF: TOM BENSON

Oysters Baked in Spinach Sauce

12 large oysters, with juice

8 oz chopped cooked spinach

½ pt white sauce

¼ tsp mixed mace and nutmeg

1 tsp dried tarragon

juice of ½ lemon

salt and pepper, to taste

1 tbsp chopped chives or parsley, to garnish

Open oysters, leave in half shell, and place in a medium-sized baking dish or on 4 individual dishes.

Gently cook spinach, white sauce, mace, nutmeg, tarragon, lemon juice, salt, pepper, and juice from oysters in a saucepan for 5 minutes. Stir well. Pour the sauce over the oysters and bake in the middle of an oven at gas mark 7 (425°F/220°C) for 10 minutes or until the sauce is bubbling. Remove from oven, sprinkle with chives or parsley, and serve.

Duckling with Apricots and Chestnuts

2 × 4½ - 5 lb ducklings

1 pt basic brown sauce

2 cloves garlic

½ tsp mixed spice

1 tbsp red wine vinegar

2 tbsp soft brown sugar or, if using tinned apricots, ½ the syrup

few drops Tabasco sauce

4 tbsp Grand Marnier

½ lb cooked chestnuts

½ lb fresh or tinned apricots, halved

Roast the ducklings in a hot oven for 45 minutes, then cut each in ½ with kitchen scissors and discard the backbones. Place brown sauce, garlic, mixed spice, vinegar, brown sugar or apricot syrup, and Tabasco in a saucepan and bring gently to a boil. Simmer for 10 minutes, strain, and add Grand Marnier.

Place duckling halves in an ovenproof dish, surround with chestnuts and apricot halves, and pour sauce *around* ducklings and *over* chestnuts and apricots. Cook in the middle of a hot oven for 10 minutes or until ducks are slightly crisp. Cook another 10 minutes, this time basting ducklings with sauce.

Serve ducklings on large, hot plates, surrounded with apricots and chestnuts. Pour any remaining sauce over ducklings.

Serves: 4

Pears in Grenadine Syrup

4 Comice pears, peeled and cored

½ pt grenadine syrup

1 bottle white lemonade, or as needed

vanilla and almond essence, as needed

2 tbsp kirsch

Place pears in a shallow saucepan with grenadine syrup and enough lemonade to cover the pears. Add a couple of drops of vanilla essence and almond essence and the kirsch. Poach the pears until they can be pierced with a skewer or the tip of a knife. (They should be nicely pink.) Remove pears from pan.

Serving suggestions: to serve pears cold, chill them in the refrigerator and serve on a bed of whipped cream. To serve pears hot, pop them in heated syrup for a couple of minutes then serve with vanilla or hazelnut ice cream or with double cream.

Serves: 4

Poissonnerie de l'Avenue

Poissonnerie de l'Avenue is owned by Peter Rosignoli, who began his career in the restaurant business in 1946 when he went to work as an apprentice in the kitchen of a restaurant in Cremona, Italy, at the age of 14. "In Italy at that time," he says, "an apprentice was paid the equivalent of two pounds a month and the work was hard, very hard. But you learned with your eyes and intuition because you wanted to progress."

And progress he did. After leaving Cremona, he worked as a waiter in grand hotels in Italy, Switzerland, and France before coming to England in 1959 to work in a famous Mayfair restaurant. He married the English receptionist of that restaurant, then the two of them bought Poissonnerie in 1962 and began the process that would turn it into one of the best known seafood restaurants in London.

Poissonnerie is a small, intimate, wood-panelled "French fish cooking" restaurant that seats 80. There is no cocktail lounge, but there is bar service at the tables. There is also a modest but excellent wine list.

The kitchen is run by Chef Roses, a native of Spain who learned classical French cooking in several top kitchens and has been at Poissonnerie since shortly after its opening. He and his associate, Chef Tomassi, cast a French touch to each seafood dish they prepare and, thereby, take what could be otherwise ordinary cuisine and make it something special.

POISSONNERIE DE L'AVENUE

**82 SLOANE AVENUE
LONDON, SW3**

01-589-2457

**LUNCH: 12:15 TO 3 P.M.
DINNER: 7 TO 11:30 P.M.
MONDAY - SATURDAY
CLOSED BANK HOLIDAYS AND
TWO WEEKS AFTER CHRISTMAS
RESERVATIONS**

**PROPRIETOR: PETER ROSIGNOLI
CHEFS: F. TOMASSI, Y. ROSES**

Coquilles St. Jacques

½ lb butter, cut in small pieces

3 tbsp finely chopped shallots

24 medium-sized scallops

1 lb chopped white mushrooms

2 glasses dry Muscadet wine

1 pt double cream

pinch of freshly ground pepper

pinch of salt

1 handful finely chopped parsley

Put a thick-bottomed saucepan on moderate heat, then add butter in small pieces and let melt. Add shallots and let cook until a golden colour. Add whole scallops and cook gently for 5 minutes. Remove scallops and reduce liquid for 5 minutes. Add mushrooms and cook another 5 minutes, then return scallops and add wine; stew for 5 more minutes. Add double cream, pepper, salt, and parsley and simmer for 5 minutes. Pour into 4 shallow dishes.

Serves: 4

Fillets of Mackerel in White Wine

½ lb butter

2 spoonfuls cooking oil, not olive oil

1 medium-sized onion, sliced very finely

2 shallots, sliced very finely

½ glass white wine vinegar

1 glass dry Muscadet wine

4 × 1 lb mackerels

2 garlic cloves, crushed

black peppercorns, as needed

1 handful chopped parsley

salt, to taste

Melt the butter in a thick-bottomed frying pan, add oil, and fry onion and shallots until golden. Add vinegar and wine and simmer for 25 minutes.

Fillet the mackerel by cutting down the backbone so each fish falls in 2. Make sure fillets are clean. Put fish into a shallow pan and pour the sauce over it. Be sure fish is completely covered by liquid. Add crushed garlic, a few peppercorns, parsley, and salt. Test seasoning; it should be nice and sharp. Let fish simmer gently for 5 minutes. Leave to cool and serve the following day. This dish can be kept refrigerated for up to 10 days.

Serves: 4

Petits Pots au Chocolat

2 pt milk

peel of 1 lemon

½ glass water and as needed

2 lb bitter chocolate, chips or broken in small pieces

½ lb sugar, caster preferred

12 egg yolks

½ glass Grand Marnier

Boil the milk in a heavy-bottomed pan and set aside.

In a clean pan, boil the lemon peel in water until it is almost reduced to nothing. Remove the peel. Add the chocolate and melt very gently (make sure it does not get too dry, add more water if necessary). Add sugar and boiled milk and set aside.

Gently beat the egg yolks and add Grand Marnier. Being sure chocolate is not too hot, add it to the egg mixture. Check for sweetness. Fill 10 small ramekin dishes up to ½ inch from the top with the mixture. Place them in a baking tin containing about 1 inch of water. Bake at 250°F (120°C) for 20 minutes, taking care that the baking tin does not boil dry. Drain the water and leave to cool. These will keep for up to 10 days in the refrigerator.

Serves: 10

Le Poulbot

Le Poulbot opened in May 1969 and is one of the "city" restaurants owned by Michel and Albert Roux. This restaurant is only open for breakfast and lunch. It has two floors: "Le Coffee Shop" is on the ground floor and serves Continental breakfasts of croissants, baked in their own bakery, and cafe au lait, from eight until ten. Simple lunches, such as Navarin d'Agneau, Blanquette de Veau, and Cassoulet ou Boudin Noir, are served from twelve noon to three p.m.

Downstairs, Le Poulbot has the successful and chic atmosphere of a first-class French restaurant, with plush upholstered cubicle-style seating, discreet lighting, prints on the walls, glistening silver plate, crisp linen, and waiters in classic livery.

The brief luncheon menu consists of original Roux creations and those of Chef Chris Oakley, along with his interpretations of dishes from a classical repertoire. The main courses include the Boudin Blanc Sauce Perigueux, the Filets de Sole Eleonora, and the Grenadin de Veau Vallée d'Auges. The salads are always very good, and the cheese board is up to the usual high Roux

standard. A list of wines in all price ranges is also available.

Almost from the time it opened, Le Poulbot was acclaimed to be one of the most outstanding restaurants in the British Isles, and today it has a star in the Michelin guide.

Le Poulbot

**45 CHEAPSIDE
LONDON, EC2
01-236-4379
BREAKFAST: UPSTAIRS 8 TO 10 A.M.
LUNCH:
UPSTAIRS AND DOWNSTAIRS TO 3 P.M.
MONDAY - FRIDAY
CLOSED BANK HOLIDAYS
RESERVATIONS
PROPRIETOR: ROUX RESTAURANTS
CHEF: CHRIS OAKLEY**

Snails Poulbot

20 hazelnuts

20 g butter

4 shallots, sliced in small pieces

3 dozen snails, cleaned and dried

1 tbsp Grand Chartreuse Verte

600 g cream

1 clove garlic, sliced in small pieces

salt and pepper, to taste

knob of butter

20 g parsley, to garnish

Put the hazelnuts on a baking tray in the oven until slightly brown. Put in a tea towel and rub together to remove skin. Chop.

Melt butter in a frying pan, add shallots, and when brown, add snails and hazelnuts. Flambé with Grand Chartreuse. Add cream and garlic and simmer slowly for 5 minutes. Add salt and pepper and knob of butter.

To serve: put 6 snail dishes under a grill to warm, then in each hole place a snail with a sprig of parsley on top.

Serves: 6

CHEF'S TIP

TINNED SNAILS CAN BE USED FOR THIS DISH, BUT THEIR TASTE IS NOT AS SHARP AS FRESH SNAILS.

Poussin Françoise

50 g red/green pepper, sliced in small pieces

250 g poultry mousse, prepared from chicken breast, egg white, and cream

30 g sweet corn

6 baby chickens, boned

1500 ml chicken stock

40 g butter

30 g flour

15 g chives

pepper and salt, to taste

knob of butter

2 tbsp cream

Mix the peppers with chicken mousse and ½ sweet corn. Divide into 6 equal portions and stuff chickens carefully

with the mixture. Put string around the chickens in 3 places to hold together, but not too tightly as they expand during cooking. Cook chickens in stock for 10 minutes. Cover pan with greaseproof paper.

Make a roux with butter and flour. Slowly add 500 millilitres stock and boil. Leave to stand. Add chives and strain. Add pepper, salt, knob of butter, remaining sweet corn, and cream. Mix the sauce well.

Remove chickens from stock, put them on their backs on plates. Remove string. Pour sauce generously over the chickens, keeping some to be served separately in a sauce boat.

Serving suggestion: serve with rice pilaff or spinach with butter.

Serves: 6

Mousse au Chocolat

4 tbsp water

125 g caster sugar

5 egg yolks

1 egg

150 g cooking chocolate, melted

100 ml double cream, beaten and refrigerated

12 macaroons

2 tbsp rum

Put water in a pan, then add sugar. When boiling, skim top with a skimmer and leave to cook until it reaches

285°F (140°C). Put into a bowl and then place the bowl in a few inches of cold water to cool the mixture.

Beat yolks and whole egg, add cooled sugar mix, and keep beating until lukewarm. Break chocolate into small pieces and melt in a bain-marie. Whisk melted chocolate, eggs, and sugar together. When smooth, add cream carefully. Half-fill 6 serving bowls with the mixture. Crumble 1 macaroon on top of each. Place remaining mousse on each, then place a whole macaroon which has been soaked in rum on top of that. Leave refrigerated for a couple of hours in the refrigerator before serving.

Serving suggestion: serve with petits fours secs.

Serves: 6

Shezan

Shezan is one of four Shezan Restaurants; this one is among London's best Indian restaurants. This 11-year-old dining establishment, located in a tiny mews near Harrods, is renowned for its outstanding cooking. It is spacious and beautifully decorated with Hala tiles from Pakistan, candlelit tables that are big and widely spaced, and comfortable brown velvet banquettes, all accented by soft lighting and Oriental background music.

From the moment you sit down in the bar, you feel that extra trouble has been taken to please you. Instead of just peanuts and twiglets to nibble, there are chick peas and green lentils that have been spiced and fried.

The family-owned business specialises in Northern Punjabi food embracing both Indian and Pakistani regional dishes, and many of them are cooked tandoori-style.

The chefs are trained in Shezan's original restaurant in Pakistan (the two other Shezan restaurants are in New York and Washington, DC). No compromise is made for western tastes; the classical Mughal recipes are served without adaptation. The flavours are gently pungent, and fresh herbs and spices are perfectly combined in such delights as Heavenly Chicken Khyberi and Seekh Kebab Mughlai (a spicy barbecued beef). Even simple accompaniments, such as nan and basmati rice, take on new dimensions of taste and texture, and the sweets are light and delicious.

Shezan

16-22 CHEVAL PLACE
LONDON, SW7

01-589-7918

LUNCH: 12 TO 3 P.M.
DINNER: 7 P.M. TO 12 A.M.
MONDAY - SATURDAY
RESERVATIONS

PROPRIETOR: CHOUDHURY SHAHNAWAZ
CHEF: PHILIP GOMES

Shish Kabab Kabli

2 tbsp mustard paste or powder

1 tbsp white pepper

1 tbsp salt

½ tbsp red chili powder

1 tbsp paprika

1 tbsp garlic powder

1 tbsp ginger powder

5 fl oz Worcestershire sauce

5 fl oz salad oil

juice of 6 lemons

6 lb beef, cut in small cubes

2 onion slices

small whole tomatoes, as needed

2 pieces capsicum

butter, as needed

white pepper and caraway seeds, to taste

To prepare the marinade: mix all the spices with the Worcestershire sauce, salad oil, and lemon juice, then dip the meat in it. Cut onion slices, tomato, and pieces of capsicum. Put 1 cube of meat, then onion, then another cube of meat, then tomato, then capsicum onto skewers and marinate for 3–4 hours. Barbecue skewers on charcoal in a *tandoor* (clay oven). Just before serving, garnish with butter and sprinkle with white pepper and caraway seeds.

Serves: 6

Gosh Kata Masala

1 × 3 lb shoulder of lamb

4 small cartons yogurt

1 tsp red chilis

1 small garlic, chopped

1 small ginger, chopped

1 tbsp ground white pepper

1 tsp *zeera* (fried aniseed)

1 whole cinnamon stick

salt, to taste

½ lb *ghee* (Indian butter)

2 fl oz cream

Chop the meat into pieces and mix with yogurt, chilis, garlic, ginger, white pepper, zeera, cinnamon, and salt. Put a pan on high heat with the *ghee*, then put everything into the pan. Stir the meat until the butter settles on top of it, close the lid and let simmer for 10 minutes until water evaporates. Add cream to get flavour and colour.

Serves: 6

Kulfi

1 pt milk (full cream)

3 tbsp sugar

4 pieces almond, crushed

4 pieces pistachio nuts, crushed

chopped almonds and pistachios, as needed

rose water, as needed

Bring the milk to a boil and leave it on low heat to thicken and dry. Once milk has thickened, remove it from heat, add sugar, and let cool. Once cold, add crushed almond and pistachio nuts, put into a mould, and let freeze overnight.

To serve: slice kulfi into thin slices and sprinkle chopped almonds and pistachios with a little rose water on top.

Serves: 6

Tante Claire

Tante Claire, a small, warm and very cosy restaurant in Chelsea, was named after an aunt who enjoyed cooking and good food.

Owner/Chef Pierre Koffmann, who was born in the South West of France, attended the École Hotelière de Tarbes and spent several years working in different restaurants in France, Switzerland, and England before opening Tante Claire in 1977.

Chef Koffmann imports most of the ingredients used in his kitchen from France and, with his French kitchen team, produces imaginative cooking with unusual recipes, most of them created by himself. He says, "I enjoy cooking and mainly cook what I like and what I believe my clientele will like, not what they want," and he seems to be right because his two most popular dishes are the "Pieds de Cochon aux Morilles" and "L'Andouillette aux Fruits de Mer," both his personal favourites. Tante Claire's wine cellar, with over 100 different French wines, and the cheese board, with all cheeses being made in the traditional way in France by a Maître Fromager, are also very noteworthy.

Chef Koffmann's main project for the future is the opening of a bigger restaurant that will provide his clientele with more ambiance and his staff with more working room. But Tante Claire will always maintain the standards of cooking, quality, and personal service for which it has become justly renowned.

Tante Claire

**68 ROYAL HOSPITAL ROAD
LONDON, SW3**

01-352-6045

**LUNCH AND DINNER: MONDAY — FRIDAY
RESERVATIONS**

**PROPRIETOR/CHEF
PIERRE KOFFMANN, M.C.G.B.**

Salade de Homard aux Fines Herbes

1 medium-sized lobster

2 tbsp olive oil

   vinaigrette, for seasoning

1 avocado pear

1 chopped shallot

1 tsp parsley

1 tsp tarragon

1 tsp chives

1 head lettuce

225 g red salad ("raddichio")

100 g cooked French beans

1 breast of chicken

   butter, to fry

1 peeled tomato

   seasoning, to taste

Roast the lobster in the oven with olive oil. Put the vinaigrette with ½ avocado, shallots, parsley, tarragon, and chives in the liquidiser for a few seconds. Dress the salads in a large bowl. Cut the lobster into small pieces and put on top. Slice the breast of chicken and fry it in butter. When cooked, add to the salad and lobster. Add tomato and seasoning.

Serves: 4

Pieds de Cochon aux Morilles

4 pigs trotters, boned

1 breast of chicken

   butter, to sauté

1 small onion, chopped

20 dried morels, cleaned and soaked in water

200 g calf sweetbreads, blanched and cut in pieces

   port, as needed

100 g cubed carrots

100 g cubed onions

   veal stock, as needed

   knob of butter

Braise the trotters in a slow oven for 3 hours while preparing the stuffing. Fry the breast of chicken in butter, then cut in cubes. In a separate pan, fry the onion in butter without colouring. Add the morels, then the sweetbreads, and leave to cook for 10 minutes. Deglaze pan with a drop of port, reduce heat, and add the cubed breast of chicken. Cook together for 3 minutes then set aside to cool.

When the trotters are cooked, remove them from the oven and put each, wide open, on a piece of tin foil and let cool. When cool, stuff with the chicken preparation, then roll them in the tin foil. Let sit for at least 2 hours.

Put cubed carrots and onions in a saucepan, put the trotters on top, and cook in the oven for 15 minutes at gas mark 7 (425°F/218°C). When cooked, deglaze with a glass of port and some veal stock. Remove the trotters, add a knob of butter to the sauce, then pour the sauce on top of the trotters and serve.

Serves: 4

Feuilleté aux Poires

200 g puff pastry dough

1 tin preserved pears, sliced

200 g caster sugar, caramelised

   fresh cream, optional

Roll the pastry for 2 minutes, cut 4 pieces into the shape of a pear, and lay them on a baking tray. Refrigerate the tray for 10 minutes, then bake for 10 minutes at gas mark 7 (425°F/218°C) and then for an additional 10 minutes at gas mark 5 (390°F/200°C). When cooked, put the sliced pears on top of the pastry and pour the hot caramel on top of it.

Serving suggestion: serve with fresh cream.

Serves: 4

Thomas de Quincey's Restaurant

Thomas de Quincey's Restaurant, which opened in the summer of 1977, is situated in the 18th century dwelling of the author whose name this restaurant bears. The restaurant is the picture of elegance. When you enter through the cocktail lounge, you are greeted by a 20-foot bar, Victorian furniture, cream wood panelled walls, and an oil painting of Thomas de Quincey himself.

The dining area decor is mainly grey brick walls, a wooden ceiling, and a small bricked area containing an abundance of plants. The walls are covered with 18th and 19th century prints and Victorian oils. Apart from the picture lights, the dining area is lit by gas wall bracket lights; at night, the lights are dimmed and silver and crystal glass candle holders are placed on the tables. The tables are each covered in a gold tablecloth. Brass place settings, silver cutlery, Wedgewood china, silver cruets, and vases with fresh flowers complete the setting. Customers sit comfortably in padded bentwood chairs.

There is an upstairs room with a glass roof used for private parties.

The proprietors have succeeded in providing a marvelous milieu in which to enjoy the French cuisine capably prepared by Chef Bird. This is evidenced by the throngs of local patrons, mostly professionals, who fill the restaurant daily.

Thomas de Quincey's Restaurant

**36 TAVISTOCK STREET
LONDON, WC2**

01-240-3972

LUNCH: MONDAY - FRIDAY,
12:30 TO 3 P.M.
DINNER: MONDAY - FRIDAY,
6 TO 11:15 P.M.
AND
SATURDAY, 7 TO 11:30 P.M.
RESERVATIONS

PROPRIETORS:
K. JONES, A.F. WEGRZYNEK
CHEF: A. BIRD

Turbot Pâté, Sauce Vert

4 ×   4 oz fillets fresh turbot

Dry Sack sherry, enough to cover

basil, chervil, and oregano, to taste

3   lb sole fillets

2   egg whites

lobster eggs, as needed

1   large lobster tail, finely chopped

salt, cayenne pepper, and nutmeg, to taste

1½   pt cream

3   oz white of leeks, julienne

3   oz celery, julienne

3   oz carrots, julienne

2   oz leaf spinach

butter, to sauté

1   oz lobster meat

1   oz pistachio nuts

1   oz diced truffle

1   oz chopped fresh tarragon

½   oz chopped fresh parsley

½   oz chopped fresh chives

1   pt thick mayonnaise

⅓   pt whipped cream

1   oz finely chopped fresh spinach

Marinate the turbot fillets in sherry, basil, chervil, and oregano for 24 hours.

To prepare lobster mousse: pass the sole through a mincer or slow speed robot coupe, add egg whites, lobster eggs, chopped lobster, salt, cayenne pepper, and nutmeg. Pass everything through a fine sieve. Beat over ice while adding cream. Chill.

Sauté the leeks, celery, and carrots. Open the marinated turbot fillets lengthways and lay the sautéed strips of vegetables in them. Sauté the spinach in butter and season with nutmeg. Line a terrine mould with the sautéed spinach. Layer the bottom of the terrine with ½ inch of the lobster mousse, lay 2 turbot fillets on top, then cover with more mousse. Sprinkle lobster meat, pistachio nuts, and diced truffle on top. Smooth over with mousse. Place another layer of turbot in terrine and cover with the rest of the mousse. Place terrine in a shallow dish of water and cook in a moderate oven for about 45 minutes.

To prepare sauce vert: mix tarragon, parsley, and chives and squeeze through a muslin cloth. Fold the green juice into the mayonnaise and some whipped cream. Finish by adding chopped herbs and fresh finely chopped spinach. Serve with turbot pâté.

Paupiette de Veau Farci Loverdos

1½   lb sole

6   whites of fresh scallops

2   oranges

1½   fl oz orange curaçao

1   egg white

¾   pt double cream

6 ×   3½ oz escalope of loin or silver side of veal

butter and olive oil, to sauté

½   oz Normandy butter

½   oz caster sugar

To prepare the mousse: pass the sole and whites of fresh scallops through a mincer. Put into a bowl and stir in the zest of 1 orange, 1 ounce of curaçao, and the egg white.

When well mixed, pass through a sieve into a bowl over ice. Then mix in cream.

Season the veal and beat to 4 by 5 inches. Lay a heaped tablespoon of mousse onto each piece of veal. Roll into a cigar shape and hold in place with 2 cocktail sticks. Lightly sauté in butter and olive oil for 2 minutes, place in a covered pan, and place in oven for about 5 minutes at 400°F (205°C). Remove from pan and place on a serving dish.

Strain off fat from pan and deglaze with juice of 1 orange, remaining curaçao, veal juice from pan, and Normandy butter. Cut 1 orange into segments and place on the serving dish. Pour sauce over. Cut the orange skin into julienne-sized strips. Crystalise the skin in caster sugar and water and use as a garnish.

Serves: 3

Tiberio Restaurant

Tiberio Restaurant, named after the Roman Emperor Tiberius, is an impressive restaurant haven situated in the heart of fashionable Mayfair. It is one of 12 restaurants owned by Mario & Franco Restaurants, Ltd. The atmosphere is delightfully intimate and yet, through the effect created by the vaulted ceiling and white arched walls, retains an air of spaciousness. Every aspect of this elegant restaurant has been skillfully balanced so as to ensure the absolute comfort of the diners.

One of the restaurant's special effects is an intriguing mural consisting of solidified lava from Mount Vesuvius. Another particularly interesting feature is the transparent rose-tinted screen that divides the restaurant from the kitchen through which guests may gaze at the brigade of chefs who, with tireless enthusiasm, create superb Italian culinary masterpieces in the *haute cuisine* tradition.

Maître chef de cuisine, Maresca Alessandro, who was formally trained in several restaurants and hotels in Italy, has been associated with Tiberio for some time. One of his most recent achievements was becoming "Pasta Champion 1980." The service, headed by Basilio de Colle, is unobstrusive; the waiters are friendly, efficient, and noticeably well co-ordinated to help create the relaxed and welcoming ambiance.

Tiberio also offers a comprehensive wine list, a cocktail lounge, and live music for dancing after 11:30.

TIBERIO RESTAURANT

**22 QUEEN STREET
MAYFAIR, LONDON, W1**

01-629-3561

**LUNCH: 12 TO 3 P.M.,
MONDAY — FRIDAY
DINNER: 7 P.M. TO 2:30 A.M.,
MONDAY — SATURDAY
RESERVATIONS**

**PROPRIETOR: MARIO & FRANCO
RESTAURANTS, LTD.
CHEF: MARESCA ALESSANDRO**

Paglie e Fieno Aurora (Noodles with Cream Sauce)

100 g Parma ham

28 g butter

124 ml double cream

70 g peeled tomatoes (4 medium-sized)

salt and pepper, to taste

500 g green and white noodles

100 g grated Parmesan cheese

Slice the ham into fine julienne and sauté in butter over low heat. Add double cream and peeled tomatoes. Stir and simmer for 3−4 minutes, then season to taste with salt and pepper.

Cook the pasta *al dente* in boiling salted water for about 5 minutes. Drain and rinse with hot water and place into a serving dish. Pour the sauce over the pasta and stir until thoroughly mixed. Sprinkle generously with grated Parmesan cheese and serve immediately.

Serves: 4

CHEF'S TIP

ENSURE THAT THE PASTA AND VEGETABLES ARE COOKED AL DENTE — IT IS IMPORTANT NOT TO OVERCOOK. THIS ALSO APPLIES TO THE VEAL WHICH NEEDS TO RETAIN MOISTURE.

Scaloppine di Vitello alla Sorrentina

12 × 40 g small veal scaloppines

salt and pepper, to taste

100 g plain flour

28 g butter

70 g peeled and finely chopped tomatoes (4 medium-sized)

84 ml dry white wine

12 × 20 g slices mozzarella cheese

1 sprig parsley, chopped

Gently flatten the veal slices to equal thickness and size. Season the veal and coat on both sides with flour.

In a small pan, heat a little butter and cook the tomatoes for 5 minutes, then season to taste. Melt the remaining butter in a large shallow pan, add the veal, and cook slowly until golden on both sides. Remove veal from pan and set aside. Add white wine to pan and simmer until volume of liquid has been reduced by about ⅓.

On top of each scaloppine, position 1 slice of cheese and place under a hot grill until cheese has melted. Remove from grill and arrange on a large hot serving dish. Garnish each scaloppine with a teaspoon of the chopped tomato and carefully pour the wine sauce from the pan around the edge of the serving dish. Sprinkle with chopped parsley and serve immediately.

Serving suggestion: serve with either new potatoes or sauté potatoes and haricots verts and broccoli spears.

Serves: 4

Wine: *white wine, Pino Grigio Grave del Friuli*

Coppa Delizia Tiberio (Strawberries and Zabaglione)

1 lb ripe strawberries

2 fl oz maraschino

6 egg yolks

1 oz granulated sugar, and as needed

3 fl oz Marsala wine

½ pt whipped double cream

½ oz plain chocolate, flaked

Hull and clean the strawberries and place in a large bowl. Sprinkle with maraschino. Reserve until required.

To prepare zabaglione: in a separate bowl (copper if possible), place egg yolks, sugar, and wine and whisk over a hot bain-marie on low heat. Continue to whisk until mixture becomes a creamy, consistent texture. Be careful not to overcook. Remove from stove, whisk a small amount of sugar into the double cream, and add to the zabaglione mixture, blending thoroughly. Transfer to a clean bowl and chill in the refrigerator for at least 20 minutes.

To serve: spoon a portion of strawberries into individual serving dishes (small coupes) and pour the cold zabaglione over the top, completely covering the strawberries. Sprinkle with chocolate flakes and serve.

Serves: 4

Wine: *Amaretto de Saronna*

Tiger Lee Restaurant

Tiger Lee Restaurant is a classy, two-year-old Cantonese restaurant located on Old Brompton Road. Mr. Tiger Lee, one of the owners, began his restaurant career at London's Trader Vic's as a barman. Later, he moved on to several other restaurants, learning more and more about the business at each new job.

Chef Cheong Hong met Tiger Lee on one of those jobs. Hong was born in Canton, China, and first became interested in cooking as an art form at the age of 17. After a year's apprenticeship at a local seafood restaurant, he travelled to Hong Kong where he studied at the Hong Kong Catering Institute for four years. He then worked for five years at an exclusive Hong Kong seafood restaurant and emerged as somewhat of an expert on exotic seafood preparations as well as a specialist of Ching Dynasty Banquets, which sometimes take weeks to prepare. Chef Hong then moved to England in the hopes of someday introducing his high class Oriental cuisine to the West.

Tiger Lee Restaurant opened in March 1979. The decor is simple and uncluttered, with soft lighting, champagne and celadon colours, plush armchairs, crystal glassware, silver service, and the sounds of running water emanating from the four stocked fish tanks, which are looked after by manager Stanley Lau.

**251 OLD BROMPTON ROAD
LONDON, SW5**

01-370-2323

**DINNER 6 P.M. TO 1 A.M. EVERY NIGHT
RESERVATIONS**

**PROPRIETORS: TIGER LEE,
CLAUDIO CASSUTO
CHEF: CHEONG HONG**

Crispy Stuffed Eel Rolls

1 ×   2 lb eel

2   oz ham, smoked preferred

3   oz bamboo shoots

1   oz ginger, sliced finely into 2 in sticks

     whites of spring onions, sliced into
2 in strips, to taste

20 ×   2 in slices coriander stalks or sprinkling of
freshly ground white pepper

8   oz self-raising flour

12   fl oz water

2   fl oz vegetable oil, and as needed to sauté

1   small coffeespoon salt

Bone the eel by slicing through the underpart in a "V" shape and extracting bone. Flatten the eel, then use a sharp knife to slice flesh sideways into 2 inch strips without the skin (about 15–20 strips). Cut the ham into ¼ inch strips, 2 inches long. Cut the bamboo shoots the same way.

Fill the eel slices with a mixture of ham, bamboo shoots, ginger, onions, and coriander and roll tightly to seal. Make a batter by mixing the flour, water, oil, and salt together well. Heat a sauté pan with 2 inches of oil until sizzling, then reduce heat to half flame. Dip the eel rolls into batter, then drop into the pan and cook until golden. Serve whilst very hot and crispy.

Serves: 6

Wine: *Pouilly-Blanc Fumé, 1978, Jide Castellac or Sauvignon*

Stuffed Fish

1   lb trout or bass

7   fl oz water

1   tbsp plain flour, and as needed to dust

½   egg white

1   flat coffeespoon salt

2   oz shelled prawns, finely chopped

     finely chopped spring onions and fresh
coriander leaves, to taste

     vegetable oil, to fry

1   large dried black Chinese mushroom

2   tbsp oyster sauce

1   flat coffeespoon caster sugar

1   finely chopped spring onion

½   coffeespoon finely chopped fresh ginger

1½   coffeespoons cornflour

1   spoon vegetable oil

     finely chopped crisp lettuce, to garnish

Scrape off scales and bone the fish by opening the stomach through the underside and removing flesh, bones, and inside gills. Incise edges of fish ¼ inch from opening in a downward direction, being careful to keep clear of skin. Cut with a sharp knife through the incision and gently pull away from skin. Remove flesh, leaving only complete head and tail and skin of body.

Scrape flesh from bones with a fork and chop flesh finely. Mix into a large bowl with 3 tablespoons water, plain flour, ½ egg white, and salt. Add prawns and beat together for 1 minute. Use your hands to blend the mixture and beat against inside of bowl for 5 minutes until it feels tender and starts to stick. Add finely chopped spring onions and coriander leaves to taste. Turn fish gently inside out and dust with flour, then return as before and fill with mix until firm and to exact fish shape. Dust outside with flour and deep fry in vegetable oil. After oil is sizzling, reduce to low heat, cover, and cook for 20 minutes until golden.

To prepare sauce: soak mushroom in hot water for 15 minutes then chop finely. Place mushroom, oyster sauce, sugar, spring onion, coriander (to taste), remaining water, ginger, and cornflour in a pan. Heat and stir until mixture rises. Add vegetable oil, stir again quickly, then remove from heat.

Slice fish into ½ inch slices, pour sauce over sliced fish, and serve piping hot on a garnish of chopped crisp lettuce.

Serves: 6

Wine: *Vouvray, still or sparkling Marc Bredif*

La Toque Blanche

La Toque Blanche is an intimate, little French restaurant that is now 18 years old. Its one narrow room, with a raised section and bar at the rear, is softly lit and quietly decorated in grass wallpaper. The tables are laid with fine gold-rimmed china on crisp white linen, with a fresh flower or two and a candle on each.

The chef/proprietor, Charles Giovagnoli, who has been in the culinary business for more than 28 years, prepares authentic French dishes with flair and expertise; his sauces show particular skill.

The menu includes an appetising list of specialities that certainly live up to their promise. For example, the trout flambéed in Pernod and herbs on a rack over a fire of dried fennel and served with rosemary, butter, and a herb sauce is superb. It is called Truite Flambée Vieille Provence.

Mr. Giovagnoli is also renowned for his dessert crepes, especially for his Crepe au Fruits de Mer and Crepes Suzette. The cheese board is always exceptionally well stocked with more than 20 varieties of cheese.

The service, by waiters in dinner jackets, is courteous, sensitive, and skillful.

La Toque Blanche

21 ABINGDON ROAD
LONDON, W8

01-937-5832

LUNCH: 12:30 TO 1:45 P.M.
DINNER: 7 TO 10:45 P.M.
MONDAY - FRIDAY

DINNER RESERVATIONS

PROPRIETOR/CHEF:
CHARLES GIOVAGNOLI

Les Langoustines à Ma Façon

100 g carrots, diced

100 g onions, diced

1½ kg crayfish tails

chopped parsley, to taste

brandy, to flame

white wine, as needed

500 ml milk

cream, as needed

salt and pepper, to taste

75 g butter

75 g flour

Put the carrots and onions in a pan with the crayfish tails; heat, then flame with brandy. Add some white wine, milk, cream, and salt and pepper. Knead the butter and flour together to make *beurre manié*, then use it to thicken the sauce. Let cook for 10 minutes.

Serving suggestion: serve with rice.

Serves: 4

Truite Flambée Vieille Provence

10 g fennel seeds

4 × 300 g trout

8 fennel sticks

55 ml Pernod

20 g Herbs de Provence

3 anchovy fillets

10 French capers

1 hard-boiled egg, yolk only

3 tbsp olive oil

Put the fennel seeds in the trout and grill them until done. Place the trout in a dish with the fennel and flame with Pernod. Prepare a sauce by crushing the herbs, anchovies, capers, and egg yolk together, then add oil.

Serving suggestion: serve with new potatoes.

Serves: 4

Le Mont Blanc

100 g vanilla ice cream

550 ml cream

1 tbsp sugar

150 g sweet chestnut purée

55 ml Calvados

roasted flaked almonds, to garnish

Divide the ice cream into 4 serving dishes. Whip ¾ cream with sugar and add it to the chestnut purée; put into the dishes. Add Calvados to the remaining cream and put into the dishes. Sprinkle almonds on top and serve.

Serves: 4

Tower Hotel, The Princes Room

The Princes Room of the **Tower Hotel** is a name that lends itself to the history of the area in which this fine restaurant is to be found.

With a fully glazed floor-to-ceiling front, it offers the most superb views of Tower Bridge and the historic River Thames meandering by. It is a perfect setting for that important business lunch, a relaxed away-from-the-office break, or a romantic dinner.

The choice is yours from a superbly presented menu, ranging from a table d'hôte luncheon for those with limited time to the sit back and relax á la carte menu. The restaurant manager, Mr. Ken Hassall, and his professional staff will treat you in the manner shown to kings and queens of the past.

On Sunday, sit down to a royal feast of Henry VIII Sirloin of Beef carved for you in the traditional manner or let esteemed Chef de cuisine Peter Ricks prepare his own specialities for you.

In the evening, you can sit back and look at the romantically lit Tower Bridge. The River Thames will carry you away to the sound of harp music played live while you dine in the fashion and comfort you deserve.

You can be sure, unlike at the Tower of London in the past, that you will not pay with your head for such an enchanting atmosphere.

THE TOWER HOTEL

ST. KATHERINE'S WAY
LONDON, E1

01-481-2575

LUNCH: DAILY 12:30 TO 3 P.M.
DINNER: MONDAY - SATURDAY
6:30 TO 11 P.M.
SUNDAY 6:30 TO 10:30 P.M.
RESERVATIONS

PROPRIETOR: MICHAEL ROBERTS
CHEF: PETER RICKS

Espadon au Poivre (Peppered Swordfish)

2 oz crushed white peppercorns

2 fl oz cognac or Armagnac

2 × 8 oz swordfish steaks, fresh or frozen

salt, to taste

1 fl oz oil

2 oz butter, and as needed

1 oz chopped shallots

4 fl oz double cream

3 fl oz reduced veal stock or thick veal gravy

Soak peppercorns in some of the cognac for 1–2 hours before using to reconstitute them

Season fish with salt and liberally cover with peppercorns, pressing well into flesh. Heat oil and butter in a heavy-bottomed sauté pan and shallow fry fish. Allow to colour golden brown. Remove to a serving dish and keep warm.

Discard burnt oil from pan, add a little fresh butter, and cook shallots without colouring. Add cognac, flame, and reduce by ½. Add cream and veal stock and reduce until sauce is correct consistency and colour of *café au lait*. Pour over fish and serve immediately.

Émincé de Caneton aux Trois Citrons

2 large oranges

2 lemons

2 limes

1 × 5-6 lb fresh duckling

arrowroot, as needed

4 oz sugar

4 fl oz wine vinegar

4 fl oz port wine

Thinly peel the skin from 1 orange, 1 lemon, and 1 lime, and cut into very fine strips (use a zester if possible). Blanch in boiling water and set aside. Reserve juice from fruit. Peel remaining fruit, remove segments for garnish, and set aside.

Stuff duck with orange, lime, and lemon peel and trimmings. Roast duckling, keeping it slightly underdone. Allow to cool. Remove flesh from carcass, taking skin from leg and breast. Cut meat into oblique slices and lay in a serving dish and keep warm.

Make a thickened gravy (*jus lie*) using the carcass and trimmings from the duck and thicken with arrowroot.

Place sugar and vinegar in a heavy-bottomed saucepan and reduce until you have a caramel. Add wine and reduce by ½. Add 3 ounces *jus lie* and fruit juice and allow sauce to cook. Adjust seasoning and consistency if necessary.

Coat the duck portions with sauce. Garnish with alternate segments of orange, lemon, and lime. Sprinkle with the fruit zest and serve very hot.

Ananas Surprise (Pineapple Surprise)

1 very small baby pineapple

1 kiwi fruit

3 oz fresh strawberries

2 oz caster sugar

2 fl oz kirsch

1 scoop lemon sorbet

Remove the top from the pineapple with a small portion of pineapple attached. Reserve to use as a lid.

Carefully remove the flesh from inside of the pineapple, using a grapefruit knife, leaving the skin in 1 piece.

Cut the pineapple, kiwi fruit, and strawberries into fairly small dice. Marinate together with sugar and kirsch. Chill the fruit and pineapple case before serving.

Place a scoop of lemon sorbet in the bottom of the case. Pile the marinated fruit on top and replace the pineapple lid. Serve with crushed ice. (Decorate with spun sugar, if desired.)

Les Trois Canards

"*Son ambiance Francaise, sa bonne table et son service amical*" — there is no better way to describe **Les Trois Canards.** Situated in that part of Knightsbridge where the road narrows and the shopfronts retreat, Knightsbridge Green, as it is called, is a passageway lined with shops and eating places of which this restaurant is a part.

The menu at Les Trois Canards is a mixture of well-known traditional French dishes and original offerings presented by Chef Jean-Louis Genety, whose speciality is duckling. Le Canard a l'Etouffe en Croute and Magret de Canard au Poivre Vert are but two of his many creative preparations. Other dishes to try should include Gateau d'Epinards aux Crevettes, which is an oven-baked mousse of spinach served with prawn sauce, and the Truite Soufflée à la Cressonnette.

Their latest addition to the menu is L'Assiette Garnie, which would be better described as a one-course meal and which is proving very popular, especially at lunchtime for those who wish to have a simple, comparatively quick, and very reasonably-priced lunch.

To complement your meal, the restaurant offers a modest, but comprehensive, wine list from which to choose, or a quality house wine is available.

LES TROIS CANARDS

**14 KNIGHTSBRIDGE GREEN
LONDON, SW1**

01-589-0509

**MONDAY - FRIDAY:
LUNCH 12 TO 2 P.M.
DINNER 7 TO 10 P.M.
SATURDAY:
DINNER 7 TO 10:30 P.M.
RESERVATIONS**

**PROPRIETORS:
A. de FROBERVILLE, P. SAUZIER
CHEF: JEAN-LOUIS GENETY**

Vegetable Terrine with Fresh Tomato Sauce

600 g fresh vegetables: beans, carrots, red peppers, spinach, mushrooms, etc. to choice

salt, as needed

lemon juice, as needed

12-15 fonds (bottoms) of artichokes

1 tbsp Dijon mustard

500 ml double cream

3 eggs

20-25 g aspic jelly

pepper, to taste

1½ kg tomatoes, skinned and seeded

5 cloves garlic

200 g shallots

parsley, to taste

100 ml vinegar

400 ml oil

cayenne pepper, to taste

(Choose vegetables bearing in mind that colour is important in the final presentation.) Cook vegetables in boiling salted water with some lemon juice. Do not overcook them. Boil artichokes in water with a lot of lemon juice until very soft. Drain and cool artichokes, then mash and mix well with mustard, cream, eggs, aspic jelly, juice of 1 lemon, and salt and pepper, to taste.

Line an earthenware terrine with foil, then fill with artichoke mixture and vegetables, not mixed together but in a pleasing arrangement. Cook in a bain-marie in the oven at 300°F (150°C) for 40–45 minutes. Cool and refrigerate for at least 12 hours.

To prepare fresh tomato sauce: crush tomatoes with garlic, shallots, parsley, and vinegar. Whip in oil, then add salt, pepper, and cayenne pepper to taste.

To serve: cut terrine in slices and serve with sauce.

Serves: 10

Magret de Canard au Vinaigre de Jeres

1 × 200 g breast of duck

3-4 shallots, finely chopped

50 ml Jeres vinegar

50 ml cognac

veal stock, as needed

30 g butter

salt and ground pepper, to taste

Cook the duck on high heat on its side to release as much fat as possible, then turn over and cook a little longer but keep meat undercooked and still rare. Remove from pan. Slice all extra fat and skin off, cut skin into small pieces, and cook in fat until crisp and brown. Pour off fat and leave crisped pieces in pan. Add shallots and brown gently. Add vinegar, cognac, some veal stock, and reduce. Add butter.

Slice duck and arrange meat on a hot plate. Remove duck skin from sauce and pour sauce over duck meat. Season with salt and pepper and serve.

Serves: 1

Wine: *Santenay Maladine, 1977*

Bavarois au Chocolat

150-200 g cooking chocolate

water, as needed

juice of 1 lemon

peel of ¼ orange, finely cut

100-150 g butter

3 eggs, separated

150 ml Grand Marnier

15-20 g caster sugar

400-500 ml double cream

1 box ladyfinger biscuits

juice of 3 oranges

2 peeled and grated apples

Melt chocolate with a very small amount of water over gentle heat. While chocolate is melting, mix ½ lemon juice, orange peel, butter, 3 egg yolks, Grand Marnier, and sugar together. Whip cream and add to chocolate when it has cooled. Beat egg whites and fold carefully into chocolate and cream mixture. Put biscuits into a mould, pour Grand Marnier syrup over it, then spoon chocolate and cream mixture over all and leave at least 12 hours.

To serve: slightly warm the outside of the mould and turn onto a serving dish. Serve bavarois with a fruit sauce made by mixing orange juice, remaining lemon juice, and apples together.

Serves: 10

Waltons
of Walton
Street

Waltons of Walton Street is an eight-year-old restaurant situated in the fashionable London district of Chelsea. It is well-known for its modern interpretation of many Old English recipes and its many innovative offerings, including Whipped Camembert Mousse; Sole with Orange and Cream Sauce; Veal Paupiettes filled with spinach and smoked ham; a yogurt, mushroom, and celeriac salad; and Cream Cheese Pie — to cite just a sampling. All are expertly prepared by Chef Shamus Barrett, who was Waltons' sous-chef before becoming chef de cuisine.

The restaurant's high society clientele is regally enveloped in opulent elegance: the walls are covered in silk and dark mirrors, and the lamplit tables, each adorned with Georg Jensen cutlery and Royal Copenhagen china, are well spaced for privacy. The service is top class.

Waltons is also known for its extensive wine cellar that is rated internationally as one of the most outstanding available in all of Great Britain. The wines are French and German and featured are 90 chateau bottled clarets and more than 40 Burgundies. Choices from an extensive list of champagnes, liqueurs, and vintage cognacs are also available.

WALTONS OF WALTON STREET

**121 WALTON STREET
LONDON, SW3**

01-584-0204

**7 DAYS FOR LUNCH: 12:30 TO 2:30 P.M.
MONDAY - SATURDAY FOR DINNER:
7:30 TO 11:30 P.M.
RESERVATIONS**

**PROPRIETOR: WALTONS
RESTAURANTS, LTD.
CHEF: SHAMUS BARRETT, M.C.G.B.**

Crab and Gruyère Quiche

8 oz shortcrust pastry

4 oz fresh crabmeat

4 oz grated Gruyère cheese

6 eggs

1 pt double cream

    mace, salt, and pepper, to taste

    watercress, to garnish

Line an 8 inch flan ring with shortcrust pastry. Mix the crabmeat and cheese together, then distribute it evenly into the flan ring. Beat the eggs, then add cream and seasoning. Pour over crab and cheese mix and bake in oven at gas mark 6 (400°F/205°C) for about 45 minutes. Garnish with watercress and serve.

Serves: 8

Wine: *Gewürztraminer, 1978*

Pork Fillet with Prunes

1 large pork fillet, trimmed of fat

    seasoned flour, to dust

4 oz butter

10 prunes, stoned

1 tbsp finely chopped onion

1 port glass non-vintage port

½ pt double cream

    seasoning, to taste

    knob of butter

    parsley, to garnish

Cut the pork fillet into 8 pieces and flatten with a metal bat or wooden mallet. Coat with seasoned flour and fry lightly in heated butter, first sealing on both sides (should only take 1 minute). Garnish with prunes, then place in oven in a warmed dish while preparing the sauce.

Remove excess butter from the pan, add onion and port and reduce. Add cream and season to taste. When sauce thickens, remove from heat, add knob of butter for brightness, and pour over meat. Serve garnished with chopped parsley.

Serves: 4

CHEF'S TIP

BAT OUT PORK FILLETS AGAINST THE GRAIN OF THE MEAT USING A SMALL METAL BAT OR A WOODEN MALLET. THIS APPLIES TO ALL MEAT TO AVOID IT BECOMING TOUGH AND SINEWY.

Wine: *Hermitage La Chapelle, 1975*

Waltons' Apple Tart

½ lb butter

½ lb caster sugar

4 eggs

1 tbsp vanilla essence

½ lb ground almonds

    raspberry jam, as needed

1 sweet paste flan case

2 apples, sliced thinly

To prepare filling: cream butter and sugar together until white. Add eggs and vanilla essence. Fold in ground almonds.

Smooth a thin layer of jam on the base of the flan. Fill with the ground almond mixture and arrange the apple slices on top. Bake for approximately 45 minutes at 350°F (177°C). Serve.

Serves: 6

The Waterside Inn

The Waterside Inn at Bray is the latest acquisition of Michel and Albert Roux. It is set in delightful surroundings, on the banks of the River Thames, near Windsor. The restaurant looks out onto the river through the weeping willows, which are floodlit at night.

The interior is decorated in pastel pinks and greens, giving a bright and sunny atmosphere. Everything in the restaurant is special, from the little choux canapes served with apéritifs to petits fours with coffee, as well as the impeccable service and the excellent cooking.

The meals at Waterside are all prepared by the esteemed, award-winning Chef Michel Roux. Most of the dishes on the menu are Roux creations. They include a masterly fish mousse and rich, flavoursome shellfish bisque, among the starters, all admirably designed to whet the appetite before such beautifully sauced and garnished main courses as veal kidneys in sweet and sour sauce, lamb cutlets with sorrel sauce, or venison in a well reduced cream sauce with morels. The sweets are just as delightful, whether a simple sorbet or a delicately balanced confection such as sable aux poires.

Only three months after opening, The Waterside Inn was acclaimed by the gastronomic press. It is now one of four restaurants in Britain to rate two stars in the Michelin Guide.

The Waterside Inn

FERRY ROAD
BRAY, BERKSHIRE
0628-20691
LUNCH: TUESDAY · SUNDAY,
12 TO 2 P.M.
DINNER: TUESDAY · SUNDAY,
7:30 TO 10 P.M.
CLOSED SUNDAY EVENINGS FROM
NOVEMBER TO EASTER
AND 4 WEEKS FROM 27 DECEMBER
RESERVATIONS
PROPRIETOR: ROUX RESTAURANTS
CHEF: M.A. ROUX, M.C.G.B.

Cervelas de Brochet Vallée de l'Adour

300 g pike meat

1½ egg whites

1 litre double cream

salt and white pepper, to taste

100 g Parisian mushrooms, sliced

205 g butter

10 g green peppercorns

120 g sausage skin (pig intestines)

300 g white part of leek, sliced thinly

200 g bread crumbs

Mix pike meat with egg white in a mixer. Mix a couple of times and strain. Put mixture in a bowl and place on ice. With spatula, mix in ½ the double cream, gradually add salt and pepper, then place in refrigerator. Sauté mushrooms for 1 minute in 5 grams butter in a frying pan. Keep in a cool place. Mix pike mousse, green peppercorns, and mushrooms together.

Place sausage skin in water then hang. Knot 1 end. Stuff the skin with mousse, then knot other end with piece of string. Pierce skin all over with a needle to prevent bursting. Divide sausage into sections by tying with string, but not too tightly or sausage could split while cooking. Put hot salted water in a large pan. When water reaches 150°F (80°C), put in sausage for 15 minutes. Remove carefully and place carefully in iced water.

Melt 100 grams butter in frying pan on low heat. Add remaining double cream, let simmer. Add salt and leeks. Cook until crispy, then remove and keep warm.

With a sharp knife, remove skin of sausage but don't destroy shape. Roll in bread crumbs, place on baking tray, pour 100 grams melted butter on top. Leave in oven for 7 minutes at 345°F (190°C). When half-cooked, turn.

Put leeks on plate, place sausages carefully on top, and serve immediately.

Serves: 10

Veal Chops Boucanière

50 g flour

1 egg

125 ml milk

salt and pepper, to taste

100 g butter

60 g sweet corn

3 bananas

pinch of icing sugar

4 × 200 g veal chops

20 g fresh ginger, very finely grated

3 tbsp raspberry vinegar

200 ml veal stock

25 g powdered coconut

Make a batter by mixing flour, egg, and milk in a bowl. Add salt and let rest in a cool place 1 hour. Melt ½ teaspoon butter in a frying pan, add ¼ pancake mixture and ¼ sweet corn. When half-cooked, turn and cook other side.

Make 3 more pancakes. Set aside on a plate.

Peel and slice bananas into 1 centimetre thick pieces. Place on butter-coated baking tray. Sprinkle with icing sugar and cook in hot oven 2–3 minutes.

Melt 2½ grams butter in frying pan. Cook veal chops 2–3 minutes on each side. Centre of chops should be slightly pink. Keep in a warm place.

Remove fat from pan. Add ginger and leave for 1 minute. Add vinegar and reduce. Add veal stock and reduce by ½ to syrup consistency. Mix together with remaining butter, chopped in pieces, salt, and pepper. Strain and keep sauce warm.

Place 1 corn pancake on each plate, sprinkle with coconut, and place chop on top. Put the 4 plates in the oven for 2 minutes at 340°F (170°C). Arrange the banana around the edge of each plate, pour sauce over veal, and serve.

Serving suggestions: serve with gratin dauphinois or savoyard, or purée de panais.

Serves: 4

Plumber Manor

Plumber Manor has been a country home of the Prideaux-Brune family since the early 17th century and is now being run as a "Restaurant with Bedrooms" under the personal supervision of Richard and Alison Prideaux-Brune.

The Manor makes a perfect halfway setting between London and Cornwall and is within easy reach of Bath, Salisbury, Sherborne, Bournemouth, and the historic splendours of Longleat, Stourhead, and Wilton. The coast is less than 30 miles away, and several golf courses, fishing on the Stour, and riding are all close at hand.

There are six very comfortable bedrooms, all with private bathrooms, that are accessible from a charming gallery hung with portraits of the family.

The restaurant at Plumber Manor, part of which is in the elegant old drawing room, seats 70 and provides an exceptional standard of cuisine and wines. The cuisine is Anglo/French and is administered by Chef Brian Prideaux-Brune, Richard's brother. Brian trained extensively in London and has created many of the items appearing on the menu. The wine list offers a comprehensive choice of French and German vintages, most at reasonable prices.

The restaurant, which opened in 1973, is actually made up of three separate dining rooms that have been designed to afford guests with a maximum amount of comfort. The colour scheme of blue with light blue linen on large tables and the paintings hanging on the walls add to an already pleasant eating atmosphere.

PLUMBER MANOR

**STURMINSTER NEWTON
DORSET**

0258-72507

**DINNER: TUESDAY — SUNDAY
RESERVATIONS**

**PROPRIETOR: RICHARD PRIDEAUX-BRUNE
CHEF: BRIAN PRIDEAUX-BRUNE**

Paupiettes of Smoked Salmon
with Avocado Fromage

2 ripe medium avocados, peeled, stoned,
and chopped roughly

juice of 1 lemon

¼ lb cream cheese,
Philadelphia preferred

generous dash Worcestershire sauce

1 tsp finely grated onion

salt and pepper, to taste

½ pt double cream

24 slices smoked salmon, each 3 by 4 in

sprigs of watercress, to garnish

lemon wedges, to garnish

To prepare avocado fromage: purée the chopped avocado with lemon juice until smooth. Add the cream cheese gradually and blend until smooth. Transfer to a large bowl, then add a generous dash of Worcestershire sauce, the grated onion, and a good seasoning of salt and pepper. Whisk the cream until thick, then fold in. Check and adjust seasoning if needed. Cover the bowl with cling foil and chill for 15–20 minutes.

Put a dollop of the avocado fromage in the centre of each slice of smoked salmon and roll up carefully. Place 3 paupiettes on each place, garnish each with a sprig of watercress and wedge of lemon and serve.

Serves: 8

Chicken Indienne

8 good-sized chicken breasts, boned

4 small bananas, finely sliced

24 white grapes, halved and pitted

4 tbsp crushed hazelnuts

2 oz butter

12 fl oz basic curry sauce

8 fl oz double cream

Remove the fillet (the underside flap) from the chicken breasts, then pound (not too vigorously) each until flat. Flatten each fillet. Stuff each breast with ½ banana, 6 grape halves, and ⅛ hazelnuts. Place fillet on top and fold the ends over to make a rectangular parcel.

Place the breasts, rounded side up, close together in a shallow roasting tin in which the butter has been melted. Bake in a preheated oven at gas mark 5 (375°F/190°C) for 20–25 minutes, basting frequently, until cooked through and golden brown.

Make up the curry sauce or use prepared sauce and whisk in the cream. Transfer chicken to a shallow flameproof dish and pour the sauce over. Put over gentle heat until bubbling and slightly thickened. Remove from heat and serve.

Serves: 8

Athollbrose Plumber Manor Style

¾ pt whipping cream

clear honey, to taste

whisky, to taste

2 tbsp flaked almonds

Whip the whipping cream until thick. Gently fold in the clear honey and whisky to taste. Add the flaked almonds. Put into glass bowls and chill. Serve cold.

Serves: 4

Le Talbooth Restaurant

Le Talbooth Restaurant, owned by Gerald Milsom, is a 16th century house perched on the banks of the River Stour, and it has a private view of Dedham Vale. With its timber frame and overhanging willows, the building looks like part of the archetypal Constable painting, and in fact, he did paint the scene. The painting now hangs in the National Gallery of Scotland.

The structure has only recently become a fully-fledged restaurant. It began as a tea shop, but gradually Mr. Milsom has built it up, renovating and rebuilding, to make it the restaurant it is today. Le Talbooth now has a riverside dining room and bar, a new dining room (which blends in beautifully with the existing building), and two upstairs rooms available for private lunches and parties.

The young chef, Sam Chalmers, runs the kitchen with expert efficiency, which is probably due to his calm temperament and ability to inspire confidence and respect. He and his sous-chefs are creating a new, lighter style of cooking. They are building up a repertoire reflecting this change in emphasis, and new dishes are constantly being tested and perfected.

The heavily beamed restaurant is luxuriously furnished, and this complements the fine English and French cooking of Chef Chalmers.

Le Talbooth

GUN HILL
DEDHAM, COLCHESTER
ESSEX

0206-323150

LUNCH: 12:30 TO 2 P.M.
DINNER: 7:30 TO 9 P.M.
DAILY
RESERVATIONS

PROPRIETOR: GERALD MILSOM
CHEF: SAM CHALMERS, M.C.G.B.

Soufflé Talbooth

2½ oz butter

¼ lb button mushrooms, finely diced

¼ lb smoked haddock, Finnan haddock preferred

¼ pt single cream

salt and pepper, to taste

pinch of cayenne pepper

1 oz flour

8 fl oz milk

1 oz Parmesan cheese

4 egg yolks

5 egg whites

To prepare the filling: melt 1 ounce butter in a medium saucepan and add mushrooms. Cook until mushrooms have softened and darkened in colour. Flake the haddock, taking care to remove all bones. Add haddock and cream to pan and blend well. Season to taste with salt and pepper and add a pinch of cayenne pepper. Simmer gently over low heat for about 10 minutes. Divide among 4 large ramekin dishes (4 inches in diameter), then set aside.

Preheat oven to gas mark 7 (425°F/220°C).

In another saucepan, melt the remaining butter. Stir in flour and cook for 1–2 minutes. Blend in the milk and cook over moderate heat, stirring frequently until mixture thickens. Simmer for about 5 minutes, then add cheese. Blend well, then let cool slightly. Slowly beat in the egg yolks, one at a time. Whisk the whites until very stiff and fold in lightly. Pile on top of the partially filled ramekins. Put ramekins into the preheated oven and bake for 12–15 minutes or until golden brown. Take out and serve at once.   Serves: 4

Suprême de Volaille aux Épinards

2 oz butter

2 shallots, peeled and chopped

4 oz mushrooms, cut into small dice

1 fl oz dry white wine

salt and pepper, to taste

4 oz fresh spinach, washed and stalks removed

4 chicken breasts

Put 1½ ounces of butter in a small frying pan, heat, and when foaming, add shallots. Sauté until shallots soften, then add mushrooms and continue cooking until they have darkened. Add wine and continue cooking for about 5 minutes. Season to taste with salt and pepper. Blanch the spinach in boiling salted water for 2 minutes, then refresh under running cold water and drain well. Set aside.

Preheat oven to gas mark 8 (450°F/230°C).

Carefully bone chicken breasts and tuck a large dollop of mushroom stuffing in between the fillet (or flap) and the main part of the breast. Wrap each one in several spinach leaves, then wrap again in a parcel of foil. Place in a buttered dish and bake for 15–20 minutes in the preheated oven. Take out, remove foil, and serve at once.

Serves: 4

Iced Strawberry Soufflé

100 g sugar

3 eggs, separated

2 leaves gelatine

200 g strawberry purée

300 ml cream

Beat sugar and egg yolks until pale. Dissolve gelatine. Pour on puréed strawberries and continue to beat. Whip cream and whites separately. Add dissolved gelatine and fold in cream, then whites. Pour into a mould. Place in deep freeze. Take out 1 hour before serving and decorate as desired.

Serves: 4

Chewton Glen Hotel

The **Chewton Glen Hotel** is a luxurious privately owned country house hotel set in 30 acres of parkland on the fringe of the New Forest. It is only a half mile from the sea and is situated between Christchurch and Lymington.

The original house was built in 1732, and in 1837, it was bought by Colonel George Marryat. His brother, Captain Frederick Marryat RN, stayed at the house in the 1840s and gathered material for his famous novel, *The Children of the New Forest*. After a succession of owners, the house became a hotel in 1962. The Skan family bought it in 1967 and have developed and improved the hotel since then. It now has 55 beautifully appointed bedrooms and suites, as well as the Marryat Room Restaurant, renowned for its delicate French cuisine and impeccable service.

The oak-panelled restaurant has a warm, relaxed atmosphere. French windows open onto a terrace and gently sloping lawns. The room is candlelit in the evenings, and both table d'hôte and à la carte menus are offered for lunch and dinner. Chef Christian Delteil expertly prepares his French dishes in the style of *la nouvelle cuisine* where the emphasis is on light sauces with subtle flavours. The wine list is very extensive, with more than 200 choices in a wide price range covering every region of France as well as several other major wine producing countries.

Chewton Glen Hotel

NEW MILTON, HAMPSHIRE
04252-5341
BREAKFAST, LUNCH, AND DINNER
DAILY
RESERVATIONS
PROPRIETOR: MARTIN SKAN
CHEF: CHRISTIAN DELTEIL

Médaillons de Volaille aux Girolles

4 chicken thighs (not drumsticks)

1 egg white

800 ml double cream

salt, to taste

120 g girolle mushrooms, finely sliced

100 g butter, and as needed

4 chicken breasts

pepper, to taste

500 ml chicken stock, and as needed

100 g chopped shallots

1 soupspoon Noilly Prat vermouth

Remove meat from bones of chicken thighs and mince in a chopping machine. Pass through a sieve and place in a bowl on ice. Add egg white and beat together with a wooden spoon for 3–4 minutes. Add 500 millilitres double cream and beat again for 3–4 minutes. When mousse thickens, season with salt. Toss mushrooms in ½ the butter and add to mousse.

Take the small fillets from underneath each breast, flatten with a bat or large knife, and set aside. Cut a slit in each breast along its length, halfway in depth. Open slit to make a pocket and season with salt and pepper. Fill pockets with mousse of chicken and girolles using a piping bag and tube. Fold over the edges of the breasts to enclose the mousse and seal over with the previously flattened fillets. Cook slowly over low heat for 10–12 minutes in a pan with the remaining butter and some chicken stock.

To make the sauce: sweat the shallots in a little butter for 1 minute, then add vermouth and remaining chicken stock. Reduce by ⅓, then add remaining double cream. Bring to a boil and reduce further to make a smooth sauce. Season with salt and pepper.

Remove bones from chicken breasts. Cut each into 4 medallions, or slices, cutting on the slant across the width of the breast. Arrange the medallions on a plate showing the chicken with the stuffing. Pour sauce around the medallions and serve.

Serving suggestion: serve with fresh noodles flavoured with basil.

Serves: 4

Wine: *Chateau de Selle Rose, Domaines Ott*

Pêches au Sauternes

6 large peaches

1 bottle Sauternes wine

475 g caster sugar

1 stick vanilla

1 kg raspberries

juice of ½ lemon

300 ml double cream

230 g plain flour

340 g icing sugar

250 g unsalted butter

8 egg whites

2 drops vanilla essence

Blanch peaches in boiling water for 1 minute, then remove and drain. Peel peaches, place in a thick saucepan, and cover with Sauterne. Add 300 grams caster sugar and vanilla stick and cover pan with greaseproof paper. Heat and simmer without boiling until small bubbles are released from the peaches. Turn off heat and let peaches cool in the wine.

To prepare *coulis de framboises* (raspberry sauce): mash raspberries finely in a blender, then pass through a fine strainer. Add 150 grams caster sugar and the lemon juice and mix well.

To prepare *mousse de framboises:* whip the double cream and the remaining caster sugar until thick. Add 3 tablespoons of the coulis de framboises and fold in carefully.

To prepare *panier à tuile* (biscuit baskets): mix the flour and icing sugar together. Beat butter and egg whites together in a bowl. Add the flour and sugar mixture to the butter and egg whites, add the vanilla essence, and fold together without overmixing. Lightly grease a large baking sheet with some butter. Pour separate tablespoons of the mixture on the sheet with a gap of 3 inches between each spoonful. Bake in a medium oven at gas mark 4 (360°F/180°C) until a light brown colour.

Whilst biscuits are hot, place each one over a cup or small bowl and shape to make a basket. (Do this quickly before biscuits cool.) Each one should have a flat top to help it stand firmly. When baskets are cool, remove them from the moulds. Place a little mousse de framboises in each one. Drain the peaches for 1 minute and place one in each basket and coat with coulis de framboises. The syrup and remaining coulis de framboises can be served separately.

Serves: 6

Wine: *Picolit, Colli Orientali del Fruili*

Eastwell Manor

Eastwell Manor is set in 3,000 acres of picture book pasture and woodland in Kent. The house has been there since Elizabethan times. It passed through various hands, including those of the Duke of Saxe-Coburg and Gotha, better known as Queen Victoria's second son.

For a long time the house was almost derelict. In 1977, a Mr. Bates bought the house and land. His son, Matthew, who had been in the hotel trade for some years, having worked in the kitchens of the Savoy in France and at the Talbooth in Dedham, was keen to run the manor as a hotel, so the house was refurbished, rewired, and re-plumbed. It is now one of the most elegant country house hotels in Britain — a vision of mullioned windows and panelled halls.

The renowned restaurant seats 80 in two panelled dining rooms that have views of the gardens. The excellent cuisine is a subtle blend of French and English dishes with an emphasis on *la nouvelle cuisine* approach. The wine list has been thoughtfully compiled.

The chef is Ian McAndrew, late of the Dorchester. A disciple of the brilliant Chef Anton Mosimann, his food is light, delicious, and wholly admirable. The Terrine de Turbot aux Fines Herbes, the Game Pie, and the Supreme of Wild Duck are all outstanding. The house specialities are Émincé de Huîtres Nouveau and Jonquil Printanier, both of which appear on the page opposite.

Eastwell Manor

EASTWELL PARK
ASHFORD, KENT

0233-35751

BREAKFAST: 7 TO 10 A.M.
LUNCH: 12:30 TO 2 P.M.
DINNER: 7:30 TO 9:30 P.M.
DAILY
RESERVATIONS

PROPRIETOR: MATTHEW BATES
CHEF: IAN McANDREW

Émincé de Huîtres Nouveau

12 oz broccoli

6 fl oz fish stock

3 fl oz dry white wine

2 oz chopped shallots

8 oysters, shelled and diced

6 fl oz double cream

6 oz chanterelles

½ oz unsalted butter

Break the broccoli into fleurettes and blanch. Bring fish stock, wine, and ⅓ the shallots to a boil, add diced oysters, and poach for about 12–15 seconds. Remove oysters and reduce the liquid. When reduced, add cream and reduce until thickened. Sauté chanterelles and broccoli in butter with remaining shallots.

Pile broccoli, etc. onto a plate, add oysters to sauce to reheat them, remove from sauce when hot and pile on top of broccoli, etc. Pour sauce around the plate and serve.

Serves: 4

Wine: *Pouilly Fumé, 1978*

Suprême de Canard aux Petites Légumes

4 supremes of duck

salt and pepper, to taste

1 dessertspoon oil

3 fl oz brandy

1 oz green peppercorns

15 fl oz *jus de canard* (thickened stock made from duck carcass)

6 oz batons of vegetables: celery, carrot, turnip, and leek cut in 1¼ by ¼ in strips

1 oz unsalted butter

Season supremes and seal them in a hot pan with oil on meat side. Turn onto skin and cook about 8 minutes or until meat is still pink. Remove from pan and drain off fat, deglaze pan with brandy and peppercorns. Add *jus de canard* and batons of vegetables; reduce slightly. Season and whisk in butter. Pour sauce into a serving dish and pile vegetables together on one side of dish. Slice supremes thinly lengthways and arrange in a fan shape slightly overlapping the pile of vegetables.

Serves: 4

Wine: *Corton Charlemagne, Roland Rapet*

Jonquil Printanier

1 egg white

salt, as needed

juice of ½ lemon

4 daffodils, washed and dried

4 oz caster sugar

4 kiwi fruit, sliced

4 oz puréed strawberries

Slightly beat the egg whites with a little salt and lemon juice. White should be very, very watery. Coat the dried daffodils completely with egg white and allow to drain for a few seconds. Liquidise the caster sugar to produce a powder halfway between caster sugar and icing sugar, then completely coat the daffodils with sugar and leave to dry. Arrange the kiwi fruit in a circle on 4 dishes, top each with a daffodil, and surround it with a purée of fresh strawberries.

Serves: 4

Wine: *Perrier-Jouet, Rose, 1975*

Mallet's

When Simon Mallet and his wife started **Mallet's** restaurant three years ago, it was with the firm belief that the serious eaters had had enough of pretentious and overly elaborate places that catered more to the eye than the palate. They admit that this statement was also reinforced by the fact that they hadn't enough money to start up any other way. Nevertheless, as chef at Mallet's, Simon believes that the food is what is important. His opinion comes from experiences in the business, not simply from idealism. After studying in Lausanne, he worked for Michael Waterfield at The Wife of Bath in Wye and later for George Perry-Smith, formerly of The Hole in the Wall and now of Riverside. Both these top chefs are also subscribers to this philosophy.

Simon changes his menus, which feature mostly French provincial dishes, every week, "to stop me from getting fed up cooking the same thing too often." He also bakes his own bread every day.

The quality of the raw material is really of the essence and has to be watched constantly. Simon says that the choice of things to cook is depressingly small outside London, and much time has to be spent just finding people who can supply good products. His wine list is modest but well chosen, as are the two house wines available.

The decor of Mallet's is simple to complement the casual atmosphere; vintage jazz and old French records are played loud enough to hear but not loud enough to disturb.

Mallet's

58 QUEEN STREET
RAMSGATE, KENT

0843-52854

LUNCH: 12:30 TO 2 P.M.
DINNER: 7:30 TO 10 P.M.
TUESDAY — SATURDAY
RESERVATIONS

PROPRIETOR/CHEF: SIMON K. MALLET

Monkfish with Gruyère Cheese

monkfish tail (angler or la lotte), cubed

Gruyère cheese, cubed

egg, as needed

bread crumbs, to dust

sunflower oil, to sauté (optional)

(Adjust quantities to taste and depending on whether dish is a starter or a light lunch.)

Alternate cubes of monkfish tail (or other fish) and Gruyère cheese on wooden or metal skewers. Coat with egg and bread crumbs, then shallow fry in sunflower oil or cook in a moderate to hot oven until golden brown, approximately 10 minutes.

Serving suggestion: serve with lemon mayonnaise.

Wine: *a white Côtes du Rhone*

Pigeon Pie

2 **large sliced onions**

2 **medium sliced carrots**

6 **sliced sticks celery**

6 **oz green, streaky bacon, chopped**

3 **cloves garlic, chopped**

butter, to sauté

6 **oz whole peeled chestnuts, or tinned natural without sugar**

2 **sprigs fresh thyme**

juice of 1 lemon

seasoning, to taste

4 **plucked and gutted pigeons**

chicken stock and white wine, as needed

shortcrust pastry dough, as needed

1 **egg, beaten**

Sweat onions, carrots, celery, bacon, and garlic with butter in a heavy casserole pan until onions are transparent. Cook slowly then add chestnuts, thyme, lemon juice, seasoning, and pigeons. Add chicken stock and white wine in equal amounts to cover birds. Cook in a slow oven at gas mark 2 (320°F/160°C) for 2½ hours. Let cool, then remove pigeons, strip carcasses, and cut flesh into strips. Strain vegetables and reduce liquid at fairly high heat until it thickens.

Mix all the vegetables and cut pigeon together and put into 4 small pie dishes. Cover with liquid, put shortcrust pastry on top, then brush with beaten egg. Replace in oven on medium heat until pastry is cooked and brown.

Alternate serving suggestion: when pigeons are cooked in the casserole, they can be served straight from the pan with just salad and potatoes.

Serves: 4

Wine: *Beaujolais or a red Rhone, Fleurie*

Walnut and Treacle Tart

4 **whole eggs**

1½ **lemons**

7 **fl oz golden syrup**

7 **fl oz black treacle**

10 **oz walnuts, approximately**

1 × 8 **in blind baked shortcrust pastry case**

Beat eggs to break albumen until well mixed. Add grated lemon rind, being careful not to get any pith in the mixture. Mix in syrup and treacle. Put walnuts in pre-cooked flan case, making sure there are no holes in the pastry.

Pour the syrup mixture over the walnuts and cook for 30–40 minutes in a medium oven until just firm in the middle.

The Toastmasters Inn

The Toastmasters Inn was purchased by the Ward family in 1964. The property at that time was known as the Royal Exchange and was a simple public house catering to the inhabitants of Burham, a 19th century industrial village. The name of the establishment was changed by the present owner's father, an internationally known Toastmaster.

After extensive alterations, the restaurant was opened in 1969 and has since achieved acclaim for the imaginative and inventive use of high quality raw materials in the preparation of the dishes featured on the short but frequently changed menu.

Presentation of the finished dish has always been of paramount importance, and the kitchen brigade of Chef Peter Chapman, Paul Duval, and Mark Clayton, displays considerable artistry in this direction and most dishes are arranged in the kitchen to this end.

The interior of the Inn is plainly but attractively decorated, and it is accented with prints and paintings by eminent local artists and a collection of wine- and food-related antiques.

The wine list has been the subject of particular praise over the years and is perhaps the most comprehensive in the South of England. Some of the wines date from the last century.

The Toastmasters Inn

CHURCH STREET
BURHAM NEAR ROCHESTER
KENT

MEDWAY 61299

LUNCH: TUESDAY — FRIDAY,
12 TO 2 P.M.
DINNER: TUESDAY — SATURDAY,
7 TO 10 P.M.
RESERVATIONS

PROPRIETOR: GREGORY WARD
CHEF: PETER CHAPMAN

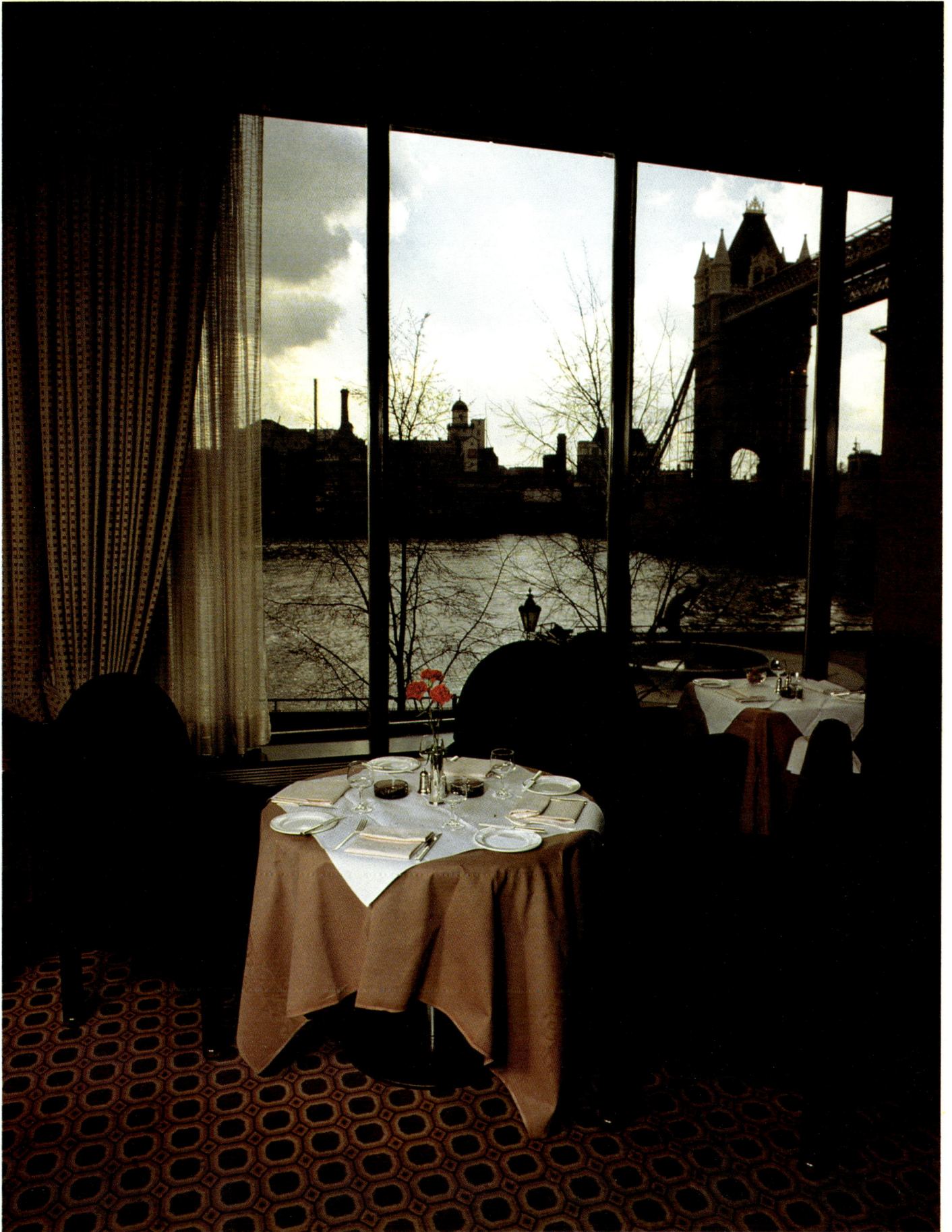

Tower Hotel   The Princes Room

Rookery Hall

The Elms Hotel

Lythe Hill Hotel   Auberge de France

Le Mariage de Fruits de Mer

8 large fresh scallops, cut in strips, with coral cut in half

200 g fresh salmon, cut in strips

25 ml raspberry or sherry vinegar

juice of ½ lemon

½ bunch chives, chopped

salt and freshly ground pepper, to taste

2 ripe green avocado pears, skinned and stoned

125 ml fresh natural yogurt

cress, to garnish

Place sliced scallops and salmon in a bowl. Add vinegar, lemon juice, and chopped chives. Season with salt and pepper. Mix well and leave to marinate for at least 10 minutes. Purée the avocado flesh; then mix in yogurt, season, and spread evenly over the centres of 4 chilled plates. Arrange the marinated fish into even mounds in the centre of the avocado purée. Garnish the rim of the plates with the halved coral and place a fine rim of cress around the avocado perimeter.

Serves: 4

Suprême de Pintade Farci aux Pruneaux d'Agen

100 g minced guinea fowl, from the legs of 4 guinea fowl

80 g Agen or touraine prunes, stoned and cooked in black tea

salt and freshly ground pepper, to taste

4 French guinea fowl breasts

⅛ litre red Burgundy wine

2 tsp chopped prunes

500 ml guinea stock, made from bones and well reduced

10 ml prune eau de vie or cognac

20 g cold unsalted butter

small spring onions, baby silverskin onions, and shallots, to garnish

butter, as needed

Mix the first 3 ingredients together to make the stuffing. Cut a small pocket into each guinea fowl breast, season, and fill with the mixed stuffing ingredients (leave the prunes whole). Wrap breasts in foil and roast for 8–12 minutes at 480°F (250°C).

To prepare the sauce: reduce the red wine and chopped prunes in a saucepan on top of the stove. Add stock and reduce further. Remove foil from guinea fowl breasts and flame in the prune de vie or cognac. Add resulting pan juices to the sauce and remove from heat. Add cold butter slowly and adjust seasoning to taste.

Sweat the spring onions, baby silverskin onions, and shallots in butter. Arrange the breasts and hot vegetable garnish on heated plates and cover with sauce.

Serves: 4

Les Fruits Exotiques au Safran

5 egg yolks

70 g sugar

500 ml milk

saffron, as needed

minimum of 10 exotic fruits: mango, papaya, guava, lychees, fig, kiwi, prickly pear, kumquat, etc.

To prepare *crème anglaise au safran:* cream the egg yolks and sugar together. Heat the milk, then add to the egg mixture. Return to heat and gently cook until it thickens. Do not boil or it will curdle. Add the saffron in sufficient quantity to colour and flavour.

Prepare the exotic fruits and, where possible, cut into large, neat shapes.

Pour the sauce onto a large ovenproof serving plate and arrange the fruits decoratively on the top. Warm through in a hot oven, then glaze under the grill and serve.

The Wife of Bath

The Wife of Bath restaurant was opened in 1963 by Michael Waterfield. The building is small and plainly decorated and furnished, but with character and charm.

Brian Boots joined the restaurant soon after as a waiter, and in 1965, Robert Johnson came in as a part-time waiter in the evenings. Towards the end of 1971, Mr. Waterfield invited the two others to join him as partners; Boots would run the restaurant and Johnson would join Waterfield in the kitchen. By 1975, Mr. Waterfield had slowly begun to withdraw, and in 1978, he became a sleeping partner, leaving Boots and Johnson to run the restaurant.

Their staff in the bar, restaurant, and kitchen is composed mainly of local people, and most have been with the restaurant since the beginning. This is something that the regular customers much appreciate; the owners have created a family atmosphere in which the people are always familiar.

The menu, featuring mainly French cuisine, is small, yet imaginative. It changes weekly in order to present selected seasonal dishes using fresh game, salmon, and vegetables. The restaurant also offers homemade pâtés, terrines, sorbets, and ices. Of particular note is the use of freshly picked flowers in the preparation of some of the dishes. There is a modest wine list and several house wines to choose from as well.

The Wife of Bath

**4 BRIDGE STREET
WYE, KENT**

WYE 812540

**LUNCH: 12 TO 2 P.M.
DINNER: 7 TO 10 P.M.
TUESDAY — SATURDAY
RESERVATIONS**

**PROPRIETORS:
BRIAN BOOTS, ROBERT JOHNSON
CHEF: ROBERT JOHNSON**

Fleurs de Courgettes Farcies

1 lb fresh or frozen spinach

¼ lb soft cream cheese

½ nutmeg, grated

juice of ½ lemon

salt and pepper, to taste

1 bunch spring onions, finely chopped

butter, as needed

12 open courgette flowers, freshly picked

¼ oz fresh yeast

warm water, as needed

½ tsp mixed salt and pepper

2 tbsp olive oil

¼ lb plain flour

lager, as needed

lemon wedges, to garnish

Chop the spinach lightly and add to cream cheese, nutmeg, lemon juice, and salt and pepper to taste. Sweat onions in butter until soft and add to mixture. Fill flowers with mixture, gently close petals around flowers and refrigerate.

To prepare batter: melt yeast in a little warm water. Add salt, pepper, and oil. Make a well in the flour, add mixture and stir. Thin to coating consistency by adding lager. Leave for at least 1 hour. Batter should then be of a consistency to coat a finger dipped in it. If too thick, add more lager. Dip courgette flowers in batter and deep fry at 320°F (160°C) until golden brown. Serve with lemon wedges.

Escalopes de Dinde aux Trois Épices

6 spring onions

1½ oz butter

1½ oz flour

1½ pt dry white wine

¾ oz cumin seeds, powdered

¾ oz cardamom seeds, powdered

1½ oz coriander seeds, powdered

½ pt chicken stock

1 garlic clove, crushed

salt and pepper, to taste

12 slices fresh turkey breast

seasoned flour, to dust

butter, to sauté

½ pt double cream

Sweat spring onions in butter until soft, then add flour and mix. Add wine, spices, stock, and seasonings. Cook thoroughly.

Dust turkey with seasoned flour and gently cook in a little butter until brown; turn over, then add onion, spice, and wine mixture. Allow to cook a few minutes, then add cream. Allow sauce to brown slightly and thicken. Serve at once. Serving suggestion: serve with new potatoes and vegetables or salad.

Serves: 6

Elderflower Sorbet

¾ pt fresh lemon juice

zest of 1 lemon

7 oz sugar

1¼ pt cold water

6 large elderflower heads

2 egg whites

Add lemon juice, lemon zest, and sugar to the water. Submerge elderflower heads in liquid and bring heat slowly up to just below boiling. Leave to cool, then strain off flowers. Either churn in an ice cream maker or freeze, constantly stirring until frozen. Whip egg whites and fold into sorbet just before serving.

Serves: 6

Lythe Hill Hotel, Auberge de France

The **Lythe Hill Hotel** is a beautifully timbered, 14th century farmhouse that is now a supremely comfortable country hotel with a glowing reputation for good food.

In its elegant restaurant, **Auberge de France,** you can enjoy the finest dishes and wines of France. Here the soft lighting reflects on copper pans and silver candelabras. The oak beamed and panelled dining room, with picture windows overlooking the gardens and one of the finest views in Surrey, is a truly romantic setting. There is also an intimate bar overlooking the hotel's own terrace and lake.

Chef Bernard Guillot, who is originally from Lyon and has been at Lythe Hill for five years, expertly prepares not only the classic dishes, but also his own specialities. It is French cooking at its best. There is an extensive à la carte menu, and some of the dishes are cooked right at the table.

The wine list includes a good choice of imported as well as English wines, and the excellent house wine is bottled in France exclusively for the Auberge de France.

Raymond Winiecka, managing director of the Lythe Hill Hotel since 1971, can be justly proud of the warm atmosphere and superb cuisine of this lovely French restaurant.

Lythe Hill Hotel

**PETWORTH ROAD
HASLEMERE, SURREY**

0428-51251

**OPEN MID-FEBRUARY TO CHRISTMAS
LUNCH: WEDNESDAY - SUNDAY,
12:30 TO 2:30 P.M.
DINNER: TUESDAY - SUNDAY,
7:30 TO 11 P.M.
RESERVATIONS**

**PROPRIETOR:
HASLEMERE HOTELS, LTD.
CHEF: BERNARD GUILLOT**

Grenadin de Veau Jeannette

butter, to sauté

8 medallions of veal, 100 g each

seasoned flour, to dust

1 glass white wine

2 tsp tomato purée

½ tsp chopped tarragon

300 ml Hollandaise sauce

4 fresh artichoke bottoms, warmed

500 g duxelles of mushrooms, heated

2 tbsp chopped fresh parsley

Melt butter in a sauté pan. Dip the medallions in seasoned flour and colour in the butter for 6–8 minutes, depending on the thickness of the medallions. Remove medallions from pan and keep warm. Drain fat from pan and de-glaze pan with white wine. Reduce by ⅔ until slightly thick. Stir in the tomato purée and tarragon, then gently blend in the Hollandaise sauce.

Fill the warm artichoke bottoms with the hot duxelles of mushrooms. Dress neatly in a dish with the veal, then coat the medallions with the sauce. Finish with chopped parsley and serve immediately.

Serves: 4

Wine: *Chateau Calon Segur, St. Estephe Medoc, 1970*

Supreme of Chicken Souvaroff

50 g butter

4 tbsp flour

4 × 200 g supremes of chicken

200 ml veal stock

150 ml double cream

100 ml port

100 g goose liver mousse

1 tbsp brandy

4 thin slices of truffle

Melt the butter in a sauté pan. Flour the supremes and colour in the butter for 3 minutes per side. Drain off the fat, add veal stock, cream, and port reduced by ½ to the sauce. Remove from heat and blend in the goose liver mousse with a fork. Add brandy to the sauce and coat each supreme with sauce and decorate each with a slice of truffle.

Serves: 4

Wine: *Fixin la Maziere, Domaine Marion, 1974*

CHEF'S TIP

GOOSE LIVER MOUSSE MIXED WITH HALF ITS ORIGINAL WEIGHT OF BUTTER BLENDS BETTER WITH ANY SAUCE.

Tarte Lyonnaise

200 g flour

100 g butter

25 ml water

pinch of salt

100 g fresh bread crumbs

250 ml milk

100 g sugar

30 ml kirsch

50 g ground almonds

4 egg yolks

2 egg whites, beaten very stiffly

One hour in advance, prepare shortcrust pastry with the first 4 ingredients. Roll the pastry in a flan case. Soak the bread crumbs in milk, then put bread crumbs and all other ingredients into the flan case. Bake for 30 minutes at gas mark 6 (400°F/205°C).

Serves: 4

Pennyhill Park Hotel

The **Pennyhill Park Hotel** is located in the heart of rural Surrey amidst the peace and quiet of more than 100 acres of magnificent gardens and parkland. Its present owner, Mr. Ian Hayton, who purchased the house and land in May 1978, cleverly preserved its country house atmosphere. The 33 bedrooms and suites, many retaining some of the original pieces they were furnished with, offer every modern comfort.

Pennyhill Park is known widely for its gardens, which are among the finest in Southern England, and for its beautifully restored Edwardian Orangery, which now houses the hotel's country club. It is a base for horseriding, fishing, clayshooting, swimming, tennis, and golf — not to forget the relaxed game of croquet no country house would be complete without.

The highly recommended restaurants are among the most noted outside London. The Latymer Room, in elegant Tudor style, offers truly superb traditional and original cuisine. In contrast, the Tamarisk Room, in the relaxed atmosphere of an indoor garden, offers an imaginative menu of reasonably priced dishes. Whatever your choice, the staff and general ambiance make you feel that you are there as a guest of a country house, rather than as a hotel visitor.

In this peaceful setting, whether on business or pleasure, it is difficult to realize that bustling London is only a mere 27 miles away.

Pennyhill Park

**COLLEGE RIDE
BAGSHOT, SURREY**

BAGSHOT 71774

**BREAKFAST, LUNCH, AND DINNER
DAILY
RESERVATIONS**

**PROPRIETOR: IAN HAYTON
CHEF: BRYAN BENSON**

Carrot and Watercress Soup

2 oz butter

¾-1 lb carrots, peeled and diced

½ lb potatoes, peeled and diced

1 large bunch watercress, finely chopped

1 small onion, finely chopped

1 oz plain flour

3-4 pt vegetable stock

salt and pepper, to taste

large watercress leaves, to garnish

Melt the butter in a large pan and add the vegetables. Cover and cook the vegetables over low heat for about 10 minutes without browning. Add the flour and cook another few minutes, stirring continuously. Gradually blend in the stock and season to taste with salt and pepper. Simmer the soup over low heat for about 20–30 minutes or until vegetables are cooked. Let soup cool, then put through a mouli or vegetable grater. Reheat soup slowly over low heat; correct seasoning if necessary. Serve the soup at once, garnished with watercress leaves.

Serving suggestion: serve a bowl of croutons separately with the soup.

Serves: 6–8

Wine: *Pouilly Fuissé, 1976*

Rosette d'Agneau Ricard

3 large carrots

2 oz butter

1 lb fresh French beans

1 whole best end of English lamb

milled black pepper and salt, to taste

½ head of celery

1 leek

2-3 finely chopped shallots, or to taste

2 oz parsley with stalks

4 pt veal stock

1 tbsp chopped tarragon

¾ tbsp Ricard

⅛ pt cream

knob of butter

1 bunch watercress, to garnish

Wash and peel carrots and reserve the trimmings. Cut carrots Parisienne-style and sauté. Top and tail the French beans and cook. Chop beans finely, purée them, sauté them, then form into quenelle shapes and place on a silver flat.

Split lamb in 2. Trim of all fat, bone, season, and roll up. Tie up and cut into 4 rosettes from each. Reserve all bones. Sauté the rosettes and place in an ovenproof dish. Cook in oven until pink. Place on silver flat and keep warm.

Sweat the bones, celery, carrot trimmings, leek, shallots, and parsley until brown. Add veal stock and reduce by ½, strain. To the dish the lamb was cooked in, add tarragon and Ricard, then flame. Add reduced stock and reduce by ½ again. At the last minute, add cream and knob of butter.

To serve: alternate beans and carrots around the 8 rosettes of lamb on the silver flat, nap the lamb with sauce, and arrange watercress at each end of the flat.

Serves: 4

Wine: *Volnay, 1971*

Melon Cantaloup

4 whole cantaloup melons (about 12 oz each)

¼ gal water ice

4 tbsp Cointreau

1-2 drops green colouring

½ gal crushed ice

4 oz crystal violets, to garnish

8 large watercress leaves, to garnish

Cut the top open on the melons with a zigzag motion to form a crown effect. Scoop out pips, leaving centres smooth. Refrigerate for at least 2 hours. Blend water ice and Cointreau together carefully, then place in a piping bag fitted with a large nozzle. Pipe mixture into centre of refrigerated melons.

Add green colouring to crushed ice and press into ice moulds to make ice towers. Place in freezer.

To serve: place each ice tower on a small dish and carefully put the melons into each tower. Replace the lids of the melons upside down and arrange the violets and watercress leaves on top. Serve.

Serves: 4

Wine: *Champagne*

Gravetye Manor

Gravetye Manor is an Elizabethan manor house set in the famous gardens created by William Robinson and surrounded by 1000 acres of forest. The interior features log fires and antique furniture blended with the modern comforts of central heating, private bathrooms, etc. — all presided over by Peter Herbert, whose father and grandfather were both hoteliers. Mr. Herbert trained in Austria and France and, in the course of his training, became interested primarily in small, first-class hotels and restaurants.

Gravetye Manor, indeed, boasts one of the better restaurants in all of Great Britain. It is now 23 years old and features classic French and English dishes prepared by Chef Michael Quinn. Prior to coming to the manor three years ago, Chef Quinn's experience included five years of indentured apprenticeship followed by senior positions in various first-class kitchens.

Chef Quinn's specialities include a superb Terrine de Canard with raisins, cream, and brandy, and Mousseline de Coquille St. Jacques, which is a light mousse of fresh scallops in a sauce made from freshwater crayfish and fresh fennel root, among many others.

Complementing the menu is an outstanding wine list that presents more than 350 choices from Europe's classic wine regions. The service in the restaurant is unhurried, and the entire atmosphere of Gravetye Manor is one of relaxation, space, and comfort.

Gravetye Manor

NEAR EAST GRINSTEAD, SUSSEX
0342-810567
BREAKFAST, LUNCH, AND DINNER
DAILY
RESERVATIONS
PROPRIETOR: PETER HERBERT
CHEF: MICHAEL QUINN, M.C.G.B.

Crème Topinambour

6 oz butter

2 lb Jerusalem artichokes, washed and peeled

4 oz roughly chopped celery

2 oz roughly chopped onions

2 oz roughly chopped leeks

10 fresh scallops

4 oz flour

3½ pt white stock

¼ pt double cream

pinch of fresh chives

pinch of fresh tarragon

1½ lb homemade puff pastry dough

1 egg

Melt butter in a pan and add all vegetables and 8 scallops. Sweat gently for 4–5 minutes. Add flour and cook another 2 minutes. Add stock and simmer 20 minutes. Purée contents of pan, add cream and herbs, and correct seasoning.

Poach remaining 2 scallops, allow to cool, cut into small dice, and combine in puréed mixture. Place soup in ovenproof bowls, cover each with piece of rolled puff pastry, and seal. Brush with a little egg wash and cook in a fairly hot oven about 10–12 minutes.

Serves: 8

Aiguillette de Canard au Poivre Rose

2 duck breasts (*magret de canard*)

freshly ground pepper and sea salt

oil, as needed

¼ pt dry white wine

2 measures cognac

¼ pt chicken stock

½ pt double cream

2 measures port

¾ oz pink peppercorns

6 oz fresh chanterelles, thoroughly washed

½ oz red pimentos in fine *brunoise* (finely diced)

2 oz unsalted butter

Season duck breasts with pepper and sea salt, sprinkle with oil, and cook in a preheated oven at 475°F (245°C) for 18–20 minutes. It is important to keep breasts "rosy"

To prepare sauce: reduce white wine and brandy by ½. Add stock and reduce again by ½. Add double cream, port, and pink peppercorns and reduce sauce to a coating consistency. Add chanterelles and red pimentos and cook another 2 minutes. Take sauce from stove and dress with butter. Correct seasoning.

Slice breasts along the grain after removing skin. Place sauce on a hot plate and fan slices of meat on top.

Serves: 4

Soufflé au Banane, Coulis de Abricot

2 bananas per person

melted butter, as needed

3 tbsp crème pâtissière

1 tbsp Galliano liqueur

2 eggs, separated

1½ pt sugar syrup

10 fresh apricots

4 oz caster sugar

¼ pt cold water

juice of 1 lemon

icing sugar, as needed

Cut bananas in half lengthways. Remove flesh and retain 1 boat-shaped skin half per person. Dip the 2 halves in melted butter and drain.

To prepare the soufflé: purée the banana flesh. Add the purée to the crème pâtissière and Galliano. Add egg yolks and cook. Remove mixture from stove and allow to cool slightly. Whisk egg whites until stiff, then gently fold into cooled mixture. Pipe the mixture into the banana skins and cook in a preheated oven at gas mark 5 (390°F/ 200°C) for about 18–20 minutes.

To prepare *coulis de abricot au caramel*: bring the sugar syrup to a boil. Add the apricots and simmer for 8 minutes. Drain and cool the apricots and remove the stones. Purée in a liquidiser. To prepare caramel: place sugar, ½ the water, and lemon juice in a pan. Bring to a boil and take to caramel stage. Add remaining water.

Mix the puréed apricots and caramel together. Sprinkle the banana soufflé with icing sugar, and serve the sauce in a sauceboat.

Serving suggestion: serve a sauceboat of crème chantilly separately.

Manleys Restaurant

Manleys Restaurant is located in the small West Sussex area of Storrington, nestled at the foot of the South Downs. The house was built during the reign of Queen Anne. The dining room, candlelit in the evenings, looks out onto a small courtyard, which is gently floodlit on summer evenings. In the winter, the bar and lounge, with their genuine old beams, are made cosy and warm by a huge log fire. The atmosphere is most welcoming and comfortable.

The menu is mostly classic French with a few Austrian and Swiss dishes reflecting owner/chef Karl Löderer's nationality and training. His specialities include Venison Maison, Crêpe Pêcheur, and his own Pêche Manley, among others.

Everything is cooked to order with the finest and best quality ingredients available. The menu is comprehensive and changes several times a year. On Sunday, there is a table d'hôte luncheon that has proved extremely popular. That menu changes every four or five weeks and always boasts unusual and interesting dishes.

The small, dedicated staff works well as a team and is run by manager Tom Deegan and Mrs. Löderer.

In addition to the excellent cuisine, this eight-year-old restaurant also features an above-average wine list that is worth your attention. There are also two vintage house wines from which to choose.

Manleys

STORRINGTON, WEST SUSSEX

STORRINGTON 2331

LUNCH: TUESDAY — SATURDAY,
12:30 TO 2:30 P.M.

AND SUNDAY, 12 TO 2:30 P.M.

DINNER: TUESDAY — SATURDAY,
7 TO 10 P.M.

RESERVATIONS

PROPRIETOR/CHEF:
KARL LÖDERER, M.C.G.B.

Crêpe Pêcheur

1 knob of butter

1 tbsp onions, sliced

1 small green pepper

1 small red pepper

2 tbsp double cream

1 lb mixed brown and white flesh crabmeat

2 medium-sized shallots

1 clove crushed garlic

1 dessertspoon Dijon mustard

salt and pepper, to taste

flour, eggs, and bread crumbs, as needed

oil, to fry

4 thin pancakes, prepared

To make pancake filling: heat the butter then add onions, peppers, and cream. Bring to a boil, then add crabmeat, shallots, garlic, mustard, salt, and pepper.

Fill the pancakes and fold each into a triangular shape. Dip in flour, eggs, and bread crumbs. Deep fry for 5 minutes on medium heat.

Serving suggestion: garnish with lettuce and a lemon wedge and serve with cocktail sauce.

Serves: 4

Wine: *Sancerre*

Médaillons de Chevreuil Baden-Baden

1 wine glass red wine

1 bay leaf

1 tsp crushed peppercorns

1 tbsp shallots

8 lb prime Scottish saddle of venison

ground pepper and salt, to taste

pinch of sweet ground paprika

oil, to sauté

knob of butter

2 tbsp double cream

wild cherries and chopped parsley, to garnish

Mix the red wine, bay leaf, peppercorns, and shallots together to make a marinade. Bone the venison, leaving the fillet. Trim well and marinate in the marinade for 4 days, refrigerated.

Cut 3 medallions per person, ½ inch thick. Beat out and season well with pepper, salt, and paprika. Fry quickly for 30 seconds on each side (*do not overcook*) and place in a heated dish.

Thicken the marinade with a knob of butter and the cream; reduce gently to make a sauce. Pour the sauce over the venison and garnish with wild cherries and parsley.

Serving suggestion: serve with potato croquettes.

Serves: 6

Wine: *Chateauneuf du Pape*

Salzburger Nockerln

5 egg whites

4 oz granulated sugar

2 egg yolks

1 dessertspoon flour

drop of vanilla essence

zest of 2 medium-sized lemons

zest of 1 large orange

1 oz butter

1 tbsp double cream

1 tbsp honey

1 measure rum, or to taste

Whip egg whites stiffly then add sugar gently. When sugar is dissolved, add egg yolks, flour, vanilla essence, and lemon and orange zest. Mix together evenly. Form 3 large mounds (*nockerln*) with the mixture.

Melt butter, double cream, and honey together in an ovenproof dish until warm, then add nockerln. Bake for 10 minutes at gas mark 6 (400°F/205°C).

Warm the rum in a ladle and set aflame. Pour rum over the cooked nockerln and serve immediately.

Serves: 3

Wine: *Muscadet de Beaumes de Venise, chilled slightly*

The Sundial Restaurant

The Sundial Restaurant is a 17th century cottage that has been converted into a comfortable French-style auberge restaurant. It is owned and run by Guiseppe and Laurette Bertoli, who 14 years ago began to provide customers with inventive dishes together with polite but informal service.

Fresh ingredients, in general, are delivered daily, and Chef Bertoli personally selects the provisions according to the season. Specialities are created with imagination, according to the occasion, and to individual taste. This is why all the orders are taken by Chef Bertoli; this enables him to discuss the menu and to recommend the specialities available to his customers.

Laurette Bertoli is the perfect hostess, and she also advises customers in their choice of wines.

The restaurant is set in a typical Sussex village, where one can witness beautiful, unspoilt views, in the midst of a very natural garden where customers can stroll at their leisure. In the front and to the side of the restaurant, two ter-races provide a picturesque location for an apéritif and an unhurried lunch on a warm summer's day.

In the evening, the garden and terraces are lit by old-style lamps that emit an inviting glow on this unique setting.

The Sundial Restaurant

GARDNER STREET
HERTSMONCEUX, EAST SUSSEX
HERTSMONCEUX 2217
LUNCH: TUESDAY - SUNDAY,
12:30 TO 2 P.M.
DINNER: TUESDAY - SATURDAY,
7:30 TO 9:30 P.M.
RESERVATIONS
PROPRIETOR/CHEF:
GUISEPPE BERTOLI

La Terrinette de Crabe Frais

water, as needed

bouquet garni: 2 bay leaves and 2 sprigs thyme

1 carrot

pinch of salt

1 small onion

juice of 1 fresh lemon

1 × 3-4 lb large crab

3 tsp powdered aspic jelly mixed with ⅓ pt hot water

1 gherkin

drop of Tabasco sauce

2 measures brandy

1 egg yolk

1 tsp tomato purée

salt and pepper, to taste

⅓ pt fresh cream

To prepare court-bouillon: half fill a casserole large enough to hold the crab with water, add the bouquet garni, carrot, pinch of salt, onion, ½ the lemon juice and bring mixture to a boil. Reduce heat to the minimum, add the crab, and allow to simmer 15–20 minutes. Remove the crab and let it cool.

Dress the crab and separate the white flesh from the brown. Put all the brown flesh and a little of the white flesh in a liquidiser along with hot liquid aspic jelly, remaining lemon juice, gherkin, Tabasco, brandy, egg yolk, tomato purée, salt, and pepper. Liquidise the mixture at high speed to a creamy consistency. Turn the liquidiser down to a lower speed and add the cream slowly. When all is mixed well together, remove and pour ½ the mixture into a square dish, spread the rest of the white flesh of the crab on top, and gently pour the remaining mixture over all. Place the terrine in the refrigerator for 3–4 hours.

Serving suggestion: serve with hot brown toast and butter.

Serves: 6

Coeur de Filet d'Agneau en Feuilleté

1 whole loin or best end of English lamb

oil and butter, as needed

pinch of mixed herbs

2 sprigs rosemary

2 cloves garlic

salt and pepper, to taste

1 lb fresh spinach

1½ lb puff pastry dough

2 egg yolks

milk, as needed

Skin and bone lamb, remove all fat, and retain "eye." Cut eye in half to produce 2 fillets. Heat a thick frying pan on high heat. When very hot, put in a little oil and a little butter, reduce to medium heat and add herbs, rosemary, and garlic to pan. Season the meat with salt and pepper and add to pan. Brown meat, taking care to turn it all the time until sealed, for about 60 seconds only to keep meat rare. Remove meat and let cool.

Cook spinach in very little salted boiling water with a piece of butter until it is blanched. Cool under running cold water and strain thoroughly.

Roll out puff pastry without folding, taking care it is thin and twice as large as the meat. Wrap the spinach neatly around the 2 fillets of meat. Put meat abreast, then place in middle of pastry. Beat yolks with a little milk, and with this egg wash, brush the inside of the pastry. Fold pastry over neatly and seal the edges, making a pleasing shape. Decorate with little strips of pastry. Brush thoroughly with remaining egg wash and put in a preheated 400°–450°F (205°–230°C) oven for 15–20 minutes until golden brown. Meat will be delicate and pink. Slice and serve immediately.

Serving suggestion: serve with a vinaigrette endive and watercress salad.

Serves: 6

Le Pot Blanc Glacé au Grand Marnier

6 egg whites

6 oz caster sugar, and as needed

½ pt fresh whipping cream

2 egg yolks

2 drops vanilla essence

4 measures Grand Marnier

1 tsp blanched split almonds

Put the egg whites in a mixer with ½ the sugar, turn on high speed and when it starts to thicken add the remaining sugar to produce a stiff meringue mixture. Remove all meringue and put in a clean bowl. Put cream into the mixer bowl and beat it at moderate speed, with a pinch of sugar, to make whipped cream. Add egg yolks, vanilla essence, Grand Marnier, and almonds. Stir gently with a wooden spoon and fold it together carefully with the stiff meringue. Fill 6 small soufflé pots with the mixture and freeze 6–8 hours.

Serves: 6

The White Horse Inn at Chilgrove

The White Horse Inn at Chilgrove was built in 1765 by a group of Chichester businessmen as a stopping place for travellers journeying to Chichester from Petersfield and Midhurst. Additions were made to the building 25 years ago to incorporate eating facilities. After passing through the ownership of several brewery companies in national takeovers, the Inn was bought in 1979 from Grand Met by the present owners, Barry and Dorothea Phillips.

As tenants during the previous ten years, they had concentrated on the food in the restaurant, but as owners, they have embarked on a programme of modernising the kitchens, the toilets, the restaurant, etc. — all without destroying the original character of the lovely old building.

The White Horse Inn features an excellent wine list, a small team of waiting staff (all of whom have been with the Inn for several years), and the talents of a most capable chef, Adrian Congdon. Chef Congdon previously worked on the *Queen Elizabeth* and in other establishments before joining The White Horse Inn 11 years ago. His menu consists mainly of plainly cooked local fish, game, and vegetables, and his customers now supply, as well as consume, a considerable proportion of the fresh ingredients he uses daily.

One of the Phillipses' passions is wine, and it is reflected in their excellent list of French, German, English, and California wines available for your enjoyment. There are also several fine house wines to choose from.

THE WHITE HORSE AT CHILGROVE

CHILGROVE NEAR CHICHESTER
SUSSEX

024359-219 EAST MARDEN

LUNCH: 12 TO 2 P.M.
DINNER: 7 TO 9:30 P.M.
TUESDAY - SATURDAY
RESERVATIONS

PROPRIETORS:
BARRY & DOROTHEA PHILLIPS
CHEF: ADRIAN CONGDON

Prawns Cheval Blanc

1 pt freshly made mayonnaise

2 lb unpeeled Selsey prawns, or
1 lb ready-peeled prawns

4 oz finely chopped onion

6 oz celery in small dice

6 oz tomatoes, blanched, peeled,
seeded, and finely chopped

1 heaped tbsp tomato purée

3 fl oz whipped double cream

6-8 lettuce leaves

3-4 lemons, halved

6-8 sprigs parsley

3-4 tomatoes, halved and starred

To the freshly made mayonnaise, add prawns, onion, celery, chopped tomatoes, tomato purée, and whipped double cream and stir gently to mix. Allow to stand for 2 hours in the refrigerator to thicken. Serve in wooden bowls on a large lettuce leaf and garnished with ½ lemon, sprig of parsley, and ½ starred tomato.

Serves: 6—8

Wine: *chilled German Nahe Cabinet or dry white Loire wine*

Escalope Bourguignonne

2 cloves garlic, finely chopped

4 oz butter, softened

4 oz chopped parsley

24 snails, finely diced

6 escalopes of veal cut from the rump,
about 6-7 oz each

2 egg whites

2 oz seasoned flour

½ lb freshly made white bread crumbs

4 oz clarified butter

3 lemons, halved

Mix the crushed garlic, soft butter, ½ the parsley, and snails together. Beat the veal between 2 polythene sheets until thin, taking care not to tear the meat. Spread some snail mixture on the veal, leaving an inch around the outside clear. Brush this outside edge with egg white. Fold each escalope in ½, dust with seasoned flour, brush with remaining egg white, and coat with bread crumbs.

Fry veal in clarified butter until golden (about 3 minutes on each side) and sprinkle with the remaining parsley. Garnish each with ½ lemon and serve.

Serves: 6

Wine: *chilled Beaujolais or young Côtes du Rhone*

Pineapple Tam-o-Shanter

1 × 7 oz tin of condensed milk

1 fresh pineapple, firm and not too ripe

10 fl oz double cream

1 tbsp kirsch

1 oz sugar

glacé cherries, to decorate

Place tin of condensed milk, unpunctured, in a pan of boiling water, covering completely with water. Boil for 5 hours, adding water as needed to keep covered. Allow to cool.

Peel and slice the pineapple into rings, removing the centre core with a sharp knife.

Open both ends of the tin and push out the dark brown contents. Slice with a sharp serrated knife by first dipping knife in boiling water to prevent sticking. Lay a slice of condensed milk on each slice of pineapple.

Whip the double cream with kirsch and sugar until thick. Pipe whipped liqueur cream around each pineapple slice to decorate, top with glacé cherries and serve.

Serves: 6

The Hole in the Wall Restaurant

The Hole in the Wall Restaurant is set in the basement area of two Georgian terraced houses (circa 1790), right in the centre of Bath. It derives its name from the entrances at road level into the old coal holes under the high pavement. Originally, it was a war-time cafe run by a Mrs. Wintle, who is fondly remembered to this day by servicemen who were stationed in Bath. George Perry-Smith took over the establishment in 1951 and immediately set about making the restaurant one of the most celebrated and best-loved in the country. The current owners, Tim and Sue Cumming, began their association with The Hole in the mid-1960s when they worked for George Perry-Smith. Later, they opened their own restaurant in Salisbury, called Crane's, and after seven years, they returned to Bath to purchase The Hole.

The building lends itself very well to the business of a restaurant. There are cocktail lounges on the ground (or upper) floor, modernly but tastefully furnished. The dining room below, the real Hole, is more informal and relaxed. It has old carriage lamps, whitewashed alcoves, an open fireplace (with burning logs in the winter), and in the centre, a magnificent cold buffet spread.

The à la carte menu is short and changes every fortnight or sooner to accommodate the seasons and the availability of a varied supply of fresh fish and vegetable produce. The food is predominantly French provincial with a scattering of specialities created by Tim.

The HOLE IN THE WALL

16-17 GEORGE STREET
BATH, AVON

0225-25242

LUNCH: 12:30 TO 2 P.M.
DINNER: 7 TO 10:30 P.M.
MONDAY — SATURDAY

PROPRIETORS: A.T. & S.C. CUMMING
CHEF: A.T. CUMMING

Tartelettes aux Crabes

9 oz flour

7 oz butter

   salted cold water, as needed

4 oz finely sliced button mushrooms

3 fl oz tawny port

3 fl oz double cream

   salt and pepper, to taste

7 fl oz milk, heated

7 fl oz light chicken or fish stock, heated

1 tsp French mustard

   butter, to grease

8 tbsp crabmeat

4 tbsp grated Gruyère or Jarlsburg cheese

Make a buttery shortcrust pastry by mixing 8 ounces flour, 5 ounces butter, and salted cold water together. Set aside to rest in refrigerator.

Soften mushrooms in ½ the remaining butter, add port, and reduce to almost nothing. Stir in cream, boil briefly, season, and let cool.

To prepare Béchamel: melt remaining butter and flour together and cook without browning. Add heated milk and stock, bit by bit, until glossy between each addition. Season with mustard, salt, and pepper.

Roll out pastry fairly thin into 4 rounds and tuck into 4 greased 4½ inch fluted flan rings with removable bottoms. Line with paper or foil, weigh with beans or rice, and blind bake in a hot oven for 10–15 minutes. Trim excess pastry from rim, but leave shell in rings. Spread a tablespoon of mushroom port mixture in the bottom of each, then divide the crabmeat among each. Salt and pepper lightly, then mask with 2–3 tablespoons of the Béchamel. Sprinkle equal amounts of cheese on each. Bake 10–15 minutes in a hot oven. Disgorge from flan rings onto hot plates.

Serves: 4

Wine: *Quincy, 1979*

Stuffed Duck Breasts

2 × 4½ lb ducks

1 duck liver

4 green peppercorns

1 tbsp brandy

   salt and pepper, to taste

1 oz butter

2 oz finely chopped celery

2 oz finely chopped onion

6 oz spinach, blanched and chopped

1 tsp chopped fresh tarragon

1 egg, partly beaten

   butter, as needed

   watercress, to garnish

Fillet the ducks. Remove legs and wings. Trim excess fat and sinew from the 2 rounds of breast with their 2 fillets.

Mash the duck liver with the green peppercorns, brandy, salt and pepper. Spread on the duck fillets.

To prepare the stuffing: melt the butter, add celery, and cook for 2 minutes. Add onion and cook another 2 minutes. Remove from heat, add spinach, tarragon, salt and pepper, and the egg. Mix well, then leave to cool.

Divide the stuffing between ducks. Pin with cocktail sticks or sew up to make a "pasty" shape. With a sharp knife, lightly crisscross the breasts. Brown gently in a trace of butter on all sides to let the fat. Pour surplus off if necessary. Roast in a fairly hot oven for 15–20 minutes. Meat should still be pink. Remove thread or sticks. Carve slices across the fillets, garnish with watercress.

Serving suggestion: serve with Béarnaise sauce and broccoli and gratin dauphinois on a side dish.

Serves: 4

Wine: *claret, Chateau Cheval Blanc, 1966 or 1970*

Kumquat Sorbet

½ lb kumquats, halved

7 fl oz water

2 oz caster sugar

   juice of ½ lemon

   juice of ½ orange

2 egg whites, half whipped

In a covered pot, stew the kumquats in the water and sugar for about 15 minutes. Strain through a sieve, mashing the fruit with the back of a ladle (should yield ½ pint liquid). Add the lemon and orange juice; let cool. When cool, mix in the egg whites, churn in an ice/sorbet machine, and freeze.

Serves: 4

Wine: *Muscat de Beaumes de Venise*

Homewood Park Hotel and Restaurant

Homewood Park Hotel and Restaurant is situated in ten acres of garden and parkland just minutes away from the centre of Bath. The old house, built around 1780, is decorated in fresh light wallpapers and fabrics and period furnishings. Each of the eight lovely bedrooms has a private bath, colour television, and telephone.

Homewood Park was purchased and refurbished in 1980 by Stephen and Penny Ross, both of whom were associated with other establishments prior to this event. It was their intent from the beginning that Homewood Park would represent, equally, the finest in accommodation and dining. To that end, every effort was made to establish a quality restaurant as well as fine lodgings.

The dining room successfully conveys a private home atmosphere. It is decorated to blend in with the rest of the house. The menu features French provincial cuisine created ably by Chef Antony Pitt, whose experience includes study at a catering college and successful tenures with several well-known restaurants in the area. Some of the items listed on the menu are his own recipes; one is Terrine de Ris de Veau, and it is the house speciality.

The wine list features 70 choices from each of the leading wine producing countries, and there are five fine house wines to select from, as well.

HINTON CHARTERHOUSE, BATH

022122-2642

BREAKFAST, LUNCH, AND DINNER
DAILY
RESERVATIONS

PROPRIETOR: STEPHEN ROSS
CHEF: ANTONY PITT

Filet de Truite au Poivre Rose

3 × 6 - 8 oz pink trout

rind and juice of 1 orange

1 lemon

3 tbsp olive oil

1 small finely diced onion

2 oz caster sugar

3 tbsp pink peppercorns

Fillet the trout, leaving skin on each fillet. Lay fillets in a tray deep enough to hold liquids.

Mix the remaining ingredients together to make a marinade and then pour over trout. Leave in a cool place for 24 hours, spooning marinade over fillets 2 or 3 times. (After 48 hours trout will begin to lose its texture. Do not prepare dish too long in advance.)

Serving suggestion: serve with some of the marinade spooned over the fillets and with a crisp salad of perhaps fennel or frisee lettuce.

Serves: 4—6

Noisette d'Agneau au Beurre à l'Estragon

1 × 4 lb loin of lamb on bone

butter, as needed

4 oz softened butter

handful chopped fresh tarragon

rind and juice of 2 lemons

2 oz bread crumbs

salt and pepper, to taste

Bone the loin of lamb and tie into a tight sausage shape with string every 2 inches. Cut into *noisettes* by dividing the loin between every

string. Season, dot with butter, and roast in a hot oven for 10 minutes.

To prepare tarragon butter: beat the remaining ingredients together until combined, then shape into a cylinder.

When lamb is cooked, remove from oven and pour off excess fats. Place a slice of tarragon butter on each noisette, then return to oven for 5 minutes before serving.

Serving suggestion: decorate with fresh tarragon leaves and serve with a hot salad of broad beans with bacon and garlic.

Serves: 4—6

Almond Tart with Raspberry Purée

8 oz sweet shortcrust

4 whole eggs

12 oz caster sugar

8 oz ground almonds

2 oz flaked almonds

1 lb raspberries

6 oz sugar

Line an 8 inch flan ring with shortcrust. Beat eggs with caster sugar to ribbon stage. Blend with ground almonds, then fill the flan case

with the mixture. Sprinkle the top of the tart with flaked almonds. Bake in the oven at gas mark 5 (375°F/190°C) for 30 minutes until set.

Boil the raspberries with sugar and no water. Liquidise and sieve to remove pips.

Serve the cool tart with purée of raspberries.

CHEF'S TIP

CHECK OVEN TEMPERATURE CAREFULLY. THE TART MUST BE COOKED EVENLY RIGHT THROUGH. IF TOP IS BROWNING, COVER WITH FOIL UNTIL CENTRE IS FIRM TO THE TOUCH.

Hunstrete House

Hunstrete House is an old Georgian country manor house, dating back to the early 18th century, that is surrounded by 90 acres of its own gardens and pastures. It was converted into a small luxury hotel in 1968 by Thea and John Dupays.

The house features 20 bedrooms (each with its own bathroom, telephone, and colour television), elegant reception rooms with log burning fireplaces, conference and private dining rooms, a heated swimming pool, a tennis court, and an excellent French restaurant.

The restaurant, which features French provincial cuisine, is headed by Chef Alain Dubois. Chef Dubois is a native of Normandy and trained extensively in France.

Much of the fresh produce Chef Dubois uses in his preparations, both vegetables and fruits, is grown right on the estate grounds. He also has created many of the dishes appearing on the menu.

Chicken Breasts stuffed with Basil and Chicken Mousse is one of his favourite dishes and is considered the house speciality. Recipes for some other favourites appear on the opposite page.

The restaurant also offers a modest but adequate wine list, a fine house wine, bar service, and a cocktail lounge.

Hunstrete House

**CHEFWOOD NEAR BRISTOL
AVON**

07618-578

**BREAKFAST: 8 TO 9:30 A.M.
LUNCH: 12 TO 2:30 P.M.
DINNER: 7:30 TO 9:30 P.M.
DAILY
RESERVATIONS**

**PROPRIETORS: THEA AND JOHN DUPAYS
CHEF: ALAIN DUBOIS**

Spinach Pots

1 lb cooked fresh spinach, drained

¾ pt double cream, and as needed

2 oz chopped ham

2 oz white bread crumbs

grated nutmeg, to taste

salt and pepper, to taste

3 tomatoes, skinned and halved

4 eggs, separated

Purée the spinach with ½ the cream. In a mixing bowl, add the puréed spinach, ham, bread crumbs, remaining cream, nutmeg, and seasoning. Place the halved tomatoes into the bottoms of 6 deep ramekins, pressing down gently to cover the bottoms. Add egg yolks to the spinach mixture (if slightly stiff, add more cream). Whip egg whites until firm, fold into the spinach mixture, then spoon a generous amount into each ramekin. Place the pots into a deep baking tray, cook in bain-marie covered with tin foil at gas mark 5 (390°F/200°C) for 40–45 minutes or until spinach is firm to the touch.

When spinach pots are cool, turn onto entrée dishes and serve. Serving suggestion: serve with fresh tomato sauce.

Serves: 6

Wine: *Sylvaner Riesling*

Chicken with Lemon and Garlic

1 chicken

grated peel and juice of 1 lemon

½ glass dry white wine

2 cloves garlic, crushed

flour, to dust

salt and pepper, to taste

2 oz butter

½ c olive oil

pitted black olives, to garnish

Bone the chicken and cut the meat into bite-sized pieces; place in a bowl. Sprinkle the grated peel, lemon juice, wine, and garlic over the chicken. Stir the marinade from time to time for at least 2 hours.

Squeeze the pieces of chicken dry, dust them lightly with flour and season. Heat the butter and oil in a frying pan and sauté the chicken pieces until they are golden brown.

Serving suggestion: serve either on a bed of chopped chicory with a light French dressing or with a light tomato sauce. Garnish with pitted black olives.

Serves: 4

Wine: *a young claret or a Beaujolais*

Pear and Frangipane Tart

½ lb plain flour

6 oz unsalted butter

1 oz sugar

2 eggs

2 oz caster sugar

½ oz flour

2 oz ground almonds

1 drop almond essence

1 tbsp kirsch

1 tbsp blackcurrant jam

2 large, firm pears, peeled and cored

apricot glaze, as needed

To prepare sweet pastry: sift the plain flour onto a work surface, make a well in the centre, and put in ⅔ the butter, cut into small pieces, and the sugar. Knead together well. Add 1 egg and mix. Gradually work in the flour until it becomes a firm dough. Roll out and line an 8 inch flan ring. Chill, then blind bake for about 15 minutes at gas mark 5 (390°F/200°C) until pastry is cooked but not brown.

To prepare frangipane: cream the remaining butter and caster sugar together until soft; add the egg, work in quickly, then add flour, ground almonds, almond essence, and kirsch.

Line the bottom of the cooked flan pastry with a thin layer of jam, then the frangipane, filling ½ the flan case. Put a rough layer of 1 pear over the frangipane, then place a second layer of thinly sliced pear on top. Bake at same oven temperature for 20 minutes or until the frangipane is firm and a golden colour. Leave on the flan ring whilst cooking to avoid pastry turning too brown. When cool, brush lightly with apricot glaze and lift onto serving plate.

Serves: 6

The Priory Hotel

The Priory Hotel, owned by Mr. John Donnithorne, was converted from a private house to a hotel in 1969. This Georgian structure, built in 1835, is constructed of Bath stone in a Gothic style. It stands in two acres of garden. Although only one mile from the Abbey and the centre of Bath, it has more the atmosphere of a country house than of a city hotel.

Mr. Donnithorne, whose hotel and restaurant career began in 1949, took over The Priory two and a half years ago.

The hotel's 15 bedrooms are all individually decorated and furnished with antiques. The restaurant, whose reputation has grown rapidly since its opening in 1970, draws a clientele from a wide area. There are two separate rooms: one an imposing Gothic room with Georgian furniture and period paintings; the other is a terrace room overlooking a courtyard with an ornamented pond and fountain.

The menu features a wide variety of Continental dishes with an emphasis on traditional French cuisine. Several offerings are unique creations by experienced Chef Michael Collom, who was with the Gravetye Manor in Sussex for five years before coming to The Priory.

There is a small bar and two spacious reception rooms, one of which leads to a large terrace where guests can relax with a drink in the summer. An extensive list of French and other imported wines, most moderately priced, is available.

THE PRIORY HOTEL

WESTON ROAD
BATH, AVON

0225-331922

BREAKFAST: 8 TO 9:30 A.M.
LUNCH: 12:30 TO 2 P.M.
DINNER: 7:30 TO 9:30 P.M.
DAILY
RESERVATIONS

PROPRIETOR: JOHN DONNITHORNE
CHEF: MICHAEL COLLOM

Suprême de Pintade Rôti au Torte de Légumes

3 guinea fowl

  salt and pepper, to taste

1 egg white

½ pt double cream

½ tbsp brandy

1 lb puff pastry dough

½ lb French green beans, blanched

½ lb thinly sliced rounds of carrot, cooked

  eggwash, as needed

  stock made from bones from guinea fowl

2 oz morel mushrooms, chopped

½ pt double cream

1 tbsp Madeira wine

1 oz butter

To prepare the mousseline: remove the legs from the guinea fowl and then the meat from the legs. Discarding skin and sinew, pass this meat through a fine mincer, then through a fine sieve. Place in a bowl on crushed ice, add a little salt, and work with a wooden spoon. Add the egg white, then slowly mix in cream and brandy. Adjust the seasoning, cover, and keep cool.

To prepare the torte of vegetables: line a 6 inch flan ring with the puff pastry. Spread a layer of mousseline ¼ inch in depth on the bottom of the flan. Place a layer of blanched green beans on top, followed by the sliced cooked carrot. Repeat this until the flan is full. Roll out the remaining pastry, egg wash the sides of the flan, cover the flan and decorate the top with leaves made from the pastry.

To prepare the sauce: reduce the stock to ½ pint. Add chopped mushrooms and simmer gently for 10 minutes. Add double cream and Madeira and reduce by ⅓. Correct the seasoning. Cover with a buttered paper and put aside.

Gently roast the double breasts of guinea fowl for 15–20 minutes at gas mark 6 (400°F/205°C), basting with butter frequently. At the same time, bake the torte of vegetables and mousseline at the top of the oven for 25 minutes until golden brown.

To serve: separate the breasts of guinea fowl, place on a large round silver flat, cover with a buttered paper, and keep warm. Take the torte from the oven, remove the flan ring, and cut into 6 equal portions. Arrange in the middle of the silver flat, placing the guinea fowl around the outside. Place a small bouquet of watercress in the centre and serve sauce separately in a sauce boat.

Serves: 6

Pommes Chatelaines

1 pt dry cider

6 oz sugar

6 evenly sliced Bramley apples, peeled and cored

1 vanilla pod

  water, as needed

4 oz sultanas

4 oz butter

4 oz caster sugar

2 eggs

1 oz flour

4 oz ground almonds

3 egg yolks

1 dessertspoon Calvados

¼ pt double cream, half whipped

Boil the cider and 4 ounces sugar together for 5 minutes. Place the apples in the resulting cider syrup and poach gently for 5 minutes. Remove the apples and place on a well-buttered baking sheet at least 4 inches apart. Let cool.

Boil the remaining 2 ounces sugar, vanilla pod, and water together for a few minutes, and then soak the sultanas in it. Fill the middle of the apples with the soaked sultanas.

To prepare frangipane: cream the butter and caster sugar together until light and white. Add the 2 whole eggs slowly, beating all the time. Add the flour and ground almonds and mix well. Fill a piping bag with a large plain piping tube with frangipane and pipe just enough to cover the top of each cooled apple.

To prepare sabayon sauce: whip the syrup in which the apples were poached with the egg yolks over a gentle heat. When thick and creamy, add the Calvados. Cool, then add the half-whipped double cream.

Place the apples with the raw frangipane on top in a hot oven, gas mark 8 (450°F/250°C). The frangipane will slip down around the apples and collect at the bottom. When golden brown, remove from oven. Using a large, round plain cutter, cut around the base of each apple, lift carefully onto a hot plate, and serve. Serve sabayon sauce separately in a sauce boat.

Serves: 6

Thornbury Castle

With a history dating back to William Rufus, and associations with Henry VIII, Anne Boleyn and Mary Tudor, merely to visit **Thornbury Castle** would be enough for many people.

To those who have dined here, however, the name Kenneth Bell conjures up thoughts and recollections of memorable meals. To eat such meals in these historic surroundings, with vast fireplaces, ancient panelling, and old paintings, is an experience to be treasured for many years.

The menu, described as European, was originally based on Chef Bell's desire to run the sort of country restaurant that one might find in France, a place where one could get a good but unpretentious meal. Now, 15 years later, this remains his aim, and the dishes he cooks today are still classical and bourgeois French.

In the near future, Chef Bell intends to open five or six letting-rooms of the castle for travellers who wish to stay within walls which have looked on many of the historic and famous.

One way in which Thornbury Castle is probably unique are the grape vines that grow up to the castle walls. The wine yielded is very drinkable and is available at a modest price. In addition, there is a very fine wine cellar.

Thornbury Castle

THORNBURY, BRISTOL
0454-412647
LUNCH ON SUNDAY
DINNER: TUESDAY — SATURDAY
RESERVATIONS
PROPRIETOR/CHEF:
KENNETH BELL, M.C.G.B.

Marinated Salmon

1½ lb very fresh salmon

8 fl oz dry white wine

4 fl oz olive or walnut oil

2 tbsp salt, sea salt preferred

1 small onion, cut very finely

1 small clove garlic, cut very finely

rind and juice of 2 oranges, rind julienne

rind and juice of 3 lemons, rind julienne

grated white peppercorns or 6 green peppercorns

Cut the centre cut of the salmon and lift out the backbone. Remove skin and all bones. Cut each fillet into 4 pieces and lay them in a stainless steel, glass, or porcelain dish. Mix the remaining ingredients together to make a marinade. Pour marinade over fish, keep in a cool place, and shake occasionally. Fish is ready in 4 hours but can be kept refrigerated for 4 or more days. Serve fish covered with marinade.

Serving suggestion: serve with a light salad such as avocado and apple or a very crisp lettuce with a little grated celery.

Serves: 4–6

Wine: *dry white wine, Sauvignon or Chardonnay*

Breast of Chicken Flamed in Pernod

2 × 3½ lb chickens

2 oz clarified butter

2 fl oz Pernod

2 oz finely diced carrot

2 oz finely diced celery

2 oz finely diced white mushrooms

salt and pepper or chicken bouillon cube, to taste

6 fl oz apple juice

4-5 fl oz double cream

Remove the legs, then lift off the breasts together with the wings of the chickens. Remove the end 2 joints of the wings. Bat out the thick part of the supremes to assist cooking.

Heat the butter in a heavy sauté pan, brown 2 supremes on both sides and lift them out, then brown the other 2. Return the first 2 to the pan, flame with Pernod. Add carrot, celery, and mushrooms. Season with salt and pepper or a small bit of chicken bouillon cube. Add apple juice, cover the pan, and cook on fairly high heat. Turn the supremes over occasionally.

After 15 minutes, the chicken should be cooked through and the liquid syrupy. (Add more apple juice if it dries out during cooking; remove lid if too much liquid.) Pour cream over chicken and boil rapidly until sauce is reduced again and quite syrupy. Serve immediately.

Serving suggestion: serve with boiled new potatoes, rice pilaf, or risotto.

Butterscotch Pudding

4 oz butter

6 oz granulated sugar

1 tsp vanilla essence

2 tsp baking powder

½ lb self-rising flour

2 eggs, well beaten

6 fl oz boiling water

5 oz dried dates or raisins, chopped

flour, to dust

3 oz brown sugar

5 fl oz double cream

2 oz shelled walnuts

whiskey or rum, optional

cold double cream, as needed

To prepare the sponge: beat ½ the butter, granulated sugar, and vanilla to a cream. Mix the baking powder with the flour and add with the eggs gradually to the butter and sugar. Add boiling water. Toss the dried fruit in a little flour and add to the batter. Pour into a well-buttered or non-stick baking tin and cook in a hot oven, gas mark 4 (360°F/180°C) for about 40 minutes or until a skewer comes out clean.

To prepare the sauce: boil the remaining butter, brown sugar, cream, and walnuts. Add a little whiskey or rum if desired.

Serve slices of the hot sponge covered with very hot sauce and cold thick cream.

Wine: *a good Sauterne or Muscat de Beaumes de Venise or a sweet dessert wine*

Count House Restaurant

The **Count House Restaurant** is situated close to Lands End in the old tin mining village of Botallack. Perched high on the cliffs looking out over the Atlantic Ocean, lashed by the winter's gales, it affords superb views westward to the Isles of Scilly.

The restaurant was created out of an old tin mine workshop; its rough stone walls and high vaulted roof add to the relaxed feeling of space that diners enjoy. Tables of different styles and sizes are set well apart, adding to the informal atmosphere. Roaring log fires in the magnificent old fireplace together with subdued lighting and candles on each table give a cosy feeling on wild winter evenings.

The restaurant is now ten years old; it was purchased by its present owners, Ian Long and his wife, Ann, six years ago. Both have trained extensively with London breweries; Mr. Long has been in the trade for more than 20 years, five of which were in management, and Mrs. Long, who is the chef, worked with many highly qualified chefs.

Their dinner menu, featuring carefully chosen examples of English cuisine, is changed daily. A traditional family luncheon is served on Sundays.

A small, selective wine list is also offered. This is revised two or three times a year, and one can usually find some interesting "bin ends" available.

THE COUNT HOUSE RESTAURANT

BOTALLACK, ST. JUST
PENZANCE, CORNWALL

0736-788588

LUNCH ON SUNDAY
DINNER: WEDNESDAY — SATURDAY
RESERVATIONS

PROPRIETOR: IAN G. LONG
CHEF: ANN LONG

Sauté Garlic Prawns with Mushrooms

8 oz butter, and to sauté

8 oz peeled prawns

1 tsp marjoram

black pepper, to taste

2 garlic cloves, crushed

brown bread crumbs, as needed

8 oz sliced mushrooms

Melt the 8 ounces butter slowly. Add prawns, marjoram, pepper, and 1 crushed garlic. Allow to cook until prawns are hot, being careful not to overcook. Set aside and leave to marinate for at least 4 hours.

Fry the bread crumbs in butter with the remaining garlic. Keep warm.

To serve: melt butter with prawns in a frying pan, add sliced mushrooms, then spoon onto warm plates and top with the crisp bread crumbs.

Serves: 4–6

Wine: *Clairette Blanche, Simonsig*

Pork Tenderloin with Onion and Tomato Sauce

3 pork fillets, trimmed

8 oz smoked ham, thinly sliced

8 oz Lancashire cheese, sliced

4 oz celery and carrots, chopped

½ pt medium sherry

1 onion, chopped

2 oz butter

1 tsp basil

black pepper, to taste

4 tomatoes, skinned and seeded

Cut the pork fillets lengthways, almost through, and flatten. On the first layer, place ½ the ham and cheese, then place the second piece of meat on top. Fill again with remainder of ham and cheese. Put last pork fillet on the top and tie the whole with string at 3 centimetre intervals. Scatter celery and carrots in a baking tray, place tenderloin on top, and pour sherry over. Cover with lightly buttered greaseproof paper, then seal tray with tin foil. Bake in oven at gas mark 5 (375°F/190°C) for 45 minutes or until tender. Keep warm. Strain the sherry stock and reserve for the sauce.

To prepare onion and tomato sauce: cook onions until transparent in 1/2 the butter. Add strained sherry stock from the tenderloin, basil, and pepper. Boil until it begins to reduce. Whisk in the remaining butter at the last minute, and then add the tomato strips.

To serve: remove the string and cut the tenderloin into slices. Serve the sauce separately.

Serves: 4–6

Wine: *Vina Lanciano, Rioja Alta*

Oatmeal Meringue

8 egg whites

pinch of salt

1 lb caster sugar

2 tbsp cornflour

1 tsp vinegar

5 oz oatmeal mixed with chopped roasted nuts, grated orange peel, currants, and chopped dried apple to choice

½ pt double cream, whipped

fresh fruit, to garnish

Whisk egg whites with salt until stiff. Beat in ¾ of the sugar, a spoonful at a time, then add cornflour and vinegar. Then add the remaining sugar. With a metal spoon, fold in the oatmeal-fruit mixture. Spread onto 2 × 9 inch flan cases lined with foil. (Meringue will come away from foil when it is completely cooked.) Cook in oven at gas mark 5 (375°F/190°C) for 1 hour.

When cold, fill with whipped double cream and garnish with fresh fruit.

Serves: 6–8

Wine: *La Flora Blanche*

Riverside

Riverside is located in Helford, a picturesque village built on either side of a tidal creek off the Helford River estuary. This is the soft, sheltered corner of Cornwall, a complete contrast to the wild moors inland. There is plenty of walking and sailing, a pub, a post office, but no "bright lights." Old Celtic Cornwall, modern artists and craftsmen, lovely gardens, and fine houses, are within easy driving distance.

The proprietor/chef of Riverside is G. Perry-Smith, who began his cooking career during the Second World War "when," he says, "simplicity and good housekeeping were essential." In 1951, he opened The Hole in the Wall in Bath and stayed there until 1972. In 1974, he purchased Riverside, which features overnight accommodation and a marvellous restaurant.

The restaurant is decorated like a cottage with settings and furnishings that complement the international food, which is French provincial in approach. Rather than just providing an attractive milieu in which to eat mediocre food, Chef Perry-Smith places his emphasis on preparing tasty dishes that are simple, clean, and colourful in presentation.

Riverside also features an extensive list of wines from which to choose, and there is also a fine house wine available.

RIVERSIDE

**HELFORD
HELSTON, CORNWALL**

032623-443

**RESIDENTS: ALL MEALS DAILY,
MARCH TO OCTOBER
NON-RESIDENTS:
DINNER: TUESDAY — SATURDAY,
7:30 TO 9:30 P.M.
RESERVATIONS**

**PROPRIETOR/CHEF:
GEORGE PERRY-SMITH, M.C.G.B.**

Sole with Green Herbs and Sorrel

1 lb Dover sole

seasoning, to taste

flour, to dust

butter, to sauté and as needed

2 oz chopped fresh herbs:
thyme, parsley, lemon balm, etc.

2 oz finely chopped sorrel

2 fl oz fish stock, optional

Fillet the Dover sole, season, and flour it. Fry the fillet in butter on one side. Turn, sprinkle with chopped herb mixture and sorrel. Add a little more butter, add fish stock, if desired, and cook 1 minute longer.

Serves: 2

Wine: *Auxey Duresses, 1976*

Rabbit with White Wine and Mustard

2 × 3 lb rabbits

seasoning, to taste

flour, to dust

3-4 oz butter

½ lb fat bacon, diced

24 small onions

2-3 oz flour

½ pt dry white wine

¾ pt stock

thyme, parsley, and garlic, to taste

1 bay leaf

grated rind and juice of 1 large lemon

1 egg yolk

¼ pt cream

mustard, to taste

Joint the rabbits, then season and flour them. Fry rabbits in butter until golden, then put them in a casserole. In the same frying pan, fry the diced bacon and onions. Add flour to make a roux. Add wine, stock, thyme, parsley, garlic, bay leaf, and rind and juice of the lemon. Check seasoning, pour over the rabbits, cover, and cook gently in a cool oven (300°F/150°C) until tender. (Time will depend on size of rabbits.) Finish with a liason of egg yolk, cream, and mustard.

Serving suggestion: serve with boiled potatoes and a salad of finely sliced fennel and Chinese leaves.

Serves: 6–7

Wine: *Morgon, 1978*

Peaches with Lemon and Brandy

3 thinly sliced lemons

2 pt water

1 lb sugar

12 large ripe but firm peaches

12 tsp brandy

Cook the lemons in water and sugar for about 15 minutes to make a syrup. Blanch and skin the peaches. Poach the peaches in the syrup until tender. Lift out the peaches as they become tender. Continue to cook the syrup until it is reduced by about half or until the lemon slices look transparent. Run a teaspoonful of brandy on each peach, and pour the reduced syrup over them, including the sliced lemon.

Serves: 6–12

Wine: *Quarts de Chaume, 1976*

The Carved Angel

The Carved Angel was started in 1974 by the same partnership that opened its sister restaurant, Riverside in Helford, the same year. The links between the two houses are more in the mind and in approach to cookery than in administration; while George Perry-Smith and Heather Crosbie run Riverside, Joyce Molyneux cooks and Tom Jaine runs the front of the house at The Carved Angel.

Joyce Molyneux, together with George Perry-Smith and Heather Crosbie, was a partner in The Hole in the Wall in Bath, which Mr. Perry-Smith founded in the 1950s. She cooked there, having previously been at the Mulberry Tree in Stratford-upon-Avon and Birmingham College of Domestic Science. Tom Jaine is related to George Perry-Smith and was brought up at The Hole in the Wall. After university, he worked in archives and historical manuscripts for some years before joining The Carved Angel restaurant partnership in 1974.

The Carved Angel benefits from its proximity to the sea. The fish is fresh and often brought in by the fishermen or sportsmen who have spent the day in Start Bay, four miles down the coast. Lobster, crayfish, crab, scallops, prawns, mussels, winkles, cockles, and clams are readily available. Thus, although it did not set out to be a seafood restaurant, there is often a preponderance of fish dishes on the menu. The remainder of the menu offers a wide variety of European dishes. A good wine list and two house wines are also available.

The Carved Angel

**2 SOUTH EMBANKMENT
DARTMOUTH, SOUTH DEVON**

08043-2465

**LUNCH: 12:30 TO 2 P.M.,
TUESDAY - SUNDAY
DINNER: 6:30 TO 10:30 P.M.,
TUESDAY - SATURDAY
RESERVATIONS**

**PROPRIETORS:
JOYCE MOLYNEUX, TOM JAINE
CHEF: JOYCE MOLYNEUX**

Ceviche of Dover Sole

1   very fresh Dover sole

    lemon or lime juice, as needed

    olive oil, as needed

    chopped parsley, to taste

    salt, to taste

1   lb ripe tomatoes

½   green pepper, diced

1   tbsp grated onion

2   cloves garlic, diced

1-6 chilis, depending on strength, diced

    chopped fennel, to taste

Fillet the sole and cut it into thin strips. Place strips in a bowl and squeeze enough lemon or lime juice onto them to cover. Stir to insure juice has reached all surfaces of the fish. Leave strips in marinade for about 4 hours. Flesh is "cooked" when it has changed colour and is slightly firmer than when raw. Drain marinade, then dress strips with olive oil, chopped parsley, and salt.

To prepare sauce: peel and dice the tomatoes, then mix them with green pepper, onion, garlic, and chilis. Add 2 tablespoons olive oil and check seasoning. Add the chopped fennel and more chopped parsley.

CHEF'S TIP

ANY VERY FRESH, FIRM OF FLESH FISH, SUCH AS TURBOT, CONGER, SALMON, OR MONK MAY BE PREPARED THIS WAY.

Dartmouth Pie

2   lb trimmed leg of mutton

    salt, to taste

2   tsp black peppercorns

1   tsp blade mace

1   tsp whole allspice

2   in cinnamon stick

2   tsp coriander

1   lb sliced onions

1   tbsp flour

½   pt beef stock

5   oz dried apricots

5   oz dried prunes

4   oz raisins

    grated rind and juice of 1 orange, Seville preferred

    prepare pie crust dough

Cut the meat in small squares, season with salt, and brown it with its drippings. Whiz the spices in a coffee grinder, then add ground spices to the meat and fry again. Add onions, flour, and stock, and simmer to mix. Put the fruit into a casserole without soaking it. Add the contents of the frying pan and bring to a boil. Add the grated rind and juice of the orange. Check seasoning, then cover and cook in a cool oven, gas mark ¼ or ½ (230°–275°F/ 110°–135°C) for about 1½ hours until the meat is tender.

It is best if the pie filling is pre-cooked a day in advance to let it mature and the spices blend and soften. It can then be put in your favourite pie dish, covered with your favourite pie crust, and baked in a hot oven.

Cranberry Sorbet

    rind and juice of 1 lemon

    rind and juice of 1 orange

8   oz cranberries

1   pt water

6   oz caster sugar

1   egg white

Put rind and juice of the lemon and orange in a pot with the cranberries and water and simmer until cranberries are tender. Put through a fine sieve and add sugar. Stir until sugar is dissolved. Put mixture to freeze in a *sorbetière* or in the freezer.

When frozen solidly, thaw until just workable. Put into a mixing bowl and with a beater beat it vigorously with the egg white to incorporate air into the mixture. Return to the freezer.

Serving suggestion: serve with a simple orange salad.

Gidleigh Park

Gidleigh Park is a remote country house located in Chagford, Devon, about 200 miles from London. It is owned and operated by a charming American couple, Paul and Kay Henderson, who in 1978 purchased the then run-down property and refurbished it to its current beauty.

The Tudor-style structure sits in a magnificent setting next to the North Teign River in 30 acres of gardens and woods. Dartmoor, with its majestic open scenery and prehistoric ruins, is a little more than a mile away. The interior of the house is attractively furnished with antiques. Public rooms are all oak-panelled, and fresh flowers and open log fires appear every day.

The Hendersons had no previous experience in hotel or restaurant operations, but what they did have was extensive travelling experience, a nose for what was good or bad about a place, and a genuine empathy for the traveller and diner. Kay is the chef and specialises in mostly French *nouvelle cuisine*. Her preparations are cooked simply, but she successfully strives to enhance the natural flavours of each ingredient.

The wine list at Gidleigh Park is very extensive and includes choices of not only classical French and German wines, but also what may be the best selection of American wines in Europe.

Gidleigh Park

CHAGFORD, DEVON
06473-2367
BREAKFAST, LUNCH, AND DINNER
DAILY
RESERVATIONS
PROPRIETORS: PAUL AND KAY HENDERSON
CHEF: KAY HENDERSON

Boulestin Restaurant Français

Mallory Court Hotel

Dorchester Hotel   The Grill Room

Le Poulbot

Carrot "Timbale"

1 lb carrots, peeled and finely chopped

½ medium onion, finely chopped

2 tbsp butter

1 pinch sugar

1 tsp salt

  pinch of pepper

6 fl oz chicken stock

2 eggs

3 tbsp grated Swiss cheese

2 tbsp coarsely chopped fresh chervil
  or parsley

  beef stock, as needed

  salt and pepper, to taste

  sherry wine vinegar, to taste

4 sprigs chervil or parsley, to garnish

Cook carrots and onions in butter with sugar, salt and pepper until tender. Add chicken stock and simmer over low heat until liquid has evaporated. Allow to cool. Then, mix with eggs, cheese, and chervil or parsley. Place mixture in 4 individual, buttered ramekins, cover with foil, and place in a pan of hot water. Bake about 30 minutes at 400°F (205°C). Unmould and surround with a sauce made of beef stock, salt, pepper, and a little sherry wine vinegar. Decorate the top of the timbales with sprigs of chervil or parsley.

Serves: 4

Wine: *California Chardonnay, Mayacamas or St. Clement*

Steak with Red Wine Sauce

1 bottle dry red wine

3 c beef stock

1 tsp thyme

1 sliced onion

1 tbsp arrowroot

  boned Scottish sirloin, trimmed of fat,
  enough to serve 6

  oil, as needed

6 slices bone marrow

  parsley, to garnish

To prepare sauce: reduce wine, beef stock, thyme, and onion to half its original amount. Thicken with arrowroot. Strain sauce several times through a cheesecloth.

Cut boned sirloin into steaks 1¼ to 1½ inches thick. Over high heat, brown steaks on all sides in just enough oil to cover bottom of frying pan. Place steaks in a preheated 400°F (205°C) oven for 5 minutes (medium rare), 10 minutes (medium), or 15 minutes (well done), turning steak over halfway through the cooking process.

To serve: cover plate with sauce, place cooked steak in centre, and top with slice of bone marrow and garnish with parsley.

Serves: 6

Wine: *claret*

Frozen Vanilla Mousse with Apricot Sauce

1½ c sugar

2 tbsp water

6 egg yolks

1 tbsp plus 1 dash vanilla extract

2½ c double cream, whipped

  butter and flour, to prepare baking sheet

2 egg whites

⅓ c flour

  grated rind of 1 orange

6 tbsp melted butter

⅔ c apricot jam

⅓ c orange juice

1 tbsp lemon juice

1½ tsp grated lemon peel

To prepare mousse: bring 1 cup sugar and water to a boil and boil 3–4 minutes to make a syrup. Place yolks in bowl of an electric mixer, pour syrup on top, and beat at high speed for 10–12 minutes. Add 1 tablespoon vanilla. Fold the whipped cream into the yolk mixture, then freeze until ready to use.

To prepare pastry cup: butter and flour a baking sheet and set aside. Combine the remaining sugar and dash of vanilla with the egg whites in a bowl and beat with a whisk until the mixture is foamy. Add flour, orange rind, and ⅔ the butter, mixing well. Spread a circle about 5 inches in diameter on the baking sheet with the back of a soupspoon. Bake for about 10 minutes in a 400°F (205°C) oven. Quickly remove with a metal spatula, turn over, and press into a large cup or small soup bowl. Allow to cool.

To prepare apricot sauce: combine all remaining ingredients in a saucepan and heat, stirring until well blended.

To serve: carefully remove the pastry cup from the cup or soup bowl, fill with the frozen mousse, surround with warm apricot sauce, and serve.

The Horn of Plenty Restaurant

The Horn of Plenty Restaurant was started in 1967 by two professional musicians, Patrick and Sonia Stevenson. The restaurant is a beautiful, small country house with a view of 27 miles over the valley of the Tamar to distant Bodmin Moor.

Initially, they featured splendid fresh salmon of superlative quality, which was so readily to hand, and country dishes remembered from their travels or culled from cookery books from all over Europe. The set dinners, genuinely regional in character with appropriately chosen wines, soon caught on, and together with their very special salmon dishes (particularly the Quenelles de Mousseline de Saumon à la Crème), the restaurant soon gained an enviable reputation.

Quite early on, the Stevensons' magic with sauces became apparent — not only new ones of their own invention, but slight alterations of well-known classics that were subtly changed to suit particular dishes. The Stevensons now regularly teach weekend courses on sauce preparation.

Over the years, a vine planted in the terrace just outside the front has grown and covered the area, making a pleasant, leaf-enclosed rendez-vous for luncheon or drinks before dinner in reasonable weather.

The Horn of Plenty is an excellent example of a small family business, run by a couple with no prior restaurant operating experience, successfully attaining high standards in both the kitchen and in the service.

The Horn of Plenty

GULWORTHY
TAVISTOCK, DEVON
0822-832528
LUNCH: SATURDAY — WEDNESDAY,
12 TO 2 P.M.
DINNER: FRIDAY — WEDNESDAY,
7 TO 9:30 P.M.
RESERVATIONS
PROPRIETOR: PATRICK STEVENSON
CHEF: SONIA STEVENSON, M.C.G.B.

Quenelles de Mousseline de Salmon

1 lb raw salmon flesh

6 egg whites, approximately

salt and pepper, to taste

1 pt double cream

Liquidise the salmon with the egg whites until the mixture turns smoothly in the goblet. Add more whites if necessary. Add salt and pepper. Work the purée through a sieve to remove any bones or filaments. Beat in the cream until the mixture holds its shape again. Check seasoning. Chill.

Roll and mould the quenelles by pulling the mixture across the bowl with a hot wet spoon. Dip in simmering salted water, tap off the spoon, and poach for 8 minutes. Drain.

Serving suggestion: serve with sauce Vin Blanc.

Serves: 4

Salmon Cutlets with Sorrel Sauce

salmon cutlets, enough per person

1 handful culinary sorrel leaves

4 egg yolks

2 tbsp water

1½ lb hot, unsalted butter

2 oz unsalted butter

salt and lemon juice, to taste

Poach the cutlets lightly in salted water until still slightly pink near the bone. Lift, drain, and remove skin and centre bone. Keep warm.

To prepare sorrel sauce: simmer sorrel leaves for 15 seconds until they turn colour, then place in a liquidiser with egg yolks and water. Cover and switch on. With a ladle, slowly spoon the hot butter into the liquidiser, including some of the butter milk which will have sunk to the bottom of the pan in which the butter was heated. Regulate the thickness of the sauce with the clarified butter from the top of the pan, thinning, if necessary, with the butter milk at the bottom. Season with salt and lemon juice.

Serve the poached salmon cutlets with the sorrel sauce.

Chocolate Meringue Gâteau

9 egg whites

12 oz caster sugar

6 tsp instant coffee

1 tbsp hot water

6 oz bitter chocolate

9 oz icing sugar

18 oz softened unsalted butter

Beat or whisk 6 whites and caster sugar to make a very firm meringue mixture. Divide into 4 equal, thin rectangular shapes and bake gently overnight at the lowest possible temperature until crisp. (Meringue will keep in an airtight container for several days.)

Dissolve coffee in water and put in a bowl over boiling water. Break chocolate into the bowl. (Don't let bottom of bowl touch the water or chocolate will harden.) Stir occasionally while preparing rest of dish, but as soon as completely mixed, remove from heat and let cool, but don't let harden.

Beat butter thoroughly with a mixer or wooden spoon until creamy. Put icing sugar and remaining whites in another bowl over a pan of water. Bring water to a boil. Beat or whisk whites and sugar over boiling water until thick and glossy and leaves a trail on the surface. Beat mixture into the butter with the soft but cooled chocolate. Continue to beat until creamy and fluffy. Trim all baked meringue sheets to same size. Layer sheets and chocolate meringue mixture and coat top and sides with chocolate meringue. (Do in foil if dessert will be transferred to a serving dish.) Smooth sides and top with a warm knife and scrape with a knife. Serve chilled and sliced.

Serves: 10

The Walnut Tree Inn

The Walnut Tree Inn is situated three miles from Abergavenny on the B4521. It is a long, low Welsh building painted white and kept in character with the rural surroundings. The decor inside is mostly simple with the exception of the antique gilded pub tables and orange ladderback chairs in the Bistro Bars. The old flagstones are retained in the small bar. The dining room is similar. Flowers are always in abundance throughout the Inn.

The Inn, which is 300 years old, was originally a posting house. Then, over the years, it became a centre for cyclists, then a local pub for the surrounding rural community. Seventeen years ago, it was purchased by Ann and Franco Taruschio and it became a restaurant.

Franco Taruschio is the chef. He attended hotel school in his native Italy, then went on to work in Switzerland and France before coming to the U.K. His menu is basically French and Italian, and its items are designed to suit all tastes —from robust food to *nouvelle cuisine*—and does not forget the simple fish dishes much appreciated by those on a diet. In fact, Chef Taruschio enjoys cooking with fish most of all. His house speciality is Brodetto, a marvellous fish casserole from the Marche region of Italy.

The customers, generally speaking, are regulars who come in week after week. Even travellers from abroad come regularly. Having a regular clientele tends to create a very relaxed atmosphere that is always present at The Walnut Tree Inn.

THE WALNUT TREE INN

ABERGAVENNY, GWENT

0873-2797

LUNCH: 12:30 TO 2:30 P.M.

DINNER: 7:30 TO 10:30 P.M.

MONDAY — SATURDAY

RESERVATIONS

PROPRIETOR/CHEF: FRANCO TARUSCHIO

Bavarois de Saumon Fumé

1½ lb smoked salmon

1 c crème fraiche (fresh cream)

½ tsp cayenne pepper

juice of ½ lemon

8 tsp red salmon roe

2 lb finely chopped onion

olive oil, to sauté

2 lb tomatoes, quartered

salt and pepper, to taste

1 tsp red wine vinegar

snipped chives, to garnish

Rinse 10 ramekins with cold water; do not dry. Line with smoked salmon and trim any excessive overhanging salmon. Blend remaining salmon and trimmings in food processor with crème fraiche, cayenne, and lemon juice until smooth. Fold in salmon roe. Divide the mixture among the ramekins; gently fold over edges of salmon. Cover with a piece of grease-proof paper, then a sheet of tin foil. Refrigerate until ready to serve.

To prepare tomato sauce: fry onions in a little olive oil until golden. Add quartered tomatoes and stir fry until puréed. Season with salt and pepper and red wine vinegar. Sieve the purée.

To serve: tip cold bavarois out of ramekins, pour tomato sauce on top, and garnish with snipped chives.

Serves: 10

Mignons de Veau à l'Orange et Poivres Verts

4 tbsp butter

2 tbsp granulated sugar

juice and rind of 2 oranges

salt and pepper, to taste

12 × ½ in slices fillet of veal

1 tbsp olive oil

Grand Marnier, to flame

2 tsp green peppercorns

2 tbsp Grand Marnier

¼ pt good rich veal stock

orange segments and watercress, to garnish

To prepare orange sauce: melt ½ the butter in a saucepan, add sugar, and stir continuously until the sugar and butter is golden and syrupy in texture. Prepare a handful of julienne strips from the orange rind and add them and the orange juice to the caramel mixture. Cook, stirring continuously until sauce thickens. Season.

Season the veal, sauté gently in oil and ½ the remaining butter until brown on both sides but pink in the middle. Flame veal with Grand Marnier. Transfer to a serving dish and keep warm.

Crush the green peppercorns with Grand Marnier and add to juices in the pan. Simmer a few seconds, then add veal stock and reduce by ⅔. Stir in orange sauce. Simmer for 2–3 minutes. Stir in remaining butter and correct seasoning.

To serve: arrange mignons on a serving dish. Top each one with 2–3 orange segments and spoon sauce over.

Serves: 4

Honey and Brandy Ice Cream

6 eggs, separated

½ pt clear honey

5 fl oz brandy

½ pt whipped double cream

½ lb icing sugar

Beat egg yolks and whites separately until thick, then mix together. Mix the remaining ingredients together and fold into the egg mixture. Freeze for 6 hours.

Yields: ½ gallon

The Drangway Restaurant

The Drangway Restaurant, opened nearly six years ago by Colin Pressdee, is situated in the oldest part of Swansea. Its decor combines old and new, as does the cuisine. The modern ground floor restaurant is bottle green and bentwood, with soft shades of brown and cream, blended nicely together with a whitewashed cellar which is little changed from how it has been for more than a hundred years.

The food served is based on pure simple freshness of ingredients, cooked in the appropriate manner, whether *nouvelle* or *ancienne*. Post-Christmas pheasants are braised, but they are finished in the touch of the lighter style of the new cooking, whereas the freshest sea bass or brill or turbot is treated with all the delicacy that it deserves.

The menu offered changes with the seasons and the availability of the produce, as well as with the ever open ideas of the proprietor and chefs. The newest recipes, such as Terrine of Woodcock with Port and Blackcurrant Sauce and Hot Oyster and Avocado Salad, are supported by well-proven favourites such as Fillet of Beef "en chevreuil," Norfolk Duck au Poivre Vert, and Turbot au Beurre Blanc.

A fine selection of wines complements the menu. They range from a superb Muscadet Sevre et Maine Sur Lie and a Vinification Personelle Rhone to Corton Charlemagne and Clos de la Roche 1971 at the top end of the range.

DRANGWAY RESTAURANT

**66 WIND STREET
SWANSEA, WEST GLAMORGAN**

0792-461397

LUNCH: 12 TO 2:15 P.M.
DINNER: 7:30 TO 10 P.M.
TUESDAY — SATURDAY
RESERVATIONS

PROPRIETOR: COLIN PRESSDEE
CHEFS: BRYAN WEBB, COLIN PRESSDEE

Braised Pheasant with Leeks and Juniper

2 large cock pheasants, plucked, drawn, and hung for 5-7 days

oil, as needed

1 medium onion, finely chopped

1 carrot, finely chopped

2 sticks celery, finely chopped

3 large leeks, diced

salt and pepper, to taste

500 ml red Rhone wine

500 ml good veal or lamb stock

bouquet garni: fresh parsley, thyme, bay

10 juniper berries

20 ml oil

40 ml wine vinegar

1 whole medium leek (white and green parts), cut julienne

50 ml good L.B.R. port

20 pink peppercorns (*Baies rose*)

Trim pheasants of excess fat in body cavity. Heat a little oil in a cast-iron pan and seal pheasants thoroughly, turning carefully, until entire outside is light golden brown. Remove from pan and keep warm.

Add mirepoix (onion, carrot, celery) to the same pan and cook for 2 minutes, then add leeks and cook another 2 minutes over brisk heat. Season with salt and pepper. Add red wine and reduce to ½, then add stock, bouquet garni, and juniper berries. Return pheasants to cooking pan, check seasoning, cover and cook in a slow oven, gas mark 3 (340°F/170°C) for 1 hour until tender and legs separate easily from the body of the birds. Remove birds from oven, cut each into 4, and keep warm. Pour off all fat from pan. Remove bouquet garni. Puree sauce then press through a sieve to make a smooth sauce.

In a clean saucepan, combine oil and wine vinegar, heat, and add julienne of leeks. Stir for about 1 minute over brisk heat until leeks are just cooked (green parts will remain very crunchy). Drain off and arrange julienne around and over pheasant pieces.

Add port and pink peppercorns to the sauce, heat through and simmer for 1 minute. Pour over pheasants and serve immediately.

Serves: 6–8

Wine: *Burgundy — Aloxe Corton, Chassagne Montrachet, Morgeot, or Beaune Clos des Mouches*

Soufflé Glacé aux Marrons au Coulis de Fraises

6 egg yolks

550 g sugar

200 ml water, and as needed

200 g egg whites

250 g tinned chestnuts in syrup

20 ml dark rum

500 ml cream

250 g fresh strawberries

100 ml strawberry syrup

20 ml eau de vie kirsch, optional

Whip egg yolks until light and stiff. Cook 150 grams sugar with a little water until just before caramelisation. Stir into whipped yolks. Repeat with the egg whites: whip until stiff, add 200 grams sugar cooked with water. (This must be done in 2 stages or sugar mix may set hard.)

Purée the *marrons* (chestnuts) with their syrup and the rum until smooth. Whip the cream until *au ribbon* stage (thick but flowing). Fold ½ the cream into the chestnut purée. Reserve remaining cream.

Fold egg yolk mix into egg white mix, then fold all into the remaining cream. Fold in the purée of chestnuts. The soufflé should be of even consistency but do not overstir. Pour mix into either one 2 litre mould or into several individual moulds and place in freezer until set. (About 4 hours for small moulds, 24 hours for large mould.)

To prepare strawberry purée: boil remaining sugar and water, add fresh strawberries and strawberry syrup, and cook, covered for 2–3 minutes. Purée the fruit and liquid in a liquidiser, press through a sieve to remove seeds, and allow to cool. Stir in eau de vie kirsch if desired.

To serve: turn out the soufflé glace onto a plate. Decorate with pieces of *marron glace*, surround with strawberry purée, and serve immediately.

The Bell Inn

The Bell Inn is owned and operated by Michael Harris, his wife, Patsy, and his mother, Mrs. Daphne Harris. The establishment dates back to 1650 when it was an old coaching inn, providing rest and refreshment for weary travellers.

The Inn offers primarily French-style cuisine with some traditional English dishes prepared by head chef Jack Dick, a Bavarian who received his training in many great European hotels. He and his sous-chef, Manuel, also train young chefs from all over the world. Cooking is a vocation and an art in Chef Dick's kitchen.

Michael Harris, himself, trained at the Lausanne Hotel School and has a passion for good wine, so not surprisingly he is in charge of the cellar. He buys and bottles a wide range of wines under his father's name, Gerard Harris. These include some interesting and lesser known wines from Beaujolais, Loire, and the petits chateaux of Bordeaux.

The interior of the restaurant is decorated in elegant green with candles, silver, and cut glass.

A cobblestone courtyard leads out to the Old Brewery opposite The Bell which was converted some years ago to provide additional hotel accommodations. The original stables and malt houses now form an attractive group of cottages round the cobbled yard.

THE BELL INN

ASTON CLINTON, BUCKINGHAMSHIRE

0296-630252

LUNCH: 12:30 TO 1:45 P.M.
DINNER: 7:30 TO 9:45 P.M.
DAILY
RESERVATIONS

PROPRIETOR: MICHAEL HARRIS
CHEF: JACK DICK

Avocado Salad with Vinaigrette Dressing

wine vinegar

olive oil

finely chopped gherkins

capers

skinned tomatoes

garlic and seasoning, to taste

1 avocado per person

lettuce

To prepare vinaigrette dressing: mix together ⅓ wine vinegar to ⅔ olive oil, then season with finely chopped gherkins, capers, skinned tomato, garlic, and other seasoning to taste.

Halve and peel each avocado and lay the 2 sections flat side down. Using a sharp knife, cut through, drawing the knife at an angle. Press gently with the flat of the hand to fan out the cut slices. Do the same with the other halves. Arrange on lettuce and serve with dressing.

Wine: Pinot Blanc d'Alsace, Hugel, 1978

Roast Aylesbury Duck with Apple Sauce

1 × 5 - 6 lb duck

salt, to taste

1 apple

oil, to grease

½ onion

2 large cooking apples, peeled, cored, and sliced

5 fl oz white wine

1 tbsp sugar, or to taste

Wash and dry the duck, sprinkle with salt, inside and out, and put 1 apple inside. Grease a baking tin with very little oil and put duck in, on its side, together with giblets and wing tips.

Roast in a fairly high oven for 20 minutes, turn onto the other side for another 20 minutes, and turn breast up for the last 20 minutes. Baste at intervals throughout. Remove duck from pan and keep hot.

Pour off excess fat from pan, then slice half an onion into pan. Cook gently on top of the stove, together with the giblets, until the onion is soft and golden brown. Drain off fat and put remaining sediment with onion and giblets through a fine sieve. Keep hot.

Cook the 2 apples gently in white wine with a little sugar, then purée them and serve with the duck.

Serving suggestion: serve with boiled new potatoes and young courgettes.

Serves: 2

Wine: Chateau Talbot, 1967

Sorbet Crème de Cassis

½ lb sugar

½ pt water

1 lb blackcurrants

1 squeeze of lemon juice

2 fl oz crème de cassis

2 egg whites, stiffly beaten

Make a syrup of the sugar and water. Add blackcurrants and cook gently in the syrup un-til soft. Add a squeeze of lemon juice and crème de cassis. Liquidise and pass through a sieve. When cool, fold in the stiffly beaten egg whites.

Fast freeze by placing mixture in a shallow metal tray in a domestic freezer. When mushy but not quite solid, remove from freezer and beat thoroughly again. Return to freezer until ready to serve.

Wine: St. Croix du Mout, Chateau Terfort, 1975

Rookery Hall

Rookery Hall, the home of Mr. and Mrs. H.G. Norton, is reputedly Georgian in origin but was rebuilt in the early 19th century. It is set in 28 acres of gardens and wooded parkland. Poised on a hill overlooking the green Cheshire plain, it is one of the finest country houses in the area.

The architecture is impressive, in the style of a grand chateau. Baron Von Schroeder, who owned it at the turn of the century, was responsible for the substantial additions that give it an unusual Continental, baronial character, making it almost unique in Britain today.

The cuisine is entirely 20th century, with Mrs. Jean Norton personally presiding over the kitchens. The lofty panelled dining room of this lovely country mansion makes a splendid baronial setting for her imaginative cooking. The wine list is Harry Norton's special interest and hobby. He offers a choice from around 500 bins and more than 20 vintage ports.

The Nortons' aim and obsession is to restore the house to its former dignity as a refuge for people of good taste who prefer and appreciate the relaxed atmosphere of gracious living.

Rookery Hall

WORLESTON
NEAR NANTWICH, CHESHIRE

0270-626866

NON-RESIDENTS:
DINNER: TUESDAY — SATURDAY
RESIDENTS: ALL MEALS DAILY
RESERVATIONS

PROPRIETORS: H.G. & JEAN NORTON
CHEF: JEAN NORTON, M.C.G.B.

Jean's Green Oysters

24 medium to large oysters
3 oz butter
1 finely chopped onion
1 finely chopped tender celery stalk
3 oz flour
1½ pt hot milk
1 bay leaf
   freshly grated nutmeg, to taste
4 tbsp dry white wine
1½ oz grated Parmesan cheese
   ground white peppercorns, to taste
   lemon juice, to taste
   pinch of salt
1 lb fresh spinach, finely chopped
6 tbsp double cream
2 egg yolks, beaten
   melted butter, as needed

Prepare oysters and retain cleaned shells. Melt butter in a thick saucepan. Add onion and celery and cook over low heat until onion is soft but not browned. Remove pan from heat, stir in flour, return to heat, and cook gently through. Add ¼ milk, heat to boiling point, and stir vigorously. As sauce begins to thicken, add remainder of milk, stirring constantly with a wooden spoon until sauce bubbles. Add bay leaf, nutmeg, white wine, 1 ounce Parmesan cheese, white pepper, a few drops lemon juice, and salt, then simmer gently for 15 minutes. Stir in chopped spinach and adjust seasoning. Remove bay leaf and leave sauce to cool. Add double cream to beaten egg yolks, then stir into warm sauce.

Position oyster shells on mounds of rock salt on a baking tray. Return cleaned and bearded oysters to shells and cover each one with sauce. Sprinkle remainder of cheese on top and brush with melted butter. Bake in a hot oven at gas mark 4 (360°F/180°C) until golden brown, about 10 minutes.

Serves: 6

Wine: *Corton Charlemagne, Bonneau de Martray, 1973*

Grouse and Rump Steak Pie

3 fresh, plump, young grouse
12 oz rump steak
12 oz streaky bacon
   flour, as needed
   seasoning, to taste
2 large onions, roughly chopped
   freshly ground black pepper, to taste
2 c red wine
2 c chicken stock
30 small shallots
6 oz button mushrooms
   cooking oil, as needed
   pinch of nutmeg
1 bay leaf
4 hard-boiled eggs, quartered
   chopped fresh parsley, as needed
2 lb flaky pastry
1 egg yolk plus little milk for egg wash

Clean and skin grouse, then joint birds into 6 portions (6 breasts and 6 legs). Leave flesh on bones. Trim steak and slice into medium-sized pieces. Cut bacon in thin strips. Dust grouse legs in seasoned flour and fry with grouse giblets, rump steak trimmings, and onions. Add seasoning, pepper, red wine, and stock. Simmer 1½–2 hours then strain liquor and reserve.

Gently brown breasts, rump steak strips, bacon, shallots, and mushrooms in cooking oil, then place everything except shallots and mushrooms in a casserole dish. Pour over the reserved liquor, adjust seasoning, and add bay leaf. Cover and bake in oven at gas mark 6 (400°F/205°C) for 15 minutes, then reduce oven to gas mark 3 (325°F/165°C) and bake another hour.

Remove dish from oven, add shallots. Cover and return to oven for another 10 minutes. Remove from oven and cool. Place breasts in a pie dish. Spread rump steak, shallots, and mushrooms evenly around the grouse and separate each portion with egg quarters. Sprinkle with a small amount of parsley and add liquor from casserole dish. Top with rolled pastry and brush lid with egg wash. Cook for 20 minutes at gas mark 5 (375°F/190°C), but place foil over pastry after 15 minutes to prevent burning.

Serves: 6

Wine: *Chambertin Cuvée Héritiers, Latour, 1973*

The Fox and Goose Inn

The Fox and Goose Inn was built in the year Henry VIII came to the throne — 1509. Church authorities in the 16th century allowed church-goers to eat and drink in the naves of churches. Abuses of the privilege eventually resulted in inns being built by church authorities — The Fox and Goose was one of these.

The "Church House" or Guildhall, now The Fox and Goose, is still owned by the church. A noble building of mellow brickwork, its north front is in the churchyard. On the front the carved date 1616 indicates when the house was enlarged. Oak timber in the original North East part of the Inn is decorated with two carved figures, one of an Abbot and the other of St. Margaret.

The dining room is simple and cottage, with beams and a log fire, and the food is served informally. The ingredients are beautifully fresh. Local game is a speciality, and the pike for the famous quenelles is caught by Mr. P. Clarke. The dishes are imaginative and excellently cooked by Mrs. Clarke and her son Adrian.

An extensive international list of wines is available featuring predominantly French vintners.

Fox & Goose

FRESSINGFIELD
DISS, NORFOLK
037986-FRESSINGFIELD 247
LUNCH: 12 TO 1:30 P.M.
DINNER: 7 TO 9 P.M.
DAILY
CLOSED 21 TO 28 DECEMBER
RESERVATIONS
PROPRIETORS: MR. & MRS. P.H. CLARKE,
MR. A.P. CLARKE
CHEF: A.P. CLARKE

Crêpes aux Fruits des Mer

4 oz plain flour, sifted

¼ pt water

¼ pt milk

2 eggs, one separated

2 fl oz olive oil

salt, to taste

2 medium-large onions, chopped medium-fine

6 calamari, sliced thinly, leave tentacles

3-4 cloves garlic

½ pt fish stock

½ pt dry white wine

3 × 15½ oz tins Italian tomatoes

6 medium-sized king prawns

6 langoustini

6 scallops

12 oz fresh prawns

½ pt double cream

4 sprigs parsley

black pepper, to taste

1 tbsp sugar

To prepare crepes: put flour in a mixing bowl. In a measuring jug, put water, milk, 1 egg, 1 egg yolk, salt, and ½ the olive oil. Turn on mixer to top speed, then quickly add ingredients in jug and allow to beat for 1 minute. Put a small frying pan on moderate heat and gently rub some butter in it. Cover base of pan with batter. Cook each crepe until lightly browned, turn, and just seal the other side (pancake must remain supple).

To prepare filling: put onions in pan on a moderate-slow heat with remaining olive oil in it. Fry for 5 minutes, then add garlic, fish stock, wine, and tomatoes. Let simmer 1-1½ hours, stirring occasionally until mixture is thick and fairly dry. Increase heat and add all fish at once. Cook rapidly about 5 minutes. Remove from heat and allow to cool slightly.

Put 6 crepes into 6-inch oval dishes so they are left hanging half in and half out. Divide fish evenly among the dishes. Place pan with filling back on high heat, add cream and parsley, and cook until cream has thickened. Add salt, pepper, and sugar to taste. Pour sauce over fish and fold pancake over the top. Place in oven at gas mark 6 (400°F/205°C) for 15 minutes or until bubbling.

Serves: 6

Cailles aux Juliennes de Légumes, Sauce Madère

2 oz butter

2 tbsp olive oil

12 plump quails

5 oz coarsely chopped onion

4 oz sliced celery

6 oz mushrooms, sliced medium

5 oz carrot, julienne

2 oz parsnip, julienne

2 oz turnip, julienne

1 pt chicken stock

1 pt Madeira wine

pinch of salt and pepper

2 oz French beans

2 oz peas

parsley, to garnish

In a large pan, place butter and olive oil and sauté the quail quickly to brown but not cook them. Place quail in a roasting tin. In the quail juices, gently cook the onion, celery, mushrooms, carrot, parsnip, and turnip, uncovered, for 10 minutes. Add the stock, wine, salt, and pepper. Cover and cook for a total of 15 minutes (until tender). After vegetables have been cooking for 3 minutes, put quail in oven, preheated to gas mark 7 (425°F/220°C), and cook for 20 minutes. At the end of 10 minutes of cooking the vegetables, add French beans to that pan. After 12 minutes, add peas. Remove quail from oven and vegetables from heat. Neatly arrange the vegetables on a large hot serving dish and place quail on top. Keep in a warm oven. Boil the stock left after you've removed the vegetables until reduced to a thick glaze. Correct the seasoning. Gently coat the quail with the glaze and sprinkle with parsley to garnish.

Serves: 6

Frais de Bois Ice Cream (Strawberry Ice Cream)

13 fl oz water

13 oz sugar

13 fl oz frais de bois liqueur

2 lb strawberries

2 pt double cream

Boil water and sugar together until reduced by about ¼. Add liqueur. Liquidise strawberries, then put them through a very fine sieve to remove all pips. Beat cream until thick but not whipped. Beat cream into strawberry mixture and freeze. Stir about every hour until frozen. Keep frozen until serving.

Serves: 6–8

Les Quat' Saisons

Les Quat' Saisons opened in Oxford on 19 July 1977. This pretty little French restaurant, which has had numerous accolades bestowed on it, offers warm, friendly atmosphere, superb cuisine, and efficient, professional service. The restaurant is air conditioned and also features smoke filters, indirect wall lighting, candles, French prints on the walls, lace and flowers on the tables, etc.

The menu features contemporary seasonal cuisine prepared by Chef/Patron Raymond Blanc, who received no formal training but possesses a unique natural flair for cooking and an admirable, philosophical perspective of the restaurant and its goals. His description of Les Quat' Saisons cannot be bettered:

"La cuisine . . . Every happy instant is celebrated at the table, which is such a wonderful symbol of happiness, friendship, love . . . We are a Family restaurant well aware of the expectations of the guest and what we have to achieve. What a wonderful and most pleasing feeling of achievement to see the little miracle of the contentment of the guest . . . that is the soul of our Team, the real meaning of our work.

"Of course, the stone base is the cuisine, the seasons playing the most vital part in the choice of dishes, bringing new colours, flavours, and taste . . . new ideas, teasing your imagination . . . there is the sense of renewal and happening."

Les Quat' Saisons Restaurant Français

272 BANBURY ROAD
SUMMERTOWN, OXFORD

0865-53540

LUNCH: 12 TO 2 P.M.
DINNER: 7 TO 10 P.M.
TUESDAY - SATURDAY
RESERVATIONS

PROPRIETOR/CHEF:
RAYMOND BLANC, M.C.G.B.

Pigeonneau de Bresse et son Voie au Vieux Madère

2 chicken livers

4 young, plump pigeons from Bresse with 4 livers

1 tsp foie gras

100 ml milk

100 ml cream

1 egg

salt and pepper, to taste

clarified butter, and as needed

1 tsp goose fat

1 tsp butter

20 g shallots

20 ml xeres vinegar

60 g mushrooms, cut finely

50 ml ruby port

100 ml dry old Madeira wine

2 tbsp demi-glace or 4 tbsp clear chicken stock

2 tbsp truffle juice

pinch of sugar

juice of ¼ lemon

To prepare gâteau de foie: liquidise the chicken and pigeon livers with foie gras, milk, cream, and egg until a smooth texture is obtained. Pass the mixture through a sieve, then season with salt and pepper. Add clarified butter and deep freeze for 1 minute, then take out. Butter some little moulds and place the mixture in them. Cook in a bain-marie for about 20 minutes at 310°F (155°C), then leave in the bain-marie to keep warm while preparing the pigeons.

To prepare pigeons: singe the pigeons, then season them with salt and pepper. Place them, breasts down, in a sauté pan with the goose fat and sear for 1 minute until golden. With a brush, butter them all over and place in a 450°F (230°C) oven for 10 minutes, basting occasionally. Remove them from the oven; the flesh should be pink. Remove the fat.

Set the pigeons aside, propped on their ends against the side of a dish to allow the flesh to relax and the juices to run from the birds. Then, remove the wings and legs, then carve the body of each bird, separating the breast from the backbone, and place the meat back in the dish. Season again.

To prepare the sauce: cut up the backbones and necks and sauté them in butter with the shallots in the same sauté pan previously used. Deglaze with the vinegar and reduce completely. Add mushrooms and cook for 1 minute. Deglaze with port and reduce by ½. Add Madeira and reduce by ½ again. Add the demi-glace and truffle juice. Bring to a boil again, and then pass through a fine strainer, pushing with a wooden spoon to obtain as much sauce as possible. Season to taste, then add sugar, lemon, and the juices released from the pigeon flesh. (Sauce should have a light consistency.)

To serve: slide a spatula against the moulds to free the gâteaux. Turn each onto a warm plate, giving a shake to help the mousse out. Pour the sauce on a serving plate, then arrange the breasts, legs, and wings in a decorative manner on top. Place the meat on top of the sauce and serve.

Serves: 4

Wine: *Chiroubles, Georges Passot, 1976*

Feuilleté aux Poires "William"

8 rounds of puff pastry (10 cm in diameter, 2 mm thick)

30 g caster sugar

1 tbsp unsalted butter

4 tbsp crème pâtissière, not cold

1 tbsp plus 1 dash of Pear William liqueur

1 tbsp whipped double cream

4 William pears, ripe but firm

lemon juice, as needed

½ litre syrup at 80°F (28°C)

icing sugar, as needed

fresh raspberry sauce, prepared

Two hours beforehand: line the pastry rounds and put them on a baking tray. Sprinkle them with sugar. Bake in a 450°F (230°C) oven for 8 minutes until the sugar caramelises and forms a golden crust. Remove from the oven and cool.

To prepare mousseline crème: cream the unsalted butter and whisk in the crème pâtissière. Add 1 tablespoon liqueur and fold in the whipped cream. Cool for 1 hour.

Peel the pears, wash and rub them with lemon, and remove the cores. Poach in syrup for 40 minutes, simmering gently, until they are cooked and slightly crystallised. Drain, cool them, then slice the pears into segments. Add a dash of liqueur.

To assemble: sprinkle 4 rounds of puff pastry with icing sugar. With a piping bag, spread 1 tablespoon of mousseline crème on the other 4 rounds. Place half the pear segments on them, spread the remaining crème on top, and put the sugar sprinkled rounds on top of all. Smooth the sides with a palette knife.

Place the feuilletés onto cold plates and surround with a fresh raspberry sauce. Serve immediately.

Serves: 4

Restaurant Elizabeth

Antonio Lopez, owner and chef of the famed **Restaurant Elizabeth** opposite Christ Church College, is a man big in stature and in heart. That he has been offering gourmet dishes for more than 20 years to a clientele that is not only academic but knowledgeable about food and wine speaks volumes about the standards he maintains.

The Elizabeth is a small, panelled restaurant with beamed ceilings and subdued lighting. Señor Lopez's white-jacketed staff, most of whom are Spanish, are attentive and add that little something special to the service that is sometimes missing even in grander establishments.

The kitchen is headed by Chef Salvador Rodriguez, who was a friend of the Lopez family since childhood and trained under their tutelage. His menu presents Continental cuisine that is both traditional and experimental. The Ttoro Soup, which is a kind of bouillabaisse finished with aioli, croutons, Parmesan cheese, and parsley, is a dish typical of the Basque country from whence both he and Señor Lopez originate. It is delicious and well worth trying.

The wines are excellent and, whilst not inexpensive, show an understanding and enthusiasm not often found. But, as the proprietor says, "The colleges in Oxford have some of the best cellars in England, so my standards have to be high."

Restaurant Elizabeth

84 ST. ALDATES
OXFORD, OXFORDSHIRE
0865-42230
LUNCH: SUNDAY, 12:30 TO 2:30 P.M.
DINNER: MONDAY — FRIDAY, 6:30 TO 11 P.M.
AND SUNDAY, 7 TO 10:30 P.M.
RESERVATIONS
PROPRIETOR: ANTONIO LOPEZ
CHEF: SALVADOR RODRIGUEZ

Ttoro Soup

2 pt water

1 lb fillets of white fish, bones reserved

olive oil, as needed

1 large leek, sliced

1 large carrot, chopped

1 green pepper, sliced

3 tomatoes, peeled and chopped

pinch of saffron

salt and pepper, to taste

3 tbsp brandy

croutons fried in butter, to garnish

4 tbsp aioli mayonnaise

4 tbsp Parmesan cheese

parsley, to garnish

Make a fish stock by boiling water with fish bones. Strain after 30 minutes. Put a coffee cupful of oil in another pan and sweat the leek, carrot, and pepper for 10 minutes. Add tomatoes and cook another 5 minutes. Add to stock and simmer for 30 minutes.

In a separate pan, sauté the fish in 3 tablespoons oil very rapidly for no more than 1 minute, add brandy and flame. Strain the thick stock and add the fish pieces. Do not cook further. Season to taste.

To serve: add croutons, aioli, and Parmesan, then sprinkle with chopped parsley.

Serves: 4

Rice in Paella

3 tbsp olive oil

½ lb chicken

1 lb mussels

½ lb scampi

1 clove garlic, finely chopped

3 tomatoes, peeled

1 small green pepper

1 small red pepper

8 oz rice

1½ pt chicken stock

pinch of saffron

salt and pepper, to taste

Heat the olive oil in a paella pan; once oil is hot, brown the chicken and then take it out. Add mussels and scampi and heat until mussels open. Remove scampi and mussels, return chicken to pan, then add garlic, tomatoes, and peppers. Cook gently until chicken is tender. Add rice and stir; add chicken stock. Check that it's well mixed, then add saffron and leave on heat for 15 minutes.

Return scampi and mussels to the pot and leave on heat another 5 minutes. Remove pan from heat and leave to rest for 5 minutes. Do not stir until on table for serving. Season with salt and pepper.

Serves: 6

Oeufs à la Neige (Snow Eggs)

4 eggs, separated

2 oz sugar

1 pt milk

½ pt double cream

1 small stick cinnamon

2 cloves

4 drops vanilla essence

peel of ½ lemon

½ tsp ground cinnamon

Beat egg whites until frothy. Add ½ the sugar and continue beating until whites become stiff. Put milk, cream, cinnamon stick, cloves, vanilla, and lemon peel in a large pan and bring to a boil. Once milk is boiling, shape the whites into egg shapes (collops) with 2 dessertspoons and gently cook in the milk (they cook very quickly). Put collops on a large plate.

Once all egg whites are cooked, beat egg yolks with remaining sugar, then pour in boiling milk, stirring all the time. If the desired consistency is not reached, return the creamy mixture to the pan and heat very slowly, continually stirring, until it is reached. Do not allow to boil or it will curdle. Pour mixture over the collops and allow to cool. Sprinkle with ground cinnamon prior to serving.

Serves: 4

La Sorbonne Restaurant

The building that **La Sorbonne Restaurant** occupies is better known as Kemp Hall. It was built in 1637. Situated on High Street in the centre of Oxford, it must count as one of the best preserved and least altered examples of 17th century domestic architecture in the city. The exterior of the building is distinguished by five gables of various sizes, a timbered framework, and overhanging upper stories. The interior is still in an excellent state of preservation as well, with its many original fireplaces, doorways, and a fine carved staircase.

The building became the site of La Sorbonne in September 1966, when the lease was acquired by M. Andre Chavagnon. Since then, it has become one of the finest restaurants in the county, providing a menu of a range and quality with which few others can compare.

Andre Chavagnon began his apprenticeship at age 14 at the Grand Hotel in Roanne. After three years, he went on to work in Vichy, Cannes, and Paris, gaining experience in all types of cuisine. He came to England in 1956 and has remained here. When he opened La Sorbonne, he had only one waiter; today, there is a large service and kitchen staff to cater to discriminating diners from all over the world. The original waiter, Alain Desenclos, is still serving today.

La Sorbonne

**130A HIGH STREET
OXFORD, OXFORDSHIRE**

0865-41320

**LUNCH: 12 TO 2 P.M.
DINNER: 7 TO 11 P.M.
MONDAY — SATURDAY
RESERVATIONS**

PROPRIETOR/CHEF: A.P. CHAVAGNON

Le Rable de Lièvre Sauce Poivrade

1 pt red wine

1 French onion

2 carrots

1 bay leaf

1 sprig fresh thyme

½ oz crushed black pepper

1 clove garlic

2 tbsp vegetable oil

  salt, to taste

1 tsp natural green pepper

1 tbsp red wine vinegar

1 × 8 lb hare

2 oz fresh butter

2 French shallots, finely chopped

3 tbsp double cream

1 tbsp redcurrant jelly

2 tbsp brandy

  boiled new potatoes, to garnish

½ oz finely chopped parsley

To prepare marinade: mix red wine, onion, carrots, bay leaf, thyme, black pepper, garlic, ½ the vegetable oil, salt, green pepper, and vinegar together. Cut legs from hare. Marinate back or saddle (le rable). After 3 days, heat ½ the butter and remaining oil. When very hot, cook saddle for 10 minutes, turning it frequently. Remove meat and drain oil from saucepan. Strain marinade.

To prepare sauce: add remaining butter, shallots, 6 tablespoons of marinade, and green pepper to oiled saucepan. Heat until reduced by ½. Add cream and jelly. Reduce again for 2 minutes.

Bone hare into long thin slices, then replace it in its original form, keeping meat pink. Pour brandy on top and place in hot oven for 2 minutes. Remove from oven and cover with sauce.

To serve: garnish with potatoes and sprinkle with parsley.

Serves: 4

CHEF'S TIP

ALWAYS GIVE YOURSELF PLENTY OF TIME WHEN PREPARING A MEAL. ALWAYS THINK ABOUT WHAT YOU ARE DOING TO MAKE SURE YOU DO NOT MAKE MISTAKES.

La Tarte aux Pommes Flambée au Calvados

250 g sieved plain flour

120 g caster sugar

3 drops vanilla essence

150 g butter

2 egg yolks

1 egg white

200 ml water

  pinch of salt

500 g best cooking apples, peeled and cored

300 g granulated sugar

100 ml water

  butter, as needed

200 ml Calvados

Prepare pâté sable by mixing first 8 ingredients together. Refrigerate approximately 4 hours. When chilled, roll out pastry and line a 20 cm dish (about 2.5 cm deep). Prick base with fork. Place a layer of greaseproof paper on base and cover with baking beans. Bake blind for 20 minutes at 350°F (175°C). Allow to cool.

To prepare filling: cook 300 grams apples with ½ the sugar in water. Reduce until purée is a golden colour. Allow to cool.

Slice remaining apples in fan-shaped slices. Fill tart base with cooled apple purée. Decorate top with apple slices. Dot with butter. Sprinkle with remaining sugar and brown under a moderate grill for 2–3 minutes.

To serve: pour flamed Calvados over and serve warm.

Serves: 4

Wine: *Calvados*

Mallory Court Hotel

Mallory Court Hotel is a country house hotel set in ten acres of garden-like grounds. Built in 1915, it was once the luxurious home of Sir John Black of Standard Motors. This small private hotel is now owned by Allan Holland and Jeremy Mort who, five years ago, purchased the property and converted the house. Both owners have had prior management experience: Mr. Holland in the retail business and Mr. Mort in the hotel trade in both Switzerland and the U.K.

A main attraction of Mallory Court is its restaurant. Its decor is highlighted by fine oak panelling and enormous open fireplaces, both of which add to the intentional warmth of the place.

Mr. Holland is the chef, and his modest but comprehensive menu reflects his preference for *la nouvelle* French cuisine. Therefore, the accent is on lighter and more imaginative cooking. Chef Holland also goes to great lengths to present each dish in as uncluttered and as appetising a fashion as possible.

There is no bar area, however, there is bar service at the table. There are also 100 bins of carefully selected French and German wines, most priced in the medium to expensive range, from which to choose to complement a most rewarding dining experience.

Mallory Court

HARBURY LANE, BISHOPS TACKBROOK
LEAMINGTON SPA, WARWICKSHIRE

0926-30214

LUNCH: 12:30 TO 2 P.M.,
SUNDAY — FRIDAY
DINNER: 7:30 TO 10 P.M.,
MONDAY — SATURDAY
AND SUNDAY FOR RESIDENTS ONLY
RESERVATIONS

PROPRIETORS: ALLAN HOLLAND,
JEREMY MORT
CHEF: ALLAN HOLLAND, M.C.G.B.

Suprême de Volaille Jacqueline

8 oz raw, skinned, and boned duck flesh

1 egg white

½ tsp salt

pinch of white pepper

8-10 fl oz double cream, chilled

¾ pt chicken stock

6× 6-7 oz chicken suprêmes

4 fl oz red port

½ pt double cream

lemon juice, as needed

salt and white pepper, to taste

1 oz butter

2 oz flaked almonds sautéed in butter until golden

6 thin slices truffle

sprigs of fresh chervil or parsley, to garnish

To prepare duck mousse: purée the duck flesh either in a food processor or by mincing then pounding flesh in a mortar. Slowly beat egg white into the purée. Pass through a fine drum sieve into a basin, put basin on ice, and refrigerate for 1 hour. Lightly whip chilled double cream until it begins to thicken, then gradually beat cream into duck mousse over ice with a wooden spoon until mixture looks light and mousse-like. Season with salt and white pepper. (If mousse seems too firm, add more cream.) Cover the basin and refrigerate.

Make a slit on the top of the breasts lengthways to form a small pocket. Fill pocket with some duck mousse, but do not overfill as mousse will swell during cooking. Place filled suprêmes in a lightly buttered sauté pan and pour cold chicken stock in. Cover pan, bring slowly to simmering point, and poach suprêmes very gently for about 8-10 minutes or until just cooked. Remove suprêmes; cover and keep warm while finishing the sauce.

To prepare sauce: pour port into the pan with the stock and boil down rapidly over high heat until well reduced and syrupy. Add cream and reduce briefly until sauce has a coating consistency. Remove from heat and add lemon juice and seasoning to taste. Swirl in the butter. Pass sauce through a very fine strainer.

Arrange the suprêmes in the centre of a serving dish or on individual plates and coat with the sauce. Sprinkle with almonds and garnish with truffle slices. Surround dish with sprigs of chervil or parsley.

Serves: 6

Crème Brûlée aux Mandarines

6 mandarins

1 pt double cream

8 egg yolks

2 oz caster sugar

2 tbsp Mandarin Napoleon liqueur

soft light brown sugar, as needed

With a very sharp, small knife, remove rind and pith from mandarins and cut out the segments. Divide segments, without membrane, among 6 small ramekins, arranging them on the bottom of the dishes.

Rinse a heavy saucepan with cold water and leave wet. Pour in double cream and heat to just below simmering point over low heat. In a separate bowl, beat egg yolks and caster sugar together until thick and pale in colour. Slowly pour hot cream onto yolk and sugar mixture, stirring slowly. Blend in liqueur.

Rinse out a saucepan and leave wet. Pour in custard mixture and, over very low heat or a pan of simmering water, cook custard, stirring continuously with a wooden spoon. (Make sure to scrape bottom of pan to prevent custard catching.) Continue stirring until mixture thickens sufficiently (until it leaves a trail when you lift out the spoon) but *do not boil*. Strain custard into ramekins and allow to cool. Refrigerate at least 6 hours or overnight.

An hour before serving, preheat grill and sprinkle an even layer of sugar (about ¼ inch thick) over the top of the custards. Place ramekins in a shallow tin filled with ice cubes and place under hot grill until sugar melts and caramelises (only a few moments). Remove from grill and allow to cool, but do not refrigerate.

Serves: 6-8

CHEF'S TIP

IF MANDARINS ARE NOT AVAILABLE, ORANGES CAN BE SUBSTITUTED. IN THAT CASE, ADD A SPOONFUL OF GRATED RIND TO THE CUSTARD AND USE GRAND MARNIER INSTEAD OF THE NAPOLEON LIQUEUR.

The Elms Hotel

The Elms Hotel & **Restaurant** is housed in a Queen Anne country house built in 1710 and is situated in 15 acres of parkland and formal gardens amidst the beautiful rolling Worcestershire countryside. There are croquet and putting lawns and tennis courts for guests to enjoy, as well as lounges and bedrooms that are furnished with antiques and have welcoming open log fires that burn all the year round.

The Regency-styled **Brooke Room Restaurant** has a 1981 addition — a delightful room continuing the furniture and decor of the old. Its main feature is a long series of arched windows that afford a fine view of a floodlit raised garden. The restaurant is renowned for the very high standard of Continental and British cooking set by Chef Murdo MacSween, who is a devoted exponent of *la nouvelle cuisine*.

Guests are offered a small à la carte menu together with a table d'hôte menu for lunch. In the evening, a most interesting menu is offered, the price of the main course determining the cost of a four-course meal. The dinner menu is altered at regular intervals, and in addition, every day there are at least two different hors d'oeuvres and entrées to choose from. Of particular note is the sweets trolley; throughout the winter months, a different hot English pudding is served every day. There is also an excellent wine cellar that boasts a particularly fine selection of clarets.

THE
ELMS HOTEL

ABBERLY NEAR WORCESTER
029921-GREAT WHITLEY 666
BREAKFAST, LUNCH, AND DINNER
DAILY
PROPRIETOR: DONALD CROSTHWAITE
CHEF: MURDO MacSWEEN, M.C.G.B.

Terrine de Saumon et Turbot au Safran

125 g salmon

½ tsp salt

2 turns of a pepper mill

1 egg

125 g turbot

½ tsp salt

2 turns of a pepper mill

1 egg

500 scant ml cream

melted butter, as needed

blanched spinach leaves, as needed

100 ml dry white wine

1 heaped tbsp chopped shallots

50 ml fish stock

250 scant ml whipping cream

pinch of saffron mixed with a little white wine

½ tbsp lemon juice

salt and pepper, to taste

parsley, to garnish

To prepare the mousse: blend salmon, seasoned with salt and pepper, in a liquidiser for 3-4 minutes. When fish is a smooth purée, add whole egg and blend another minute. Put container in refrigerator for 30 minutes to firm mixture. Repeat the same steps for the turbot. Return salmon mixture to the liquidiser, add ½ the cream, and blend for several seconds. Do the same for the turbot mixture. Preheat the oven to gas mark 7 (425°F/220°C). Brush interior of terrine with melted butter and line with blanched spinach leaves. Fill bottom half with salmon mousse, put turbot mousse on top, cover with spinach leaves, and cover with the buttered lid. Cook in a bain-marie for 30 minutes.

To prepare saffron sauce: bring wine and shallots to simmering point in a small saucepan and reduce, uncovered, until 3-4 tablespoons remain. Add fish stock and whipping cream and boil until reduced to ⅔ of original volume. Strain sauce onto the saffron, add lemon juice, and season. Keep warm in a bain-marie.

When terrine is cooked, turn out onto a cutting board, divide into 6 portions, and put onto 6 hot plates. Pour saffron sauce generously around each slice, garnish with parsley, and serve.

Serves: 6

Wine: *Chablis*

Côtelettes d'Agneau Farcie en Croûte

6 large lamb cutlets

salt and pepper, to taste

25 g butter

2 tomatoes, peeled, seeded, and finely chopped

150 g finely chopped mushrooms

100 g finely chopped ham

1 tbsp chopped parsley

400 g frozen puff pastry

1 egg yolk

2 tbsp water

Season cutlets with salt and pepper, brush with melted butter, and grill on both sides until half-cooked.

To prepare stuffing: put tomatoes into a basin with mushrooms, ham, parsley, and seasoning. Melt remaining butter, add to mixture, and blend well.

Roll out pastry and cut 6 rectangles large enough to cover cutlets completely. Put a spoonful of stuffing on each piece of pastry and place a cutlet on top. Top with another spoonful of stuffing. Brush the edges with egg yolk and water. Fold pastry over and seal edges so each cutlet is completely enclosed. Brush all over with egg wash and bake in a hot oven, gas mark 7 (425°F/220°C) for about 15-20 minutes.

Serves: 6

Lemon Curd Tart

4 lemons, zest and juice

250 g butter

250 g sugar

3 eggs

125 g sugar

125 g butter

200 g egg

100 g bread crumbs

zest and juice of 2 lemons

1 sweet pastry case

To make the curd: whisk the first 4 ingredients together in a bowl over boiling water until thick. To make the filling: beat the sugar and butter together until white. Add eggs, bread crumbs, and lemon zest and juice. To assemble: smooth a thin layer of curd over the base of the flan. Fill to the top with lemon filling. Bake at gas mark 6 (400°F/205°C) for about 30 minutes.

Serves: 6

The Lygon Arms

The stately **Lygon Arms** has been providing hospitality for more than 400 years in Broadway, reputed to be one of the most famous villages in England. Here at the Inn, the old and the new are successfully combined to provide 20th century comforts in a unique 16th century setting that features a wealth of antiques, log fires, and oak-beamed rooms.

The setting for dinner is the Great Hall, with its barrel-shaped ceiling and oak panelling. "Now good digestion wait on appetite and health on both" is written above the entrance to the room. There is a fine cocktail bar, adjacent to the Great Hall, that features canapes and, on cold nights, hot savouries.

The Lygon Arms is situated in the centre of the Cotswolds and on the edge of the Vale of Evesham, and the menu reflects this: Cotswold Lamb and Evesham Vale Asparagus and Strawberries are offered along with choice traditional French dishes and all are complemented by an international and highly selective wine list.

Should you require a meal for a special occasion, Shaun Hill, the head chef, is glad to accommodate. Chef Hill's prior experience includes years of service at several other fine hotels before he joined The Lygon Arms. A sampling of his offerings promises to be a happy memory.

The Lygon Arms

BROADWAY, WORCESTER
0386-852255
BREAKFAST, LUNCH, AND DINNER
DAILY
RESERVATIONS
PROPRIETOR: DOUGLAS BARRINGTON
CHEF: SHAUN HILL

North Sea Fish Soup

½ lb each: turbot, cod, scallops, and monkfish

4 oz peeled prawns

lemon juice, as needed

2 pt fish stock, made from white wine, fish bones, prawn shells, and water

1 oz chopped shallot

1 oz chopped parsley

1 large tomato, skinned and seeded

½ oz potato flour

3 egg yolks

½ pt cream

salt, pepper, and nutmeg, to taste

Skin and fillet fish. Cut into large chunks and turn briefly in lemon juice to keep from discolouring. Poach fish in stock until just done. Lift fish into a tureen, add shallot, parsley, and tomato. Slightly thicken the cooking liquid with potato flour. Mix egg yolks and cream together and add to cooking liquid. Reboil. Adjust seasoning with salt, pepper, and nutmeg. Pass soup onto fish.

Serving suggestion: serve with croutons made from 2 slices of white bread.

Serves: 6

Wine: *chilled Don Zoilo Fino Sherry*

CHEF'S TIP

TAKE CARE NOT TO TEST SOUP FOR SEASONING AND TEXTURE WITH A TEASPOON OR BY DIPPING IN YOUR FINGER. WHAT TASTES FINE IN TINY AMOUNTS IS OFTEN OVERPOWERING WHEN YOU ARE TO TAKE A BOWLFUL. USE A SOUPSPOON OR A CUP.

Supreme of Hare with Horseradish

6 fillets of hare

1 drop of vinegar

1 pt good game or veal stock

4 tbsp grated horseradish

1 tbsp mustard

½ pt double cream

1 lb celeriac purée

Remove membrane from fillets. Reserve a little hare's blood mixed with a drop of vinegar. Seal fillets in a copper pan and cook slowly for about 5 minutes until pink. Remove fillets, set aside, and keep warm.

Deglaze pan with stock and allow to reduce. Add horseradish, mustard, and cream, then reboil. Finish sauce with hare's blood. Adjust seasoning. Slice fillets and arrange on top of sauce. Garnish with celeriac purée.

Serves: 6

Wine: *Aloxe Corton, Chanson Pere et Fils, 1971*

Pears in Cider

6 pears

1 pt stock syrup

1 pt cider

6 egg yolks

6 oz caster sugar

juice of 1 lemon

8 leaves gelatine, well soaked

Peel the pears without removing the stalks. Poach in stock syrup and ¼ cider until done. Allow to cool. In a double saucepan or over a bain-marie, whisk the egg yolks, sugar, remaining cider, and lemon juice. When thick, incorporate the well soaked gelatine. Arrange the pears in a crystal bowl or attractive glasses. Coat with the cider sabayon. Serve chilled.

Serves: 6

Wine: *Chateau Coutet Premier Cru Barsac, 1972*

Restaurant Croque-en-Bouche

Three years ago, Marion and Robin Jones opened **Restaurant Croque-en-Bouche**, a small, comfortable restaurant in a Victorian house, set in the lee of the Malverns with a bar overlooking the Severn valley. The Joneses offer meals prepared French provincial style. The table d'hôte menus change each week, and each dish is prepared using only the best fresh produce available.

Dinner is five courses: A tureen of soup, such as Soupe de Poisson or Soupe au Pistou, precedes a choice of starters, mainly fish. (Gravad Lax is a speciality, served with local asparagus when in season.) This is followed by a choice of main dish (the list usually highlights the local lamb and game), served with potatoes and a salad with walnut oil dressing. There is much use of fresh herbs grown in their garden. A selection of French cheeses (including four goat cheeses) and various desserts complete the meal. Sunday lunch is three courses with hors d'oeuvres as the first course.

This restaurant serves only 22 people at a sitting and is presided over by the Joneses alone.

Marion Jones is the chef; her expertise has won her numerous culinary awards. The half-dozen tables are looked after, without help, by Robin Jones. You can, therefore, count on special personal service.

RESTAURANT CROQUE-EN-BOUCHE

**221 WELLS ROAD
MALVERN WELLS, WORCHESTER**

06845-MALVERN 65612

LUNCH: SUNDAY
DINNER: WEDNESDAY — SATURDAY
RESERVATIONS

PROPRIETORS: MR. & MRS. R.G. JONES
CHEF: MARION JONES

Homard Gratinée au Porto (Lobster with Port)

2 × ½ lb cooked lobsters or equal amount crabmeat

freshly ground black pepper and salt, to taste

3 tbsp double cream

½ lb button mushrooms, sliced

1 oz butter, heated

2 tbsp port

½ pt Béchamel sauce

grated Gruyère cheese, as needed

Remove lobster flesh and coral. Slice, season with pepper and salt, and moisten with ⅓ the cream. Toss mushrooms quickly in hot butter in a pan, add port, and reduce by ½ over high heat. Remove from heat and, when cool, add remainder of cream and season. Divide mushroom mixture into 6 ovenproof dishes, add lobster, top with Béchamel sauce, and sprinkle cheese on top. Bake for about 12 minutes in a hot oven until browned.

Serves: 6

Pheasant ''Truffée'' with Tarragon

4 oz butter, softened

4 rashers smoked bacon cut into small lardons

1 tbsp chopped fresh tarragon

1 tbsp finely chopped shallot

1 garlic clove, finely chopped

salt and freshly ground black pepper, to taste

2 pheasants

1 tbsp flour

1 tbsp sherry vinegar

2 tbsp white wine

¼ pt chicken stock

¼ pt double cream

Mix the first 7 ingredients to make the stuffing. Spread the mixture inside the birds, between the skin and body, using a small spatula. Roast birds on a rack in a roasting pan near the top of an oven at gas mark 6 (400°F/205°C). Baste frequently with the flavoured butter which runs into the pan. When cooked, remove birds from oven and keep to one side covered.

Pour off all but 1 tablespoon butter. Dust flour into pan. Cook over heat gently. Add vinegar, wine, and stock. Cook for a few minutes, scraping bits from bottom of pan. Strain into a saucepan, whisk in cream, reduce to a good sauce consistency, and season.

Carve pheasants into pieces and arrange on a serving dish. Cover with the sauce.

Serves: 4–6

Reine de Saba (Chocolate Almond Cake)

4 oz softened, unsalted butter

4 oz plus 1 tbsp caster sugar

3 eggs, separated

pinch of salt

7 oz plain chocolate

4 tbsp coffee

2 oz ground almonds

¼ tbsp almond extract

2 oz plain flour

1 oz unsalted butter

4 tbsp sieved apricot jam, heated

Cream the softened butter and 4 ounces sugar until pale yellow and light. Beat in egg yolks. Beat egg whites with a pinch of salt to form soft peaks. Add remaining caster sugar. Beat until stiff. Melt 4 ounces chocolate with ½ the coffee until smooth. With a spatula, stir chocolate into butter and sugar mixture, then add almonds and extract. Fold in gently ¼ egg whites and ¼ flour. Repeat in stages until rest is folded in. Turn into an oiled and floured 8 inch cake tin, spreading mixture up to the rim. Bake in the middle of an oven at gas mark 4 (360°F/180°C) for about 25 minutes. Cake is done when puffed and needle inserted 2½ inches from the edge comes out clean. Centre should remain soft and slightly undercooked. Let cake cool in tin for 10 minutes. Reverse onto a rack and allow to cool thoroughly.

To prepare icing: melt remaining chocolate and coffee together until smooth. Whisk in the remaining butter. Allow to cool to spreading consistency. Brush cake with hot apricot jam, then allow to cool. Ice the cake using a spatula.

Farlam Hall

Farlam Hall is listed as of historical and architectural interest. In 1826, the property changed hands, and from a 17th century farmhouse, it was enlarged in stages to become a notable border manor house and the centre of a thriving local community.

John Wesley is reputed to have preached in the house. George Stephenson, of steam engine fame, stayed here; his famous "Rocket" belonged to the family, and it spent the last years of its working life on the local line before being presented to the Science Museum.

Farlam Hall stands in four acres of mature grounds with lovely trees, a stream, and an ornamental lake. It is now a country house hotel, owned and personally run by the Quinion family, that offers Cordon Bleu cooking and high standards of comfort and service. Extensive use is made of the prime local meat, game, fish, and dairy produce available. Only fresh vegetables are offered. A modest, but well selected, wine list is available.

A small bar for the use of residents and diners, three lounges, 11 spacious bedrooms, central heating, and open fires all contribute to the feeling of peace and well-being enjoyed in this fine old country house.

Farlam Hall

BRAMPTON, CUMBRIA
06976-234
LUNCH ON SUNDAY, DINNER NIGHTLY
RESERVATIONS
PROPRIETOR: ALAN QUINION
CHEF: BARRY QUINION

Savoury Spinach Tart

shortcrust pastry, enough to line a deep 8 - 9 in tin

1 pt single cream

6 whole eggs

½ tsp ground mace

1 clove crushed garlic

6 oz cooked, drained spinach

salt and pepper, to taste

Line the tin with pastry and blind bake for 12–15 minutes at 350°F (180°C).

Put all the other ingredients into a food processor or a blender and mix until smooth. Pour mixture into the pastry case and bake at gas mark 5 (375°F/190°C) for approximately 45 minutes.

Serves: 6

Wine: *Bouilly, light red*

Veal Cutlet Polonaise

3 oz strong cheese

3 oz sliced ham

6 thick veal cutlets (or pork cutlets)

¼ pt cold thick white sauce

flour, as needed

oil, to fry

white wine, as needed

salt and pepper, to taste

watercress or parsley, to garnish

Retain enough ham and cheese to cover 1 side of the cutlets; dice the rest and combine with a little of the white sauce. With a thin sharp knife, cut a slit in the cutlets. Start at the bottom of the bone and gently work the knife away, taking care not to cut through any of the outer meat. Keep the entry hole as small as possible. With a piping bag, fill the cutlets with the ham and cheese mixture. Seal the ends of the cutlets with flour. Season the cutlets, dip in flour, then fry lightly on each side and put on a tray.

Cover the cutlets with the remaining ham and cheese and put in the oven while finishing the sauce. (This lets the cheese melt.)

Tip excess fat from the pan. Swirl a little white wine into pan, add the remainder of the white sauce, and stir until smooth. Season to taste. Dress the cutlets on a serving dish, garnish with watercress or parsley, and serve the sauce in a warm sauce boat.

Serves: 6

CHEF'S TIP

PREPARE THE VEAL UP TO 12 HOURS IN ADVANCE AND REFRIGERATE. THIS HELPS PREVENT THE FILLING FROM OOZING OUT WHILST COOKING.

Toffee, Pear, and Walnut Flan

6 oz pastry, approximate

3½ fl oz milk

1½ oz plain flour

6 oz Demerara sugar

5 oz margarine

unsweetened whipped cream, as needed

4 medium pears, peeled, sliced, and chilled

4 oz chopped walnuts

Line a flan tin with pastry and blind bake at 350°F (180°C) for 12–15 minutes.

To prepare toffee: mix milk and flour in a saucepan. Add sugar and margarine and bring slowly to a boil. Leave to cool.

Put some of the cream in the base of the lined tin. Arrange the pear slices on the cream. Pour the toffee over the pears and leave in the refrigerator until cold.

Pipe toffee around the top of the flan in 2 circles, then fill in between with the chopped walnuts.

Serves: 6

Michaels Nook

Michaels Nook Country House Hotel/Restaurant is 11 years old and is, today, one of the most renowned country house hotels in England. It still retains the character and atmosphere of an elegant private home; furnishings, enhanced by an abundance of flowers and plants, reflect the taste and knowledge of the proprietor, Reg Gifford, whose reputation is also long-established in the antique world; the ten bedrooms are charmingly decorated and furnished, each with a character of its own.

Relaxed elegance is matched by no lack of sophistication in food, wine, and service in the hotel's restaurant. This small dining room is very tastefully appointed; the genuine antique wood tables are candlelit and set with silver, porcelain, crystal, and fresh flowers — all of which lend to the overall effect of warmth and comfort.

The menu features mainly traditional English dishes. Subtlety of cooking and good wines (not necessarily the most expensive) are high among Reg Gifford's priorities. Chefs Barrie Garton and Nigel Marriage work with the finest fresh produce and provide a table d'hôte menu that offers a choice in all courses. The menu changes every day.

Michaels Nook, as a whole, has attracted consistent praise, and both the food and the wine list have received some of the highest accolades. The service throughout is most thoughtful and efficient, as well.

MICHAELS NOOK

GRASMERE, NEAR AMBLESIDE
CUMBRIA

096-65496

BREAKFAST, LUNCH, AND DINNER
DAILY

RESERVATIONS

PROPRIETOR: R.S.E. GIFFORD

CHEFS:
NIGEL MARRIAGE, BARRIE GARTON

Stilton Beignets

½ pt water

4 oz butter

pinch of salt

5 oz plain flour

4 eggs

8 oz soft Stilton cheese

1 tbsp kirsch

salt and black pepper, to taste

hot oil, as needed

1 large onion

1 carton natural yogurt

¼ pt double cream

1 tbsp wine vinegar

dash of Tabasco sauce

juice of 1 large lemon

sugar, to taste

Boil the water, butter, and pinch of salt together until butter is completely melted. Add flour and beat over heat until mixture leaves the sides of the pan. Allow to cool, then beat in the eggs, one by one. Crumble in the Stilton. Add kirsch and beat vigorously until cheese is evenly dispersed. Season with pepper and more salt if desired. (It is better to over-season than under-season this dish.) Using 2 dessertspoons dipped in hot oil, mould the mixture into ovals by scraping between the spoons. Drop into hot oil (360°F/180°C) and cook for 10 minutes with as little handling as possible. When golden brown, place on absorbent paper and allow to drain.

To prepare sour cream and onion sauce: liquidise the onion, then add yogurt, double cream, wine vinegar, Tabasco, and lemon juice. Season to taste with plenty of salt, black pepper, and sugar and serve with beignets.

Serves: 9—10

Wine: *Sauvignon de Touraine, 1978—79*

Leg of Lakeland Lamb en Croûte

1 lb fresh apricots, or dried apricots soaked overnight

sugar syrup, as needed

1 large onion, finely chopped

3 oz butter

1 large bunch mint leaves, chopped

12 oz fresh white bread crumbs

2 tbsp double cream

1 beaten egg

1 leg of lamb, bone "tunnelled out" but reserved

2 small carrots, roughly chopped

1 onion, roughly chopped

2 celery sticks, roughly chopped

salt and pepper, to taste

1 lb rough puff or flaky pastry

eggwash

½ pt sherry

flour, as needed

stock, as needed

juice of 2 oranges

To prepare apricot and mint stuffing: blanch, skin, and poach the apricots in a little sugar syrup until tender. Sweat the finely chopped onion in the butter until soft but not brown. Add mint leaves, allow to soften for a minute, then quickly drain the apricots. Keeping apricots moist, roughly chop them and add to the pan and stir into the onions. Add bread crumbs and cream. Beat in the egg when mixture has cooled slightly. Season to taste with salt and pepper.

Stitch halfway up the boned leg of lamb with string and a trussing needle. Stuff with the stuffing, forcing it well into the bottom of the joint. When well filled, stitch up to the top and check for leaks. Place the bone in a roasting tray with the roughly chopped carrot, onion, and celery. In a large pan, melt a little dripping, season the joint, and brown well in the dripping, then place on the bone and cook in a hot oven, gas mark 4 (360°F/180°C) for 1½ hours. When the joint has gone cold, remove the strings.

Roll out ¾ of the pastry to a large square, egg wash the edges, place any excess stuffing in the centre and put the joint on top. Bring the corners of the pastry into the centre and trim and crimp the edges. Use the remaining pastry to decorate the joint. Allow to rest in a cool place for 30 minutes, then bake for 45-55 minutes in a hot oven, gas mark 5 (390°F/200°C). Remove from dish.

To prepare sherry sauce: place the roasting pan over high heat and fry the vegetables until they caramelise to a good brown colour. Pour off any fat, remove the bones, and deglaze the pan with the sherry. Boil over high heat to reduce the liquid. Add enough flour to form a soft roux, cook for 2-3 minutes, then pour in the syrup from the apricots and some good stock, stirring continually. As the sauce thickens, add more stock as required to form a smooth pouring sauce. Strain sauce into a clean pan, add the orange juice, reboil, and adjust seasoning. Serve in a sauceboat as accompaniment to the lamb.

Serves: 10—11

Miller
Howe

Miller Howe is an elegant country house hotel, perfectly situated in the heart of the English Lakes. Sitting on the brow of a hill, it looks over Lake Windermere to the Coniston Fells and Langdale Pikes beyond.

But, beautiful though Miller Howe is in its setting and luxurious in the manner of a fine home, it is made, more than anything else, by its people. John Tovey, the internationally famous Chef/Patron, and his staff are people whose pleasure it is to create pleasure. Their unique blend of personalities and skills create, each day, a welcoming, warm atmosphere that will make the most discerning guest feel at home.

Each evening, a different five-course English dinner is served. When the guests are seated, the house lights are dimmed, and the room is transformed into a theatre. The fare is then presented. The panache and élan of the service combine with John Tovey's very personal style of cooking to produce a brilliant result.

John Tovey has had no formal training as a chef, but he has most certainly become a professional. After ten years with Miller Howe, his enthusiasm, dedication, and attention to detail have gained him an enviable reputation. Dinner at Miller Howe is a dramatic as well as gastronomic experience.

MILLER HOWE

WINDERMERE, ENGLISH LAKES
CUMBRIA

09662-2536

DINNER: SUNDAY — FRIDAY AT 8:30 P.M.
AND SATURDAY AT 7 P.M. AND 9:30 P.M.
RESERVATIONS
PROPRIETOR/CHEF: JOHN TOVEY, M.C.G.B.

Miller Howe Utter Bliss

1 small melon

4 oz strawberries or raspberries

1 tbsp brandy

2 tbsp icing sugar

2 tbsp redcurrants, stalks removed

½ bottle chilled sparkling white wine: white Burgundy or Asti Spumanti

Slightly top and tail the melon before cutting in 2 "around the equator." Scoop out balls of melon from around the edge with a medium-sized Parisian scoop or melon baller. Return balls to original places but bottoms up.

Place melon halves on a tray, cover well, and leave until required. Liquidise the strawberries with brandy and sugar and leave to chill. Cover each serving plate with a doyley and, if available, a large fern leaf on top. At the last minute, put redcurrants into the well of the melon, lightly pour the liquidised strawberries around the balled rim, and fill the well to the brim with the sparkling wine.

Serves: 2

CHEF'S TIP

IF REDCURRANTS ARE NOT AVAIL-ABLE, USE FRESH, STONED CHERRIES.

Wolfgang's Austrian Steak

4 × 8 oz rump steaks about ½ in thick

3 tbsp plain flour seasoned with salt and freshly ground black pepper

2 oz butter, melted

6 oz finely chopped bacon

1 medium-sized onion, finely chopped

2 small carrots, finely chopped

1 pt beef stock

½ tsp allspice

½ tsp thyme

3 tbsp wine vinegar

juice and rind of 1 lemon

2 oz plain flour

½ pt double cream

¼ pt Marsala wine

Coat the rump steaks with some seasoned flour, then seal them in the melted butter in a frying pan. Transfer steaks to drain on kitchen paper. Fry the bacon in the same pan until well done, then remove from the pan. In the combined residue of original butter and bacon fat, lightly fry the chopped onion and carrot.

In a separate bowl, mix the beef stock, allspice, thyme, wine vinegar, lemon juice and rind together. Sprinkle the plain flour over the vegetables in the pan and stir vigorously to make a mixed smooth roux. Add the seasoned beef stock to the pan and stir again. Put steaks in a suitably sized flameproof casserole, pour the sauce over, and then sprinkle the bacon evenly over them. Cook in the over at gas mark 3 (325°F/170°C) for 1½ hours.

Remove the steaks from the casserole and put them back in the oven on a tray or overproof plate. Place casserole on top of the stove and add cream and Marsala to the vegetable broth. Cook, stirring continuously, until thick and well reduced. Serve sauce with cooked steaks.

Serves: 4

Wine: *Meerlust Cabernet Sauvignon, 1974*

Lemon Ice Box Pudding

6 egg yolks

8 oz caster sugar, sieved

finely grated rind and strained juice of 2 lemons

1½ pt double cream

6 egg whites, stiffly beaten

Marie sweet biscuit crumbs, enough to form base and topping.

Place yolks into a warmed Kenwood bowl. Start to whisk at high speed, adding sieved sugar little by little. When volume will increase no further, beat in the lemon flavouring. Whip the double cream lightly to just running consistency and bring the two mixtures together in a large plastic bowl with a long-handled spoon. Fold in the beaten egg whites by first incorporating ½ then the remaining ⅔.

Liquidise the biscuits and line the bases of either individual ramekin dishes or a 1 pound loaf tin. Pour the basic pudding mix on the crumbs and then coat the top quite liberally with more crumbs. Put immediately into the freezer and leave 12 hours. Remove just as you are about to serve the main course of your meal, then the pudding will be easy to cut or slice and soft, rich, and creamy to eat.

Serves: 8

Wine: *Muscat d'Alexandrie*

Sharrow Bay Country House Hotel

Sharrow Bay Country House Hotel began in 1948 when Francis Coulson found this beautiful early Victorian house superbly situated on the edge of Lake Ullswater. With the support of his father and a few hundred pounds in his pocket, he tackled converting the empty family mansion house into a small hotel. Mr. Coulson was trained formally by a French Cordon Bleu chef and obtained further experience working with colleagues in France.

In the spring of 1949, Sharrow Bay opened with six bedrooms and, as food was still being rationed after the war, a menu that was simple but honest.

In 1952, Brian Sack, who trained at the Westminster Hotel School in London, arrived on the scene, intending to stay for only a short time, but it seemed straightaway that the two men complemented one another, and it obviously was meant to be that a partnership should develop. The success of that partnership was reflected in the gradual development of Sharrow Bay into the cosy, comfortable establishment, with 29 bedrooms, 19 private bathrooms, and a first-rate restaurant, that it is today.

The restaurant features English and French cuisine and specialises in Old English roasts, local fish and fowl dishes, and traditional English puddings. An extensive wine list, highlighting French and German vintages, is also available.

Sharrow Bay

LAKE ULLSWATER
PENRITH, CUMBRIA
08536-301
BREAKFAST: 9 TO 9:30 A.M.
LUNCH: 1 TO 1:30 P.M.
DINNER: 8 TO 8:45 P.M.
DAILY
CLOSED: DECEMBER - FEBRUARY
RESERVATIONS
PROPRIETORS:
FRANCIS COULSON, BRIAN SACK
CHEF: FRANCIS COULSON, M.C.G.B.

Special Pâté Parfait

½ lb chicken livers, prepared

Madeira or port, for marinating

1 oz lard

3 oz bacon, finely chopped

1 small onion, chopped

thyme and bay leaf, to taste

1 tbsp sherry

1 tbsp port

brandy, to taste, kirsch preferred

3 tbsp double cream, optional

seasoning, to taste

melted butter, as needed

Marinate livers in Madeira for 1½ hours, turning occasionally. Drain livers. Heat lard in a small frying pan and when hot, sauté livers briefly, just long enough to brown all sides. In another pan, cook bacon and onion, add thyme and bay leaf and cook over low heat. When mixture is cooking, add livers but do not overcook; remove from heat. Put mixture, minus bay leaf, into a liquidiser or through a sieve. Add sherry, port, and brandy to taste, mix well. Add cream if dish is to be served immediately. Season to taste. Place mixture into a terrine dish and cover pâté with melted butter.

Casserole of Rump Steak Eszterhazy

1 × 2 lb rump steak

flour seasoned with black pepper, to dust

1½ oz lard

1 medium onion, chopped

1 clove garlic, minced

2 small carrots, finely chopped

3 tbsp flour, approximately

1½ pt beef stock, fresh or tinned consommé

¼ - ½ tsp allspice

3 medium bay leaves

4 peppercorns

a little thyme

1 strip of lemon peel

4 rashers lean bacon, finely chopped

chopped parsley

3 tbsp white wine vinegar

8 tbsp double cream

1 tsp lemon juice

Cut up steak, trimmed of fat and sinew, and dip pieces in seasoned flour. Heat lard and brown steak all over. Remove to a dish. Add onion, garlic, and carrot to original pan and cook about 8 minutes, stirring frequently until vegetables are lightly coloured. Remove from heat and stir in flour; continue to stir until all flour has been absorbed. Add stock and bring to a boil; stir until completely smooth. Add allspice, bay leaves, peppercorns, thyme, lemon peel, bacon, parsley, and vinegar. Return meat to pan and bring to a boil. Reduce heat, cover pan, and simmer until tender (about 50 minutes), or as desired.

Arrange steak on a dish and keep warm. Strain contents of pan, skim off any surface fat, whisk cream a little and fold in. Add a little lemon juice. Do not let boil again or it will separate.

Serves: 4

Le Gâteau Victoire au Chocolat

7 oz menier chocolate or any good dark chocolate

1 oz cocoa or unsweetened chocolate

½ tbsp instant coffee

3 tbsp boiling water

1 tbsp dark rum

3 large eggs

2 oz caster sugar

9 fl oz double cream

½ tbsp vanilla essence

butter and flour, as needed

icing sugar and whipped cream, as needed

Melt chocolate with cocoa, coffee, water, and rum. Beat eggs with sugar to a thick foam, the consistency of lightly whipped cream. Beat mixture until smooth and shiny. Beat into eggs until smooth. Whip cream to very soft peaks; whip in vanilla. Fold cream into chocolate mixture and pour into a buttered and floured cake tin about 8 inches in diameter. Place tin in a bain-marie of boiling water to come 1½ inches up the sides and bake on rack in lower middle of oven at gas mark 4 (350°F/180°C) for 1½ hours or until cake has risen, cracked slightly, and skewer comes out clean. (Cake will sink to original volume.)

Turn off oven, leave door ajar, and let cake sit in oven for 30 minutes. Remove from bain-marie and let sit another 30 minutes before unmoulding. Dust with icing sugar and serve with whipped cream.

Tarn End Hotel

The **Tarn End Hotel** stands on the banks of the 60-acre Talkin Tarn in a country park on the outskirts of Brampton, ten miles east of Carlisle. It boasts a Regency-style restaurant, a delightful cocktail bar, and six comfortable bedrooms.

A family-run business, its air of smooth efficiency reflects the professional experience of the proprietress, Mrs. M.C. Hoefkens, her son, Martin, who is a Paris-trained chef, and her daughter, Carole, who is second chef.

The restaurant boasts the most extensive à la carte and table d'hôte menus in the district, and the Hoefkenses prepare French haute cuisine to tempt the palate of the most discerning gourmet.

Daughter-in-law Jean, who runs the restaurant, will be only too pleased to give you the benefit of her wide experience in the choice of wines available, from a most comprehensive wine list, to complement your meal.

The pleasantly restful cocktail bar, with its open log fire, is run by daughter Claire, who has studied the fascinating art of mixing drinks for 25 years. She will produce "the drink for the occasion" or your own particular mix on request.

The entire hotel exudes the atmosphere of a French-style country restaurant.

Tarn End Hotel

TALKIN TARN, BRAMPTON
CARLISLE, CUMBRIA
2430 BRAMPTON
LUNCH: 12:30 TO 1:45 P.M.
DINNER: 7:30 TO 9 P.M.
DAILY
CLOSED OCTOBER
RESERVATIONS
PROPRIETOR: MRS. M.C. HOEFKENS
CHEF: M.J. HOEFKENS

Noisette of Pork

1 teacup port wine

1 tsp sugar

4 cloves

1 bay leaf

6 black peppercorns

2 whole fillets of pork, trimmed

8 - 12 large prunes cooked in water

½ teacup very thick apple purée, slightly sweetened

clarified butter, to sauté

2 measures brandy

12 round croutons, 1½ in diameter, fried in butter

1 teacup thick fresh cream

watercress, to garnish

Mix the first 5 ingredients together to make a marinade. Cut the fillets into about 1 inch thick noisettes and leave in the marinade with the prunes for 2–3 days, turning the meat occasionally.

Stone the prunes gently by splitting halfway through with a sharp knife. Fill with the applesauce purée and warm the prunes in the oven. Sauté the noisettes of pork quickly in clarified butter until golden brown on both sides, but do not overcook. Flame with brandy.

Arrange each noisette on a crouton surrounded by prunes. Deglaze the pan with the marinade and reduce to ¼. Add the cream and simmer gently until thick. Strain over the noisettes, garnish with sprigs of watercress, and serve.

Serves: 4

Wine: *Chateauneuf du Pape, 1976*

Gâteau Strega

2 oz raisins

1 oz shelled walnuts

2 measures Strega liqueur

¼ oz yeast

4½ oz sugar

⅛ pt lukewarm milk

1 whole egg

1 tsp salt

9 oz plain flour

¼ lb softened butter

½ pt milk

3 egg yolks

1 dessertspoon cornflour

3 egg whites

eggwash

water, as needed

caster sugar, as needed

Soak the raisins and walnuts in the Strega overnight.

To prepare dough: cream the yeast and ½ ounce sugar together, then add lukewarm milk, whole egg, salt, and 4 ounces flour, and mix together with a wooden spoon. Sprinkle 4 ounces flour on top. Allow to prove in a basin with a cloth cover for 20 minutes. Mix into a dough. Roll out into a rectangle and spread softened butter on half. Fold over to make a sandwich of the butter and roll out as for puff pastry (giving 4 turns, 2 at a time, and resting ½ hour between turns). Fold in a cloth and put in refrigerator overnight.

To prepare filling: boil the milk. In another pan, mix egg yolks, remaining sugar, remaining flour, and cornflour together with a whisk. Whisking all the time over a fairly gentle heat, add the boiling milk to make a smooth stiff cream. Beat the egg whites until stiff and fold into the cream, keeping it on the heat all the time. Add nuts, raisins, and Strega and leave to cool.

Roll out the dough into a circle about 16 inches in diameter, egg wash around the edge, and place the filling in the centre. Evenly draw up the dough into the centre and pinch together well, forming the shape of a pleated bun. Brush with a little water and sprinkle caster sugar all over. Bake at gas mark 6 (375°F/190°C) for about 30 minutes. Serve warm.

Tullythwaite House

The village of Tullythwaite is a picturesque hamlet of some 30 people — little changed since its first mention in 1300 A.D. — located in an unspoilt valley set between Morecambe Bay and the beauties of the English Lake District. Here, agriculture, holiday pleasures, and local community life exist happily together.

Visitors and residents alike come regularly to **Tullythwaite House**, a restaurant that enjoys a reputation for good food and a particular friendly, cosy comfort that no doubt stems from the fact that this old Georgian house is a family home and has been for several centuries. It is noted, in fact, that the property was established in 1636 as a tannery, and the original tanpits can still be seen in the cattle-grazing meadows.

Today, Proprietor Mary Johnson and Chef Barbara Johnson, both of whom came to Tullythwaite House 16 years ago, offer diners a wide variety of English dishes, some associated especially with the house, in an atmosphere of antique furnishings, old copper and brass, and pleasant gardens. Be sure to try the Roast Duckling in Orange Sauce; it's an old family recipe.

TULLYTHWAITE HOUSE

**UNDERBARROW
KENDAL, CUMBRIA**

04488-CROSTHWAITE 397

DINNER: 7 P.M.
TUESDAY — SATURDAY
RESERVATIONS

PROPRIETOR: MARY E. JOHNSON
CHEF: BARBARA H. JOHNSON

Prawn Cheesecake

8 oz savoury biscuits

4 oz melted butter

½ oz gelatine

hot water, as needed

juice of 1 large lemon

8 oz cream cheese

4 tbsp mayonnaise

1 tbsp tomato purée

¼ pt natural yogurt

¼ pt whipped double cream

8 oz prawns

watercress, to garnish

To prepare biscuit base: crush the biscuits and mix them with melted butter. Press them into a greased loose-bottomed flan tin and chill.

Dissolve the gelatine in a little hot water. When melted, add the lemon juice. Beat in the cream cheese, mayonnaise, tomato purée, yogurt, and double cream, then add prawns.

Spoon the mixture onto the biscuit base and leave to set. Garnish with watercress and serve.

Serves: 4–6

CHEF'S TIP
TO CRUSH BISCUITS: PUT THEM INTO A PLASTIC BAG, THEN ROLL OUT WITH A ROLLING PIN.

Roast Duckling with Orange Sauce

1 duckling, prepared for baking

1 tbsp flour

½ c sugar

rind and juice of 1 orange

cold water, as needed

½ pt boiling water

knob of butter

Put the duck into a roasting tin, cover with buttered, greaseproof paper, and cook for approximately 3 hours at gas mark 6 (400°F/205°C). Baste frequently to make the skin crisp.

To prepare the sauce: put the flour, sugar, and rind of orange into a pan and mix with a little cold water to make a paste. Add the boiling water and boil for 4 minutes. Add the juice of the orange and the butter and serve the sauce with the duckling.

Serves: 2

Chocolate Cream

8 oz plain chocolate

¼ pt double cream

3 tbsp rum

4 eggs, separated

whipped cream and chocolate curls, to decorate

Melt the chocolate in a basin over hot water, then add the cream and rum. Beat in the egg yolks. Whisk the egg whites until stiff, then fold them into the chocolate mixture.

Put the mixture into custard glasses and, before serving, decorate with whipped cream and chocolate curls.

Serves: 4–6

The River House

The River House was built about 1830 as a gentleman farmer's residence. Up a quiet creek, it overlooks the River Wyre with views of boats and the Bowland Fells. Although only four-and-a-half miles from Blackpool, directions are usually essential for first-time customers.

The house, which was once described as shabbily comfortable, is furnished with antiques, has a cosy bar with a log fire, and is also the home of the Scott family.

There are four guest bedrooms, one sporting a half four-poster bed. The bathroom has a hooded bath — a wonder of Victorian plumbing in regular use.

The River House was opened in 1958 by a Mrs. Scott. Nine years ago, her son, Bill, joined her. Now, with the help of his wife, Virginia, Bill runs the business and does the cooking.

"Our aim," says Bill, "is to present freshly cooked food that tastes of what it is; that is, beef of beef. Consequently, I do not cook dishes in sauce, but serve them with sauce. I believe good food presents itself, and these days, too much attention is paid to tarting up food at the expense of quality. In order to achieve this, we ask customers, whenever possible, to order their main course in advance. The last thing you taste is the pudding. It should be freshly made, not frozen or tinned. Better to have less selection."

THE RIVER HOUSE

SKIPPOOL CREEK, THORNTON-LE-FYLDE
BLACKPOOL, LANCASHIRE

0253-883497

BREAKFAST, LUNCH, DINNER
DAILY
RESERVATIONS

PROPRIETOR: THE SCOTT FAMILY
CHEF: BILL SCOTT

Crab Mousse

½ c bread crumbs

¼ c milk

⅛ c stock

½ lb dark and light crabmeat

salt and pepper, to taste

1 tsp lemon juice

½ tsp chopped fresh parsley

1 egg yolk, beaten

1 egg white, well beaten

lettuce, cucumbers, and lemon wedges, to garnish

Add bread crumbs to milk and stock and leave in a warm place for 5 minutes. Add crabmeat, salt, pepper, lemon juice, and chopped parsley. Cool slightly, then add beaten egg yolk. Fold in well beaten egg white. Pour into 4 well greased cocottes, cover with foil, and bake in a tin of water in a moderate oven for 40 minutes. Serve each garnished with lettuce, cucumber, and a wedge of lemon.

Serves: 4

Crispy Rare Noisettes with Garlic Sauce

2 middle cut loins of lamb

butter, to grease

½ pt double cream

6 cloves garlic, crushed

salt and pepper, to taste

2 tbsp brandy

Strip off outer layer of skinny tissue on lamb loins (should pull off quite easily). Cut meat off bone in one piece. Trim, leaving enough fat to wrap around eye of loin. Tie securely with string at 1 inch intervals. Cut between strings to make noisettes. Place flat on a buttered baking dish. Cook for 5 minutes in a preheated oven as hot as you can get it (500–550°F/ 260–290°C). The fat outside should be crispy and the meat rare.

To prepare sauce: reduce cream and garlic over high heat until it thickens. Add salt and pepper to taste and brandy. Pour over noisettes and decorate with sprigs of parsley.

Serves: 4

Hungarian Torte

5 egg yolks

8 oz caster sugar

2 tbsp lemon juice

½ lb ground hazelnuts

2 scant oz fine white bread crumbs

3 oz raisins

5 egg whites

sweetened fresh cream, as needed

chocolate butter icing, prepared, as needed

Beat egg yolks, gradually adding ½ the sugar until quite thick. Fold in lemon juice, ground hazelnuts, bread crumbs, and raisins. In a separate bowl, beat egg whites with remaining sugar until quite stiff, then fold in the nut mixture. Divide the mixture between two 8 inch cake tins and bake at gas mark 6 (400°F/205°C) for 30–35 minutes. Cool on a cake rack.

Sandwich the two cakes together with sweetened fresh cream and cover with chocolate butter icing.

The Bridge Inn

The Bridge Inn was a public house and brewery for almost 400 years until, in the 1940s, it began to build its present reputation as the home of one of Yorkshire's finest eating houses.

Centrepiece of the complex is the Byron Room, the actual restaurant, which was removed piecemeal from Halnaby Hall, near Darlington, and set up at The Bridge by two local craftsmen. This massive project was conceived by the owners of the Inn at the time, who decided that this historic room, in which Lord Byron dined on the first night of his honeymoon, would be perfect as their new dining room.

Dating from the early 18th century, the Byron Room is a remarkable combination of English woodcarving and Italian plasterwork. In addition to the walls and ceiling, the fireplace, windows, and doors all belong to the original room. The central wall panels contain relief portraits of the three members of the family who owned the house at the time of the room's original construction.

In the four corners of the ceiling are symbolic representations of the pleasures of the dining room: food, wine, good fellowship, and intelligent conversation. Director Donald Smiley and Chef William Bennett strive to ensure that their guests enjoy these pleasures in full measure by providing a fine selection of international dishes as well as some specialities that can only be found at The Bridge Inn.

THE BRIDGE INN

**WALSHFORD, WETHERBY
NORTH YORKSHIRE**

0937-62345

LUNCH: 12:30 TO 2 P.M.,
TUESDAY - SUNDAY
DINNER: 7:30 TO 10 P.M.,
TUESDAY - SATURDAY
RESERVATIONS

PROPRIETOR: DONALD SMILEY
CHEF: WILLIAM BENNETT

Smoked Trout and Horseradish Chantilly

½ pt fresh double cream

2 oz grated horseradish root or best horseradish sauce

juice of 1 lemon

seasoning, to taste

2 whole large smoked trout

6 large finely diced radishes

2 kiwi fruit, to garnish

Beat cream until just stiff, add grated horseradish or horseradish sauce, lemon juice, and seasoning to taste. Skin trout and remove from bone, keeping as whole as possible. Mould cream into towers in the centre of a plate. Place even-sized pieces of smoked trout around cream neatly, decorate with diced radish and roundels of kiwi fruit.

Serves: 4

Wine: *Chardonnay, Fireston, 1977*

Noisette of Lamb

8 oz butter

2 cloves garlic, crushed

seasoning, to taste

1 pair best ends of lamb, about 6 lb in weight

½ pt Noilly Prat vermouth

1 pt good thin demi-glace

1 lb tinned flageolet beans

12 white round mushrooms

Whip butter and crushed garlic with seasoning until almost white and fluffy, then roll up in greaseproof paper about the size of a ten-pence piece and chill. Split the lamb, keeping all bones, remove fat around eyepiece of meat and cut into 12 even-sized roundels. Brown bones in a saucepan and add Noilly Prat and demi-glace and cook for 2 hours. Strain sauce, add 2 walnut-sized pieces of seasoned butter and flageolet beans. Sauté pieces of lamb in a hot pan until pink, place roundels of seasoned butter on each, and brown under a hot grill.

Cover the bottom of a serving dish with the sauce, place pieces of lamb on top decorated with fluted mushrooms, and serve immediately.

Serves: 4–6

Wine: *Cuvée Latour Rouge, 1976*

Raspberry Mousse

8 egg yolks

2 oz granulated sugar

1 pt whipping cream, boiled

4-6 gelatine leaves soaked in cold water

1 lb fresh or frozen raspberries

juice of 1 lemon

8 egg whites

½ pt whipped cream

Beat egg yolks with sugar and add to boiled whipping cream. Return to heat and cook until custard is creamy but do not boil. Drain gelatine and dissolve in a hot pan. Add to egg custard and strain. Allow to cool. Liquidise raspberries and strain to remove seeds, reserving some raspberries for sauce. Add lemon juice. When egg custard is nearly set, add raspberries and lemon juice. Whip egg whites stiffly and fold into mixture. Refrigerate until set.

When mixture is set, warm a tablespoon and spoon out neat quenelles of the mousse onto plates. Decorate with whipped cream and remaining raspberries.

Wine: *Sancerre Chos du Roy Rose, 1978*

McCoy's Restaurant

Conceived in 1973, later to be born in November 1976, **McCoy's Restaurant** is the result of three brothers' aspirations, frustrations, and determination to succeed.

The building, which was built originally as a "post-house" in 1804, employs a somewhat eclectic decor, borrowing from almost every decade of the 20th century in furnishings and accessories, all of which add up to, say the owners, "a rather suave hotch potch."

This intentional, informal blend is also evident on their menu, which features selections of French, Italian, English, Indian, and other cuisines. The current owners, Peter and Thomas McCoy, are the self-taught cooks, and it is greatly to their credit that they have achieved the high standards evident at McCoy's. Of course, they did have the advantage of being born into the restaurant business and have lived in that atmosphere all their lives.

You will certainly enjoy your visit to McCoy's, whether for the restaurant or five-room hotel, as long as you can get in. The brothers say, "Steer past the only rubber-toothed labrador bitch, find the door if you can, and hope for miracles when you ring the bell."

McCoy's Restaurant

**THE TONTINE, STADDLEBRIDGE
NORTHALLERTON, NORTH YORKSHIRE**

060982-207

**BREAKFAST, LUNCH, AND DINNER
MONDAY - SATURDAY
RESERVATIONS**

**PROPRIETORS/CHEFS:
PETER AND THOMAS McCOY**

Rough Terrine of Chicken Livers and Pork

7 spoonfuls Armagnac

3 tbsp port

3 tbsp sherry

2 tsp peeled, chopped garlic

¾ oz chopped parsley

1 tsp thyme

  pinch of nutmeg

1 tsp caster sugar

2 heaped tsp salt

12 turns of the pepper mill

18 oz chicken livers, halved

7 oz pork belly, cubed

7 oz sausage meat

7 oz pork back fat for lining

4 sprigs thyme

4 bay leaves

8 oz butter

3 lb onions, thinly sliced

3 tsp salt

2 tsp pepper

11 oz sugar

1 lb dried apricots

¾ lb sultanas

14 tbsp sherry vinegar

4 tbsp grenadine

1 pt red wine

To prepare the marinade, mix the first 10 ingredients together. Place the livers, pork cubes, and sausage meat in a bowl and marinate for about 12 hours. Line an ovenproof dish (6½ by 4 by 3 inches) with pork back fat and fill to brim with mixed marinade. Cover top with fat. Put thyme and bay leaves on top. Bake for 3 hours in a bain-marie in the oven at gas mark 7 (425°F/220°C). Cool overnight in the refrigerator.

Next day, prepare apricot and onion purée. Heat the butter in a saucepan until nut brown, add onions, apricots, salt, pepper, and sugar. Cover pan and allow to cook for 30 minutes. Add remaining ingredients and cook slowly for another 30 minutes. Allow to cool. Serve the purée with the terrine.

Serves: 8

Wine: *Beaujolais, Pierre Ferrard, St. Armour, 1978*

Sole Roly Poly

1 tsp chopped chives

4 heaped dessertspoons small, shelled clams

  salt and cayenne pepper, to taste

4 peeled langoustine or jumbo scampi

4 large fillets of sole, skinned

2 hearts of lettuce cooked gently in butter

¼ pt fish fumet

¼ pt double cream

  lemon juice, to taste

Mix chives and clams with a sprinkling of salt and cayenne pepper. Lay ¼ of this mixture with 1 langoustine or scampi on each piece of sole. On top, place ½ lettuce heart. Roll up the sole around the mixture and secure with cocktail sticks.

Poach fillets gently in fish fumet. When fish are just cooked (firm to the touch), remove from pan, set aside, and keep warm.

Quickly reduce fumet to ⅛ pint approximately. Add double cream, bring to a boil, remove from heat, season with salt and lemon juice. Pour sauce over sole fillets and serve.

Wine: *White Beaune Greves, 1976*

Pool Court Restaurant

Michael Gill and his wife, Hanni, opened the **Pool Court Restaurant** some 15 years ago at Pool in Wharfedale, a small village just nine miles from Harrogate, Leeds, and Bradford. Since that time, a combination of elegant surroundings within the Georgian mansion, a balance of imaginative and classical dishes on the extensive menu, and a feeling of genuine, warm welcome have contributed to their success. Today, Pool Court is certainly one of the top restaurants in Great Britain.

Chef Roger Grime, who trained extensively in this country before coming to the restaurant 12 years ago, and his team base their cooking entirely on fresh in-season produce. The menu is changed at least weekly, offering guests a four-course meal with a choice of six or seven dishes in each section.

The restaurant is traditionally furnished in the Regency-style, and a separate dining area, known as the Cellar Restaurant, is available for private parties. It has a separate bar for informal pre-dinner drinks, an intimate atmosphere, and the same standard of cuisine and service for which Pool Court has become justly famous.

In addition to providing customers with a comfortable pre-dinner cocktail lounge, Pool Court also features an extensive wine list that offers a choice from more than 200 bins. There are also two excellent French house wines available.

Pool Court Restaurant

**POOL IN WHARFEDALE
OTLEY, WEST YORKSHIRE**

0532-842288

**LUNCH BY APPOINTMENT
DINNER: TUESDAY - SATURDAY,
7 TO 10 P.M.
RESERVATIONS
PROPRIETOR: MICHAEL W.K. GILL
CHEFS: ROGER GRIME, IAN MURRAY**

Saumon et Coquilles St. Jacques Pool Court

2 lb fresh salmon, skinned, boned and portioned

4 oz peeled carrots, julienne

4 oz leek, julienne

8 fl oz Muscadet white wine

8 fl oz fish stock

seasoning, to taste

10 oz butter

24 fresh scallops, prepared for cooking

8 lemon slices

8 oz tomato concasse (roughly chopped tomato) flavoured with lime

8 small crayfish

parsley, to garnish

Place salmon in an earthenware dish and cover with the vegetables, white wine, stock, and seasoning. Dot with 2 ounces butter, cover with foil, and bake for 30 minutes. After 20 minutes, remove foil, add scallops, replace foil, and cook for the remaining 10 minutes.

To prepare sauce: pour the juices from the fish into a pan and reduce to a jam-like consistency. Lower the heat and allow mixture to cool slightly. Gradually add the remaining butter in small pieces, whisking all the time. Check seasoning.

Place salmon and scallops in a serving dish, garnish with julienne of vegetables, lemon, tomato concasse, crayfish, and parsley.

Serves: 4

Wine: *Hermitage Blanc*

La Nectarine Christina

11 oz sugar

1 pt water

¼ pt brandy

4 large nectarines

1 egg

3 oz sifted flour

1 tsp salt

7½ fl oz milk

1 tsp brandy

1 fl oz oil, and to sauté

3 oz butter

Renshaws praline or dark chocolate, as needed

roasted ground hazelnuts, as needed

2 oz icing sugar

3 oz dark brown sugar

Dissolve 10 ounces sugar in cold water then bring to a boil. Turn off heat, skim, then add brandy. Halve and stone nectarines and put into cooling syrup to poach. When cold, take out and remove skin. Slice 4 of the 8 halves and lay them in individual fireproof oven dishes. Place remaining halves on top and sprinkle with a little brandy and some of the poaching liquid. Cover and refrigerate until ready for use.

To prepare praline crepe: beat the egg. Add flour, salt, and sugar. Beat to a smooth paste and gradually add milk, a little at a time, beating in well. Add brandy and oil. Allow to stand for 3 hours before use.

Heat a heavy-bottomed frying pan or crepe pan and brush lightly with oil. Put about 3 fluid ounces of the batter in the pan and swirl around to coat the surface. Cook on medium heat until brown, turn over, tip out, and leave to cool. Repeat until enough crepes have been made.

Melt some Renshaws praline (or chocolate) on a low heat (about blood temperature). With a palette knife, spread the praline mix very thinly over the crepe and sprinkle them with roasted, ground hazelnuts. Roll the crepes up tightly, trim off the ends, and dredge with icing sugar.

Sprinkle brown sugar over the nectarines and glaze the tops of the nectarines and crepes with a very hot brûlée iron — place under a preheated grill for 5–7 minutes. Remove and serve at once.

Serves: 4

Isle of Eriska

Isle of Eriska is housed in an old Scottish baronial country house in Ledaig. It is owned by Robin and Sheena Buchanan-Smith. The restaurant is eight years old and features traditional country cuisine prepared by Sheena.

Sheena's practical experience includes many years of country house entertaining. Her dishes do not possess the aggressiveness of the impressive giants of metropolitan renown, but rather tend toward the reflection of country house living of an earlier era.

Breakfast with its hot dishes set under silver covers, a lunch concentrating on the delights of a cold table, and the more formally set six-course dinner combine to impart the unique character of the old house, as a whole.

Despite the candlelit sparkle of crystal and silver, there is an informal sense of belonging and of a sharing of the atmosphere with fellow guests.

The service is most attentive, without being stiff, and the silk wallcoverings, light wood panels, and traditional furnishings blend well with the ease of the house and its surrounding countryside.

An extensive wine list and a cocktail lounge are available.

Isle of Eriska

LEDAIG, CONNEL, ARGYLL

0631-72-371

OPEN EASTER TO NOVEMBER
ALL MEALS SERVED DAILY
RESERVATIONS

PROPRIETORS:
ROBIN & SHEENA BUCHANAN-SMITH
CHEF: SHEENA BUCHANAN-SMITH

Eggs Dalriada

6 eggs

½ lb fresh salmon, cooked

½ pt Hollandaise sauce

   salt and pepper, to taste

½ pt dill mayonnaise

   cucumber salad, prepared

   fresh dill, to garnish

Hard boil the eggs, peel, and let cool. Mix the salmon with the Hollandaise sauce; season with salt and pepper. Halve the eggs and add the egg yolk to the salmon mixture. Refill egg halves, moulding back into shape, and arrange around the edge of a dish. Coat the eggs with the dill mayonnaise and place cucumber salad in the centre. Decorate each egg with a spray of fresh dill.

Serves: 6

Wine: *Sancerre Comte Lafond, Château du Nozet*

Roast Haunch Venison with Port and Orange Gravy

1 pt oil

   juice of 3 oranges

1 bay leaf

   salt and pepper, to taste

2 glasses port

1 onion, chopped

½ pt red cooking wine

   flour, as needed

1 × 3-4 lb haunch of venison, hind preferred

2 dessertspoons redcurrant jelly

   juice of 2 oranges

1 glass port

12 orange slices, to garnish

Mix the first 7 ingredients together to make a marinade. Pour marinade over haunch and leave for 12 hours, turning once. Cook roast in marinade for 2 hours in a slow oven, gas mark 2 (300°F/150°C). Drain roast, set aside, and pour off excess juice from roasting tin.

To make gravy: add a little flour to juice, mix well, then add jelly, orange juice, and port. Cook for 3 minutes.

To serve: decorate haunch with slices of orange and serve with gravy.

Serves: 6–8

Wine: *Bouchard, Beaune, 1976*

Highland Mist

1 lb brambles (blackberries)

8 oz sugar

   water, as needed

1 pt double cream

2 glasses Drambuie

4 egg whites

Cook almost all the brambles with sugar and a little water. Set aside to cool. Liquidise then sieve. Beat the cream until thick, add the Drambuie. Beat egg whites until stiff. Add bramble purée to cream and fold in the egg whites. Place in glasses and top with an uncooked bramble.

CHEF'S TIP

SIMPLICITY AND IMAGINATION ARE THE WATCHWORDS. YOU MUST START WITH THE BEST OF INGREDIENTS AND NEVER LOSE SIGHT OF THE ULTIMATE GOAL OF PERFECTION, HOWEVER ELUSIVE.

Wine: *White Bordeaux, Graves*

Caledonian Hotel, Pompadour Restaurant

The **Pompadour Restaurant** is a part of the famed **Caledonian Hotel**, located on Princes Street in the very heart of Scotland's capital. The hotel opened in December of 1903 and has always been the first choice for the discerning visitor to Edinburgh, both tourist and businessman alike. It is proud of its long-held reputation for providing the highest standards of comfort and cuisine in Edinburgh. Its guest register reads like a *Who's Who* in government and entertainment.

The Pompadour Restaurant, which seats 60, opened in 1953 and offers a combination of superb French and Scottish cuisine. It is a true consummation of the "auld alliance." In an atmosphere of quiet elegance of classic French decor with well-appointed tables and refined service, one can relax and enjoy good food and good company.

The extensive à la carte menu is supported by an inexpensive, well varied table d'hôte and speciality menus. The wine list is comprehensive and of excellent quality and features predominantly French vintners. There are also several house wines to choose from, and there is a cocktail lounge adjacent to the dining room.

Executive Chef Paul Rogerson and his brigade take great care to insure superb quality and presentation of the dishes and are always conscious of the importance of providing good value for good money.

Pompadour
Restaurant

PRINCES STREET, EDINBURGH

031-225-2433

DINNER: 7:30 TO 11 P.M.,
MONDAY - SATURDAY
RESERVATIONS

GENERAL MANAGER: MR. McLEOD
CHEF: PAUL VINCENT ROGERSON

CALEDONIAN HOTEL

Crêpinette de Crabe aux Ris de Veau

60 g plain flour

pinch of salt

1 egg

150 ml milk

1 tsp mixed herbs

1 tbsp oil, for frying

7 braised lamb sweetbreads

5 g butter

white meat from 1 crab

15 ml cream

25 ml Hollandaise sauce

3 warmed crab claws, to garnish

3 slices cooked courgette, to garnish

To prepare herb pancakes: put flour into a bowl, add salt and egg, and mix to a roux. Add milk slowly, mixing constantly, then add mixed herbs. Cover bottom of frying pan with oil, heat until hot, then add ⅓ the pancake mixture. Lightly brown on 1 side, flip over, and lightly brown the other side. Remove from pan and keep warm on a plate. Do same for other 2 pancakes.

Sauté sweetbreads in butter, add crabmeat, heat through, and add cream to bind. Fill pancakes with mixture and keep hot.

Coat the plate with Hollandaise and lay the pancakes in a row across the plate. On each pancake, place a warmed crab claw and a slice of remaining sweetbread and courgette.

Serves: 1

Mignon de Boeuf Glace au Coulis de Tomate

seasoning, to taste

1 medallion of beef

20 g butter, and as needed

2 tomatoes, peeled, seeded, and chopped

2 sliced leeks

double cream, as needed

1 sliced artichoke bottom

1 dessertspoon Hollandaise sauce

haricots verts (French or string beans), enough to serve 1

Season the beef, sauté it quickly in butter, and keep hot. Cook the tomatoes quickly in a little butter and keep hot. Sweat the sliced leeks in a little butter and add enough double cream to bind. Season. Lay sliced artichoke on beef and nap with Hollandaise sauce, set to glaze. Place tomato on a plate, lay glazed beef on top. Next to it, place creamed leeks with haricots verts on top.

Serving suggestion: serve with 3 pieces of dauphine potatoes.

Serves: 1

Peach Highland Cream

4 fresh peaches, peeled

whisky-flavoured syrup, as needed

raspberry sorbet, as needed

2 egg yolks

50 g sugar

2 measures whisky

whipped cream

Poach the peaches in the syrup, then chill. Cut in half and remove stone. Fill cavity with raspberry sorbet and put back together again. Make a sauce by beating egg yolks, sugar, and whisky over a basin of hot water until it doubles in volume and you can see the whisk marks in the sauce.

Put peaches in a Hock glass coated with sauce and topped with whipped cream.

Serves: 4

Prestonfield House Hotel

Prestonfield House Hotel stands in some 23 acres of its own grounds within the city of Edinburgh. The present house was built in 1687 for Sir James Dick, a close friend of King James II. The architect, Sir William Bruce, had just built the neighbouring Palace of Holyrood House. Today's Prestonfield has been subtly transformed into a country house hotel with five bedrooms and a number of very elegant public rooms, furnished with priceless antiques, Persian carpets, Chinese and Dresden porcelain, and Mortlake tapestries.

Outside, shadows of trees as old as the 17th century house still trace their patterns across its harled walls. Peacocks step diffidently across the paths, whilst pheasants and partridges still feed on the lawns, unaware that they are within a city's limits.

The relaxed and elegant dining rooms at Prestonfield glow with polished wood, silver, and glass, providing the correct setting for the French and classic Scottish cuisine perfectly prepared and presented by Chef Colin Warwick and his team.

Chef Warwick, who has been in the trade for more than 18 years, is particularly pleased to present his Wild Duck with Orange and Ginger, which is a long-standing house speciality. With 24 years experience, Manager Giovanni Fabbroni capably guides the smooth running of the entire operation. His wine cellar, incidentally, features an excellent choice of both European and Californian wines.

PRESTONFIELD HOUSE

**PRESTONFIELD ROAD
EDINBURGH**

031-667-8000

**BREAKFAST, LUNCH, AND DINNER
DAILY**

**MANAGER: GIOVANNI FABBRONI
CHEF: COLIN WARWICK**

Avocado Stilton

100 ml olive or corn oil

50 g rindless Blue Stilton cheese

juice of ½ lemon

chopped parsley, to taste

100 ml wine vinegar

½ tsp French mustard

salt and milled white pepper, to taste

lettuce, as needed

4 large ripe avocado pears

chopped parsley, to garnish

tomato, cucumber, capsicum etc. to choice

To prepare the dressing: liquidise the first 6 ingredients, then season with salt and pepper to taste.

Form a bed of lettuce on each of 8 plates. Using a stainless steel knife, halve the avocados, remove stones, then carefully peel off skin. Slice at an angle into 8 slices, taking care to retain shape of the pear. Lay slices on lettuce and, with gentle pressure, spread slices slightly. Coat with dressing, sprinkle with chopped parsley, and garnish each plate neatly with optional salad items.

Venison Chop Prestonfield

200 ml red wine

25 ml oil

2 cloves crushed garlic

1 bay leaf

1 blade mace

25 ml wine vinegar

100 g chopped onion

pinch of thyme

pinch of rosemary

½ tsp crushed peppercorns

8× 150-200 g venison chops

seasoned flour, to dust

100 ml oil

100 g butter

375 ml basic brown sauce

1 small jar redcurrant jelly

125 ml cream

8 small choux paste buns

Mix the first 10 ingredients together to make a marinade. Place the chops in the marinade at least 1 day before required (3 days would be ideal).

Drain venison from marinade. Drain liquid from rest of marinade ingredients and retain both. Season, flour, and sauté chops quickly in a frying pan with hot oil and butter. Take care to keep them frying, not stewing in their own juices. Take out when medium well done and keep warm.

Drain off any excess oil and gently fry the onion, garlic, and herbs saved from the marinade. Do not scorch. When the onion is soft, add liquid from the marinade and reduce almost completely. Add brown sauce and a dessertspoonful of redcurrant jelly and boil. Add cream and check seasoning and consistency. Add any juice or blood that has drained out of the chops being kept warm. (Optional: to increase gloss and enrich sauce, add 50 grams butter in pieces, mix in and do not re-boil.)

To serve: coat the chops with the sauce and decorate with the choux buns which have been slit and filled with redcurrant jelly.

Serves: 8

Wine: *Barolo D.O.C. Fontanafredda, Justerini & Brooks*

Chocolate Mint Mousse

350 g plain chocolate

25 g butter

60 ml water

5 eggs, separated

1 small measure brandy

50 g caster sugar

125 ml whipped cream

2 measures chocolate mint liqueur, or to taste

To prepare mousse: melt 250 grams chocolate with the butter and water and cook. Let cool. Whisk the yolks, brandy, and ½ the sugar together in a double boiler on a slow fire until light and thickened. Remove from heat and

beat until cool. Beat whites with the remaining sugar until stiff. Mix the yolk mixture into the cooled melted chocolate. Fold in the whites thoroughly. Divide between 8 wine glasses and allow to cool in the refrigerator for at least 4 hours.

Meanwhile, melt the remaining chocolate. Place a little at the bottom of 10 or 12 (to allow for breakage) small petits four cases. Using your finger, spread chocolate around the sides as evenly as possible. Repeat process to build up a cup with walls strong enough to withstand removing paper case by careful tearing.

Decorate top of mousse with whipped cream. Fill 8 of the chocolate cups with chocolate mint liqueur and place on top.

Serves: 8

Central Hotel, Malmaison Restaurant

Malmaison Restaurant was named after the charming house of Malmaison acquired by Napoleon for his wife, Josephine, that is situated about eight miles outside of Paris.

Arthur Towle opened the restaurant in 1927 in the **Central Hotel**, which was part of the largest hotel group in Europe created by the amalgamation of the Caledonian Railway Company, the London Midland, and the Scottish Railway.

When Malmaison first opened, it was a grill room with a direct entrance from Central Station, but after a few structural changes in 1935, it was changed to a high class French restaurant. Its reputation for good food, good wine, and good service survived the Second World War and the many economic ups and downs of the country. Today, it continues to be one of Britain's most critically acclaimed dining establishments.

In terms of ambiance, the restaurant boasts traditional French decor, dimmed candlelight, elegant table settings, and live piano music.

The classical French dishes are expertly prepared by Chef D.S. Cameron, whose prior experience includes tenures at the Caledonian Hotel in Edinburgh, the Ritz Hotel in London, and the Station Hotel in Perth, among others.

A particularly good selection of French clarets and good value regional wines is available, and there is a cocktail bar on the premises.

Malmaison
RESTAURANT

CENTRAL HOTEL
GORDON STREET, GLASGOW

041-221-9680

LUNCH: MONDAY - FRIDAY,
12:30 TO 2 P.M.
DINNER: MONDAY - SATURDAY,
7 TO 10:30 P.M.
RESERVATIONS

PROPRIETOR:
BRITISH TRANSPORT HOTELS, LTD.
CHEF: D.S. CAMERON, M.C.G.B.

L'Assiette de Langoustine Belle de Champs

36 pieces scampi

seasoning, to taste

½ iceberg lettuce, finely shredded

1 punnet strawberries

milled black pepper, to taste

1 tsp caster sugar

8 fl oz olive oil

2 fl oz wine vinegar

strips of truffle, to garnish

Poach the scampi in seasoned water, drain and refresh. Halve the scampi lengthways and place into a small, round earthenware dish and press. Place shredded lettuce in the centre of a round plate, then turn scampi onto it.

Purée the strawberries and add milled pepper and sugar to bring out its flavour. Whisk the oil and vinegar into the purée. Surround the bed of lettuce with the strawberry vinaigrette and garnish scampi with fine strips of truffle.

Serves: 4

La Surprise de Sole aux Primeurs

8 × 3 oz fillets of sole

seasoning, to taste

½ oz cooked and puréed *mange-tout* (sugar peas or beans)

2 oz butter, and to sauté

½ oz finely chopped shallots

¼ bottle dry white wine

¼ pt fish stock

1 pt double cream

3 oz turnips

3 oz carrots

3 oz peas

Flatten the sole fillets to double size. Season lightly and divide *mange-tout* purée among them. Roll and fold in sides to form a small parcel.

In a pan, rub ½ the butter on base and sprinkle with shallots. Place stuffed fillets with white wine and fish stock into pan. Bring to a boil. Put in a medium oven for 7–10 minutes, then remove fish.

Place pan with stock and wine on top of stove and reduce to about ¼; add cream. Season lightly and reduce again until sauce will coat the back of a spoon. Check seasoning, remove from heat until it stops boiling, then add the remainder of the butter, shaking the pan until it is mixed through the sauce.

Cut the turnips and carrots to pea size with a small scoop. Sauté them in a little butter with the peas for garniture.

To serve: pour the sauce onto a serving dish, place fish on top, and nap the sautéed vegetables over the fish.

Serves: 4

Nivingston House

Nivingston House is an elegant Scottish country house set in ten acres of grounds surrounded by the gentle scenery of Kinross-shire. This ten-year-old restaurant is owned by Colin Scott-Smith, who purchased it eight years ago. Since then, he has built up its reputation for excellent food, fine wines, and personal attention — all within the elegant and comfortable surroundings of silver, candles, and coal fires.

His chef is Bill Kerr, who has been in the business for more than two decades. Chef Kerr presents superb traditional French cuisine of the highest standard. Unlike most restaurants, he changes his luncheon and dinner menus each week, taking advantage of seasonal opportunities. He also grows many of his own vegetables and uses local produce wherever possible. Fish and other seafood are delivered regularly — direct and fresh from the west coast of Scotland.

Because of frequent inquiries for private party facilities, Nivingston House now has available a private dining room that can accommodate up to 30 guests. Special menus can be prepared by prior arrangement. In addition, there is a good selection of French, German, Austrian, Italian, Portuguese, and Pyrenean wines to choose from, and there is a cocktail lounge on the premises.

Nivingston House is only a 30-minute drive from Edinburgh, less from Perth, Glenrothes, and Edinburgh Airport.

Nivingston House

CLEISH, KINROSS-SHIRE

05775-216

BREAKFAST: 8 TO 10 A.M.
LUNCH: 12:30 TO 2 P.M.
DINNER: 7 TO 9 P.M.
TUESDAY - SUNDAY
RESERVATIONS

PROPRIETOR: COLIN R. SCOTT-SMITH
CHEF: WILLIAM KERR

Le Soufflé des Coquilles St. Jacques

10 oz finely chopped shallots

2 soupspoons dry white wine

3 soupspoons wine vinegar

6 oz butter

12 fresh scallops

2 egg whites

seasoning, to taste

4 large spinach leaves

1 pt fresh cream

4 mushroom caps, fluted

To prepare beurre blanc: put shallots, white wine, and wine vinegar in a saucepan and reduce to about 2 soupspoons of liquid. Remove from heat and add butter, little by little. Whisk vigorously all the time to obtain a light foamy mixture. Keep warm.

Remove scallops from shell and wash. Remove coral from scallops. Blend white flesh until pulp. Whisk egg whites until fluffy, add to scallop mixture, add seasoning, and put through a fine sieve. Place on crushed ice and chill. Blanch spinach leaves for about 60 seconds and place in 4 buttered dariole moulds or ramekins. Remove scallop mixture from ice and mix in fresh cream. Fill half the moulds with mixture then place a coral in centre of mould, then put remainder of mixture on top. Overlap spinach leaf. Place moulds in bain-marie and cook for 12 minutes.

To serve: turn the soufflés out of the moulds and coat each with beurre blanc. Place a fluted mushroom cap on each.

Serves: 4

Le Suprême de Pintade au Verjus de Framboises

2 × 2 lb fresh guinea fowls

3 oz nugget of butter

4 russet apples

4 oz raspberries

4 fl oz Armagnac

demi-glace, as needed

seasoning, to taste

watercress, to garnish

Skin and remove legs from birds. Fillet supreme from carcasses (save carcass trimmings for stock). Put ½ the butter in a pan and lightly cook the supremes without colouring. Cut caps off the apples and scoop out flesh carefully without damaging skin. Place raspberries in apples with a spot of butter on each and bake in oven at gas mark 4 (360°F/180°C) for 15 minutes. Add Armagnac to supremes and flame. Remove guinea fowl from pan and place on a serving dish. Add demi-glace to saucepan, finally add nuggets of butter, and season to taste. Remove apples from oven and place on serving dish. Coat supremes with Armagnac sauce and garnish with fresh watercress.

Serves: 4

Le Poire d'Avocat Nicola

2 large ripe avocados

2 fl oz orange curaçao

2 fl oz cognac

1 oz caster sugar

1 orange, skinned and diced

1 banana, skinned and diced

1 fresh pineapple, skinned and diced

1 tsp apricot purée

1 kiwi fruit, skinned and diced

toasted almonds, to garnish

Halve the avocados and scoop flesh from shells. Reserve shells for presentation. Mix orange curaçao, cognac, and sugar together to make a marinade and marinate the diced avocado, orange, banana, and pineapple in it. Leave to chill on crushed ice.

To serve: mix the apricot purée through the marinated fruits, then place mixture in the reserved avocado shells. Place sliced kiwi fruit on top and sprinkle toasted almonds on top of kiwi fruit.

Serves: 4

Index of Recipes

SWEETS

Directory of Restaurants